Clues, Myths, and the Historical Method

Carlo Ginzburg

Clues, Myths, and the Historical Method

Translated by
John and Anne C. Tedeschi

The Johns Hopkins University Press
Baltimore

Originally published as *Miti emblemi spie: morfologia e storia*.
Copyright © 1986 Giulio Einaudi editore s.p.a., Torino

Johns Hopkins Paperbacks edition, 1992
Second printing, 1992

The Johns Hopkins University Press
701 West 40th Street, Baltimore, Maryland 21211-2190

Library of Congress Cataloging-in-Publication-Data

Ginzburg, Carlo
    [Miti, emblemi, spie. English]
    Clues, myths, and the historical method / Carlo Ginzburg ;
    translated by John and Anne C. Tedeschi.
        p.   cm.
    Translation of: Miti, emblemi, spie.
    Bibliography: p.
    Includes index.
    Contents: Witchcraft and popular piety—From Aby Warburg to E.H.
    Gombrich—The high and the low—Titian, Ovid, and sixteenth-
    century codes for erotic illustration—Clues—Germanic
    mythology and Nazism—Freud, the wolf-man, and the werewolves—
    The inquisitor as anthropologist.
        ISBN 0–8018–3458–9   ISBN 0–8018–4388–X (pbk.)
        1. History—Methodology.   2. Historiography.   I. Title.
D16.G5213   1989
907'.2—dc20   89-45483

Contents

Preface to the Italian Edition

This collection, with the exception of the final essay, which is published here for the first time, consists of texts that appeared between 1961 and 1984. The subtitle reflects recent preoccupations dealt with explicitly in the papers on Freud and Dumézil. Today, the relationship between morphology and history seems to me to be the common thread (at least partially) running through the entire group. But perhaps the reader will find that these writings on such different subjects actually have little in common.

I should like to explain why they were selected and the context in which they came into being. I apologize for the partially autobiographical character of these observations. In the mid-1950s I was reading fiction; the idea that I might become a historian never crossed my mind. I also was reading Lukács, impatient with the way in which he discussed Dostoyevsky and Kafka. I thought that I would like to deal with literary texts, avoiding both the frustrations of rationalism and the mire of irrationalism. Today I find this project obviously naive in its ambition; however, I cannot forsake it. I still find myself caught up in it. The antithesis between rationalism and irrationalism recurs at the very beginning of "Clues," a piece that can be read as an attempt to justify a method of research in historical and in general terms.

An equally powerful thread of continuity binds me, despite everything, to my first relatively independent intellectual choices made in this period, choices that are not directly attributable to family background. Croce and Gramsci (that is, Croce read through Gramsci); Spitzer, Auerbach, Contini. These were the writers being discussed during those years in the review *Officina*, which I remember perusing with intense curiosity. I have never been terribly fond of Pasolini (except for a few of his films), who was one of the moving spirits of this journal; today I can see clearly, however, that the intersection of populism and stylistic criticism, typical of Italian culture in the late fifties, provided the background for my first attempt at research, "Stregoneria e pietà popolare" (1961; reprinted

here as "Witchcraft and Popular Piety"). Subsequent encounters
with people and books complicated and enriched the picture,
without, however, erasing it. Hermeneutics applied to literary texts
and, more specifically, the taste for telltale detail guided my later
in-depth work, which was mostly directed towards a totally different
type of documentation.

Among the motives impelling me towards the study of witch trials
there was also a desire to demonstrate that an irrational and (at least
for some) atemporal phenomenon – and one thus historically
irrelevant – could be studied in a rational, but not rationalistic key.
After more than twenty-five years and numerous studies devoted to
witchcraft (then definitely a peripheral subject), the polemic implicit
in this position appears to be obvious, or even incomprehensible. But
the decision to study not only the persecution of witchcraft but
witchcraft itself still appears to be both fruitful and not so patent.
(Other, more personal motives pushing me in this direction only
became clear to me later.) Even my reading of De Martino's *Mondo
magico*, which reached me through Pavese's *Dialoghi con Leucò*, seemed
an invitation to overcome by the means of concrete research the
ideological antithesis between rationalism and irrationalism.

The hypothesis formulated at the conclusion of "Witchcraft and
Popular Piety," which saw the witch trials as a clash between cultures
(as distinct from the other thesis, which viewed witchcraft as a
primitive form of class struggle), found confirmation some time later
in the Friulian materials studied in *I Benandanti* (1966; *The Night
Battles*, 1983). It was possible, then, to reconstruct a culture radically
different from our own, in spite of the intervening filter represented
by the inquisitors. But the *benandanti* ("well-farers," "do-gooders")
themselves confronted me with a new contradiction. The beliefs I
encountered in sixteenth- and seventeenth-century Friuli had
disconcerting similarities with spatially distant (and perhaps also
chronologically distant) phenomena: the myths and rites of Siberian
shamans. Could this connection be dealt with in historical terms? At
the time I thought not – and not just because of my own limitations.
Recalling an argument in Bloch's *The Royal Touch* (a decisive book
for me), I thought it possible to oppose a typological comparison
between historically independent phenomena, on one hand, and a
more strictly historical analogy on the other – and I opted for the
latter. This time the antithesis seemed insurmountable because it
was tied to an intrinsic limitation within the discipline itself. And yet I
wasn't certain that my choice exhausted the possibilities offered by

the documentation on the benandanti. For a time I toyed with the notion of presenting my work in two different forms: one concrete and descriptive, the other abstract and diagrammatic. Pulling me in the second direction was my encounter with the writings of Lévi-Strauss, specifically his *Structural Anthropology*. Even if typological or formal connections were out of bounds for the historian (as Bloch maintained), why not analyze them anyway, I asked myself?

Still today I have not been able to cope with this challenge. Nevertheless, underneath, it continued to sustain much of my work in the ensuing years. (At least that is how I see it now.) At the beginning of the 1960s, thanks to Cantimori, I discovered the Warburg Institute. My attempts to come to terms with the intellectual tradition associated with it forced me to reflect not only on the uses of figurative evidence as a historical source, but also on the persistence of forms and formulae outside the context in which they had originated. The result was "From Aby Warburg to E. H. Gombrich." My intention to study basic categories, anthropological in character, in different cultural settings – an ambitious project that ended up giving birth to a mouse ("The High and the Low") – also dates from the same period. After this failure, the old idea of transgressing the tacit boundaries of the discipline, pushing them back, presented itself in a different form. This time it was a question of restoring to the purview of history not so much obviously atemporal as apparently negligible phenomena – something resembling the witch trials. This was behind *Il formaggio e i vermi* (1976; *The Cheese and the Worms*, 1980), but also there was much else: for example, Don Milani (*Lettera a una professoressa*, 1967) and the events of 1968. But for demonstrating the significance of seemingly negligible phenomena, instruments of observation and scales of research different from the usual were needed. Thinking about the problem of detailed analysis of a microscopic type resulted in "Clues." Initially I had intended to justify my working methods indirectly by constructing a private intellectual genealogy, which would include principally a small number of books which I thought had influenced me in a particularly significant way: Spitzer's essays, Auerbach's *Mimesis*, Adorno's *Minima Moralia*, Freud's *Psychopathology of Everyday Life*, Bloch's *The Royal Touch*, all books that I had read between eighteen and twenty years of age. Then the project burst out in other directions. Once again I was tempted to analyze the object of my research (an object that seemed ever beyond my grasp because it was constantly expanding) over a long, in fact, immense sweep of time, while focusing, however, on a series of details examined close-up. I had thought of a similar telescopic and microscopic approach fifteen years earlier when I was mulling over the notion (which came to nought) of writing a book on the subject of "The High and the Low." In the meantime, however, something in me had changed.

I am well aware that I have been using ridiculously agonistic terms – "challenge," "obstacle," etc. – to describe innocuous intellectual activities. But the anguish is largely interiorized. The objections voiced within me are never the same as those of public critics. Negative reviews sometimes annoy me, sometimes make me happy; I forget them almost immediately. With the passing of time they have become more frequent, but my readers have also become more numerous and the subjects of my research, for a variety of reasons, have moved from the periphery to the center of the discipline. Contemporaneously, however, the antagonist within me has become much stronger. Once, it used to place obstacles in my way which I usually could overcome in one way or another – in the worst case, by ignoring them. But for the first time, while working on "Clues," I experienced a sensation that made itself more pronounced as the years passed: I did not know if I would side with myself or with my opponent. Did I want to broaden the horizons of historical research or tighten its boundaries, solve the difficulties tied to my work or continually create new ones?

What got me into trouble was the decision taken in the mid-seventies to return to problems associated with the benandanti and especially to one that had eluded me before: the analogy between benandanti and shamans. In the meantime, perhaps wrongly, I had become less prudent. I was no longer willing to discard a priori the possibility that resemblance implied a historical link (to be reconstructed from top to bottom). But the contrary hypothesis, of a purely typological relationship, was equally possible, and certainly more plausible. All this would require an expansion of the research to a sphere that, chronologically and geographically, was much vaster than late-sixteenth- and early-seventeenth-century Friuli. Moreover, the relationship between typological (or formal) connections and historical connections had to be confronted even in its theoretical implications.

The research on the sabbat of which I am speaking is still in progress. A number of its provisional findings are contained in a brief article not included in this collection ("Présomptions sur le sabbat,"

Annales: E.S.C., 1984). I do not rule out that even this project may be destined for partial failure. I see now, however, that in the meantime the theoretical difficulties associated with it have cropped up again on another level, in connection not with myths but with paintings.

This awareness is retrospective. I have permitted myself to be guided by chance and curiosity, not by a conscious strategy. But what appeared to be distractions (although fascinating ones) at the time, now do not seem such. What myths and paintings (works of art in general) have in common is, on the one hand, that they originated and were transmitted in specific cultural and social contexts, and on the other, their formal dimensions. That this can be illuminated by an analysis of the context is obvious (except to strict formalists): implicit references to literary texts and the reactions of the public assist us, for example, to better understand Titian's erotic paintings ("Titian, Ovid, and Sixteenth-Century Codes for Erotic Illustration"). But the prospect of peaceful collaboration suggested indirectly in that essay, on the basis of a division of labor between formal analysis and historical research, did not satisfy me on a general level. Which of the two approaches, I asked myself, has, in the last resort, greater power of interpretation?

This question, in some ways foolish, stemmed (as I think I understand now) from the research on the sabbat in which I have been stuck for so long. The documentation which I had been accumulating seemed to be forcing me to choose between a historical connection which I was not able to prove and a purely formal one which I resisted. On the other hand, a compromise solution, theoretically possible, had to be preceded (or so I thought) by an evaluation of the respective weight of the two alternatives – and thus, provisionally, by their radicalization. The contrast between external and stylistic data as elements to establish the chronology of Piero della Francesca's works (*Indagini su Piero*, 1981; *The Enigma of Piero della Francesca*, 1985) is a comparable expedient in a totally different context. The proposal for a chronology based on extrastylistic data was made necessary by the limits of my knowledge, certainly not by a prejudicial hostility of a theoretical nature. The morphological approach of a connoisseur like Morelli (which is examined in "Clues") fascinated me, as did Longhi's exceedingly more complicated one. The attempt to reconstruct otherwise unknown historical phenomena (artistic personalities, dating of art works) through a series of purely formal connections could be checked and corrected, if necessary, by the discovery of a different documentation, but its legitimacy remained intact.

I suddenly realized that in my long research on the sabbat I had been pursuing a method that was much more morphological than historical. I was collecting myths and beliefs from different cultural contexts on the basis of formal affinities. Beyond superficial similarities I recognized (or at least I believed I recognized) profound connections, being inspired more by Longhi than Morelli. The previously known historical links could not guide me because those myths and those beliefs (independently of the date in which they appeared in the sources) could go back to a much older past. I was using morphology as an instrument to probe depths beyond the reach of the usual historical methods.

I have mentioned Longhi and Morelli: but more immediately my model was and remains Propp, for reasons that are both specific and theoretical. Among the latter is his distinction, so precise and so fruitful heuristically (certainly not owed to external political pressures) between the "morphology of the folktale" and the "historical roots of fairy tales." In my plan, the work of classification should constitute a preliminary phase, meant to reconstruct a series of phenomena which I would like to analyze historically. All this unexpectedly became clear to me some years back when I stumbled on that passage in the *Notes on Frazer's "Golden Bough"* where Wittgenstein juxtaposes two ways of presenting material, one synoptic and achronic, the other based on a hypothesis of a chronological development, emphasizing the superiority of the former. The reference to Goethe (to Goethe the morphologist) is explicit, as it also is in Propp's *Morphology of the Folktale*, written in the same period. But Propp, unlike Wittgenstein, considers morphological analysis a useful instrument in historical research, not an alternative to it.

In the case of my current work on the sabbat, the integration of morphology and history is only an aspiration which may be impossible to realize. But the manner in which Propp in his *Historical Roots of Fairy Tales* (a great book despite its defects) filled the inevitable gaps in the documentation with a series of commonplaces based on a rigid evolutionism, makes clear the risks associated with an endeavor of this kind.

This digression on a still unfinished book has a single purpose: to clarify the links that otherwise might not be immediately evident between two of the essays in the collection and the others. The difficulties which continue to beset my research on the sabbat arise from the discovery, irrefutable in my opinion, of a mythical nucleus which retained its vitality fully intact for centuries – perhaps for millennia. This continuity, traceable despite numerous variations, cannot be generically credited to a tendency in the human spirit. Having discarded in advance pseudo-explanations which restate the problem ("archetypes," "collective unconscious"), I inevitably came to a critical reappraisal of Freud and Dumézil. My conclusions are partial and provisional; but a few of the implications of my work are now clear to me. In the essays presented in this volume I think I can recognize some of the stages that brought me, after many comings and goings, to the point where I am now.

Postscriptum 1989

This English edition (for which I am indebted, once again, to the ability and patience of my friends John and Anne Tedeschi) contains a previously unpublished essay, "The Inquisitor as Anthropologist," that was not included in the Italian volume. Like the essays on Dumézil and Freud, it too originated in the course of research on witchcraft that had begun many years before. The publication of *Storia notturna: Una decifrazione del sabba* (Turin: Einaudi, 1989) now closes, provisionally, a cycle of work reflected by the writings collected here.

❧ Translators' Note

We take great pleasure in bringing to the English reader a translation of Carlo Ginzburg's *Miti, emblemi, spie* (Turin: Einaudi, 1986), a selection of his essays on the broad theme of historical method, with the addition of a recent contribution, "The Inquisitor as Anthropologist," published here for the first time. Two of the pieces have previously appeared in English but in the present volume they have been translated anew.[1] The papers are arranged chronologically, by year of publication, and include Ginzburg's first essay in print, "Witchcraft and Popular Piety" (1961).

The author has not revised or updated the collection, with the exception of brief bibliographical addenda at the conclusion of most note sections. For our part, we have corrected a few errors, omitted a handful of allusions intended primarily for an Italian audience, and in the notes supplied English titles, whenever they were available, for works which the author had cited in other languages. To make the reader's task simpler, we have reduced the number of notes in the longer papers by consolidating them, but without sacrificing any of the material involved.

In our earlier Ginzburg translations (*The Cheese and the Worms*, 1980; *The Night Battles*, 1983) we made an observation about the recording of testimony in inquisitorial trials which is also valid for the first essay in this volume. The notary of the court customarily transposed direct testimony to the third person, so that questions and answers, though verbatim, read as an indirect form of discourse. Passages from these documents appear as quotations, though remaining in this indirect form, because Ginzburg simply took them as he found them in the trial records. Thus "In reply to a specific question, Chiara adds: 'After she [Chiara] had given birth to her first child, Our Lady appeared before her, beautiful ...' "

The English reader who wishes to become better acquainted with Carlo Ginzburg is invited to turn to the profile by Anne J. Schutte and the more recent interview with Keith Luria.[2] Finally, we should like to express our gratitude to the author for taking the time to read every page in this collection, so that it might reach the reader as error-free as possible, and to Carolyn Moser for her meticulous and intelligent editorial labors on a very difficult manuscript.

J.T.
A.C.T.

[1] Respectively in *Past and Present* (1976) and *History Workshop* (1980) (in an abridged version). All the essays in the Italian volume, *Miti, emblemi, spie*, had been published before with the exception of "Freud, the Wolf-Man, and the Werewolves." See the following Bibliographical Note.

[2] Anne J. Schutte, "Carlo Ginzburg," *Journal of Modern History* 48 (1976): 296-315, and Keith Luria, "The Paradoxical Carlo Ginzburg," *Radical History Review* 35 (1986): 80-87.

❧ Bibliographical Note

"Witchcraft and Popular Piety: Notes on a Modenese Trial of 1519" originally appeared as "Stregoneria e pietà popolare: Note a proposito di un processo modenese del 1519," in *Annali della Scuola Normale Superiore di Pisa: Lettere, storia e filosofia,* 2nd ser., 30 (1961): 269-87; "From Aby Warburg to E. H. Gombrich: A Problem of Method" was first published as "Da A. Warburg a E. H. Gombrich: Note su un problema di metodo," in *Studi medievali,* 3rd ser., 7 (1966): 1015-65; "The High and the Low: The Theme of Forbidden Knowledge in the Sixteenth and Seventeenth Centuries" appeared originally in English in *Past and Present,* no. 73 (Nov. 1976): 28-42, and in Italian translation in *aut aut,* no. 181 (January-February 1981): 3-17; "Titian, Ovid, and Sixteenth-Century Codes for Erotic Illustration" was published first as "Tiziano, Ovidio e i codici della figurazione erotica nel Cinquecento," in *Paragone,* no. 339 (May 1978): 3-24; "Clues: Roots of an Evidential Paradigm" appeared originally as "Spie: Radici di un paradigma indiziario," in *Crisi della ragione,* ed. A. Gargani (Turin, 1979), pp. 59-106 (and in English translations in *History Workshop* 9 [Spring 1980]: 5-36, and in *The Sign of Three,* ed. U. Eco and T. Sebeok [Bloomington, 1983]); "Germanic Mythology and Nazism: Thoughts on an Old Book by Georges Dumézil" was published first as "Mitologia germanica e nazismo: Su un vecchio libro di Georges Dumézil," in *Quaderni storici,* n.s., 57 (December 1984): 857-82; "Freud, the Wolf-Man, and the Werewolves" made its appearance originally in *Miti, emblemi, spie.* "The Inquisitor as Anthropologist" is previously unpublished.

Clues, Myths, and the Historical Method

❧ Witchcraft and Popular Piety: Notes on a Modenese Trial of 1519

An examination of the series of inquisitorial trials preserved in the Modena State Archives, and particularly the first group, ranging in date from the end of the fifteenth century to, roughly, the first half of the sixteenth, reveals an increase of trials and denunciations for witchcraft, magic, and superstition in the triennium 1518-20.[1] In this brief period there are twenty-two trials or denunciations (even the latter can be significant for the attitudes of inquisitors, since in all likelihood they were rarely made spontaneously), whereas in the quinquennium 1495-99 there were only fifteen, and in the decade 1530-39, not more than twelve.[2] Unfortunately, the fragmentary state in which this material has reached us, and especially the lacunae, some of which extend over many years and interrupt the series of trials about 1550, make it difficult to determine the reasons for this intensification of persecution and repression of witchcraft by the Modenese Inquisition. This phenomenon may be connected to the presence in Modena during this period of an inquisitorial vicar, Fra Bartolomeo da Pisa, who proved his zeal by conducting personally almost all the witchcraft cases, with only occasional and hasty participation by the inquisitor, Fra Antonio da Ferrara. This conjecture gains plausibility if, as seems likely, Fra Bartolomeo da Pisa can be identified with Fra Bartolomeo Spina, who in these very years was writing the famous treatise *Quaestio de strigibus*, which reflects in large measure the practice of witchcraft in the Emilia region – whether we suppose that Spina had a previous interest in the question of witchcraft, which would have led him in the period of his Modenese activity to step up the pursuit of the *secta maleficarum*; or, instead, that it was actual experience with witchcraft in the area that drew his attention to the problem, moving him first to repression, and to theoretical reflection afterwards.[3]

Only further study may help us answer these questions; and if the suggested identification of the provincial vicar with Spina proves to be correct, the Modenese trials constitute a precious source for study, sadly neglected thus far, of the connection between inquisitorial procedures and the doctrinal evolution of the demonology treatises. But aside from the problem of the vicar's identity, these trials are of great intrinsic interest, especially one against Chiara Signorini, a Modenese peasant woman accused of witchcraft. Her case helps to elucidate problems that are generally advanced as conjectures or plausible associations (but of a purely psychological order): the relationship between witchcraft and popular piety, the social forces behind witchcraft itself, and the imposition of inquisitorial schema on the actual phenomenon of popular witchcraft.

The first accusations against Chiara Signorini are voiced in the course of a trial against a Servite friar, Bernardino da Castel Martino.[4] On December 9, 1518, Bartolomeo Guidoni appears before Fra Bartolomeo da Pisa, vicar of the Modenese inquisitor, claiming that his sister, Margherita Pazzani, has been the victim of witchcraft for about the last five years. He suspects that the perpetrators of the crime are a married couple, Bartolomeo and Chiara Signorini, who used to live as tenants "on a certain piece of land or holdings" belonging to Margherita. It emerges that "the pair have a bad reputation in this regard" and that Chiara has declared publicly on several occasions that Margherita could not be cured "unless [Chiara] first wished it and not until [Margherita] returned her and her husband to the possessions from which Lady Margherita had expelled them."[5] Several relatives of the sick woman then came to Chiara, who told them that indeed she could cure her former mistress, but only on the condition that she and her husband be permitted to return to the land from which they had been driven. She did not conceal that she had cast a spell on the Pazzani woman. The trial notary recorded that "on account of Chiara's curses Lady Margherita was paralyzed in her arms and legs ... and it was because of such curses that she drove Chiara from her aforementioned piece of land, the latter asserting that if Lady Margherita had not chased her off, she would not have suffered such an infirmity."[6] But Chiara pledged to make her well within a month "through her prayers and her children's." So there had been the customary promise "sworn on Scripture" before several witnesses. In addition to the pledge stated above, Chiara received a garment, a sum of money, "and certain other pieces of linen."[7] Shortly thereafter Margherita Pazzani was cured. But when word reached Chiara that a maidservant "had been heard to say that because Chiara had cast a spell over Lady

Margherita she ought to be denounced to the inquisitor and be burned,"[8] Margherita was stricken anew and now had been languishing for about a year.

These were the facts narrated by Bartolomeo Guidoni, followed by accounts of Margherita Pazzani's attempts to overcome her infirmity, among which had been recourse to the magic arts of the Servite friar Bernardino da Castel Martino. In addition to exorcising her along with a group of women who were reputed to be possessed, he had not been above using wax statuettes for their therapeutic qualities.[9] Depositions against the friar continued through February 3, 1519, but there is no evidence that he was ever interrogated in person. The trial against Chiara Signorini, however, had been under way since the fifth of January.[10] The demons inhabiting the body of one of the women exorcised with Margherita Pazzani had also accused Chiara.[11] In addition, Bartolomeo Guidoni's testimony weighed heavily against her. The tribunal of the Inquisition viewed her position as extremely serious.

On January 5 Chiara Signorini is brought before the inquisitorial vicar and Tommaso Forni, bishop *in partibus* of Ierapolis and vice-vicar to the bishop of Modena, and interrogated for the first time.[12] Her arrest had been a turbulent one; she had attempted to flee, hid herself under a bed, and offered resistance. Concerning these events, which created a strong presumption of guilt in the minds of the judges, she had offered confused and embarrassed explanations: "she replied that she had been afraid they would kill her; later she said that she dreaded being taken to the prison of the inquisitors ... and also added she feared being led before the governor at the castle and being imprisoned there," even though, the notary commented, "no one has said anything to her about a jailing."[13]

Chiara begins her defense on the spot, not simply by refuting the facts, but by denying that she had received any sort of diabolical assistance in committing them. She admits that she possesses special powers, such as being able to take away or put spells on specific people. But she claims to have this ability from God "through her prayers and her children's."[14] It is God who sustains her, thereby making amends for the injustices she had suffered. She is aware that she is reputed to be "infamous and a witch by certain people." But there is a reason for it. She had been chased away "from a certain piece of land located in the villa Maiagali" owned by Margherita

Pazzani. And this had been done, she states vehemently, "against all justice and promises that the aforesaid Margherita had made": "Seized by anger she cursed Lady Margherita, and afterwards Lady Margherita fell sick: and now people believe that it was Chiara who caused this infirmity, supposing that she had cast a spell over the aforesaid Lady Margherita Pazzani."[15]

When the stricken woman's relatives had asked Chiara to cure her, she agreed, promising that she would do it within twenty days "through her prayers and her children's, provided God was willing." But in return she had exacted "cows from good stock and other animals and a garment of gray cloth," an advance of seed grain, and the assurance that she would never again be driven away.[16] Lady Margherita was cured in fifteen days, but since she did not keep her promise, "Chiara began once again to pray against her and curse her, beseeching God to take away Lady Margherita's health, and again she did indeed fall sick and become increasingly worse." And even though afterward the woman Pazzani implored Chiara to restore her health and repeated her former promises, since Chiara "had never prayed God for her from the heart, she thought, consequently, that the lady Margherita could not be cured."[17]

Thus ends the first trial session. Chiara steadfastly denies using witchcraft or other diabolical arts; and the judges, "perceiving ... that it was impossible to get at the truth through straightforward questioning about the things of which she was accused," return her to her cell.[18]

But further testimony adds to the already serious evidence against the defendant. First of all, it seems that Chiara had threatened her former mistress with these words: "You would have been better off if you had never chased me off your land; you wouldn't have this sickness that you now have," with not even the slightest allusion to the mediation (suspect in itself) of the prayer to God, as if Margherita's recovery or sickness depended on her alone.[19] In addition, Nina, a young girl raised by Margherita, had spotted Chiara Signorini one day placing near the entrance of their house certain "bewitched objects," consisting of "fragments of olive branches formed like a cross and wild vetch and pieces of human bones, and silk dyed white, presumed to be smeared with holy ointment."[20] In a face-to-face confrontation on February 11 with Chiara (who persists in denying everything), Nina firmly sticks to her story ("audaciously," the notary adds).[21] Then one of the witnesses who had gone with others to Chiara to ask her to heal Margherita reports the suspected witch's own description of how she cast a spell over her former mistress, an account which beyond question reveals a jumble of black magic.[22] Still another accuser declares that he had heard more than one person say that Chiara was a witch and that it was for this reason that she and her husband had been driven from "her piece of land."[23]

This last deposition lets us piece together the couple's real situation, and other evidence volunteered in the course of the trial helps to complete the picture. On February 12, a former mistress of Chiara's, Orsolina Malgazali, after confirming that both the accused and her husband "enjoyed a poor reputation as far as magical arts and witchcraft were concerned," states that Francesca, the daughter of Angelo Mignori, "had refused … to receive either Chiara or her husband as tenants on her land, out of fear that she might cast a spell on [Mignori's] daughter." And she herself, after having dismissed Chiara from one of her farms ("which [Chiara] took very badly"), was seized by violent pains that drove her to her bed. But she had not connected this illness with Chiara until a year later when the couple were going to be hired by Gentile Guidoni, dubbed "la Guidona," to work a piece of land "in the area of Saliceto da Panaro." At this point Bartolomeo Signorini had come forward and to her great amazement had beseeched her "not to tell anyone that Chiara had bewitched her, for fear she would not be able to take possession of that land." But Gentile Guidoni, in the end, had dismissed Chiara, and Chiara, in a fit of agitation, threatened, "I've made La Pazzana and La Malgazali pay, and now you'll pay too."[24]

Two peasants, loathed because they were suspected of practicing magic and casting spells, feared by their masters, continually being dismissed, avenging themselves for these wrongs (not only against their masters who had fired them, but also against their successors)[25] by appealing to powers which ended by turning against them:[26] this is the picture that emerges from the trial testimony. In this particular case there is no doubt that witchcraft can be considered a weapon of both offense and defense in the social struggle.[27] But the notoriety attached to witchcraft, or even the suspicion of it, could also lead to ostracism. One witness declares, perhaps with a little exaggeration, that "even those dwelling in the villa Malgazali fled, afraid because Chiara and her husband Bartolomeo were living there."[28] And then, too, odd habits and behavior easily provoked first the suspicion and later the accusation of witchcraft. A servant girl of Orsolina

Malgazali, who had lived with the couple for a while, asserts that "during that time she never saw or knew them to go to Mass." Chiara had confided to this girl that she had learned some superstitious recipes to cure livestock from a neighbor "who was always willing to teach her, no matter how many times she asked, to the very end of her life." The girl suspected that "the woman was a witch who made Chiara, as a sort of bequest, the successor to her witchcraft, in the same way as she heard others had done."[29]

In other words, it is difficult, and perhaps impossible, to say to what extent the isolation experienced by Chiara and Bartolomeo Signorini resulted from their reputation for practicing witchcraft and magic, or whether such followers of the Devil were not already to be found precisely among those outcasts existing on the fringes of human society.

In short, the evidence thus far does not tell us if the couple deliberately took advantage of their reputation, even if they did not themselves place any faith in the powers attributed to them, or whether they may have really believed in such practices and spells. The problem is not a marginal one and will not be resolved easily. Our only source is Chiara Signorini's testimony. The interpretation of these documents is made more difficult by two troubling factors – the use of torture and the interrogation technique – which we shall examine in a moment.

Let's return to the trial proceedings. On February 6 Chiara is summoned to face the vicar a second time. She denies having said that she was the cause of Margherita Pazzani's infirmity. The vicar asks her whether she ever told Margherita, "You would have been better off if you had never chased me off your land; you wouldn't have this sickness that you now have." She replies that she had indeed spoken these words, but merely as a supposition: "You would have been better off, etc., etc., then perhaps you wouldn't have this sickness that you now have." The questioning continues with this give and take, but suddenly it takes a wholly unexpected turn. Even the notary's record of these affairs, which is usually so impersonal, seems to betray a trace of astonishment:

> When, however, the discussion turned to her husband and daughter, and the vicar reproached her for teaching her daughter badly, something the vicar was well informed about, Chiara said, "It is enough to know that my daughter is not in prison." And asked how she knew this, she replied that after dinner that day Our Lady appeared before her, though she could

not see her, and Our Lady spoke these words to her: "Keep up your courage, my daughter, and do not be so afraid, because they will not have enough power to cause you sorrow"; and Our Lady herself informed her that her daughter was not in prison.[30]

Confronted by the witch's improvised, ingenuous attempt to defend herself, the vicar lets the discussion drop for the moment. The questioning in the trial resumes, now concerning the superstitious healings administered to Margherita Pazzani and the time when Chiara lived in the home of Lorenzo Malgazali. Then the vicar abruptly asks the woman if the Virgin had appeared or had talked with her on other occasions, and she replied: "Once, when she [Chiara] prayed for Lady Margherita, the Blessed Virgin herself stood before her in white vestments, and spoke to her saying, 'My daughter, do not worry whether you will be able to cure her, if she does what she promises for you. Keep on praying hard.' "[31] Fra Bartolomeo wants to know if the vision had appeared to her while she was awake. In Chiara's reply we see an earthy, peasantlike Virgin emerging, who inspires in her protegé an affectionate, almost sensual worship:

> [Chiara] replied that she was awake and praying on her knees, and the Blessed Virgin asked to be worshipped, which Chiara did, and she worshipped her kissing the ground, and bowing before her because she was comely; the Blessed Virgin was beautiful, rosy-cheeked, and youthful, and Chiara kissed her outstretched arms all the way to the neck with great reverence and happiness, and felt her to be as soft as silk and very warm.[32]

The trial resumes the next day, February 7. This third interrogation turns its attention to Chiara's visions. But the attitudes of both the vicar and the accused have hardened from the previous day. The churchman now blatantly attempts to influence Chiara's testimony, convinced that the so-called visions of the Madonna were really only diabolical hallucinations. The woman, on her part, pursues a course that she hopes offers an avenue of escape, embellishing and refining her original story. We are observing a classic example of suggestive interrogation intended to lead the defendant's responses along a predetermined course. Fra Bartolomeo's questions implicitly introduce the content of the replies; and Chiara docilely adjusts to his queries, even while adding to and elaborating upon them.

The vicar promptly asks "whether she had received revelations and if Our Lady appeared before her in visible form." Chiara replies that the Madonna had appeared before her "many times, more than a hundred times in the form of a real woman, dressed in white and with a pretty face." And "asked if our Lady always gave in to Chiara's wishes, she replies that she had always granted everything she asked":

> Interrogated if she ever prayed to Our Lady to defend her and hers, and avenge her against those people who were injuring her and hers ..., Chiara replied that the Virgin did appear before her, promising vengeance, and, in fact, did avenge her against the many who were injuring her. Standing before [Chiara] afterwards [Our Lady] spoke these words or similar ones: "I can tell you that I have punished them," and it was stated that Chiara beseeched Our Lady that those afflicted ones could be made well.[33]

The vicar's questioning becomes more subtle:

> Interrogated if at the beginning when Our Lady began to appear to Chiara ... she asked Chiara to give and offer her soul and body to her, Chiara replied that she might have been fifteen years old when Our Lady appeared to her in her home, and ordered Chiara to offer and give up soul and body to her, promising many good things, and that Our Lady would never abandon her. And Chiara had acquiesced and given her soul and body to Our Lady, kissing her gently, and throwing herself at her feet, Chiara worshipped her at the request of Our Lady. And questioned whether after she had taken a husband, he too had revelations, saw Our Lady and gave up his soul and body, she replied that even her husband Bartolomeo saw Our Lady on various occasions and paid homage to her, just as she did, offering himself to Our Lady and giving his soul and body and worshipping her, just as she had. And she was told this by her husband himself, shortly after she had taken him, and this was Chiara's own doing who had induced him to give himself to Our Lady, just as she had.[34]

In reply to a specific question, Chiara adds:

> After she [Chiara] had given birth to her first child, Our Lady appeared before her, beautiful and clothed in white, just as she had many other times, and beseeched her to offer her first-born; and this Chiara did, raising her child up in her arms and offering it to Our Lady, surrendering its soul and body; and she did this with all her children.[35]

She concluded by saying that "no one could see Our Lady except myself."[36]

The technique and objectives of this questioning are clear enough. The judge was suggesting a string of ideas – revenge on one's enemies, the surrender of body and soul, etc. – that might seem ambiguous, but which for him already possessed negative implications, and endowed the "Virgin" who had appeared to Chiara with diabolical characteristics. It is also obvious how Chiara's responses lent themselves to being interpreted in this sense (the paying of homage, the offering up of the first-born, etc.); we can almost grasp the exact effect of her words on the mind of the judge. But the complex relationship which evolved in the course of the interrogation does not end here. We have seen how Chiara adapted herself to the questioning of the vicar and submissively followed his lead, even in her efforts to save herself. But the response to the judge's suggestions in the thinking of the defendant is especially remarkable: there is a congruence between them that stands out in the ingenuous spontaneity of some of her replies (the Virgin who appears, saying, "I can tell you that I have punished them"). Far from being a mere expedient for salvation, the Virgin, whether divine or diabolical apparition, seems to have deep roots in Chiara's mind. But even if this was not the case, the deposition (however invented or insincere) still would have an intrinsic significance, since it provides us with precious, if indirect, information about a large segment of popular piety in this period. And there is more yet in the dramatic exchange and confrontation between witch and inquisitor. It is difficult to distinguish in Chiara Signorini's account between that which she invents in the hope of finding some means of escape and that which she really believes, or would like to believe: for example, the Virgin protectress in human form, as she was able to conceive her, who comes to rectify and vindicate the injustices against her, uplifting her from a dreary and miserable life.

The trial resumes on the ninth of February. For Fra Bartolomeo, evidently, the nature of the Virgin's miraculous appearances has been resolved to his full satisfaction, because he asks no more questions on the subject. After a brief exchange of words, in the course of which Chiara denies everything, he decides to proceed to interrogation with torture. But she confesses as soon as she is conducted "to the instruments of torment and bound by a rope." She admits having said that the cure of the Pazzani woman was in her hands and, "released from the rope," continues to describe the malefice she used against her former mistress.[37] But the vicar wants to know more, and interrogated if she had a sign from the Devil over the bewitching and injuring of Lady Margherita Panzana, she replied that the Devil appeared before her in the form of a youth after she had performed the previously mentioned incantation, and the Devil asked Chiara to tell him whatever she desired, since she had summoned him; and Chiara replied that she wanted him to cast a spell on Lady Margherita Panzana, because Lady Margherita had expelled Chiara from her possessions.[38]

The questions go on in this manner, following the by now familiar technique, in which the content of Chiara's replies are being implicitly suggested to her:

Interrogated if the Devil promised her to do this as long as Chiara worshipped him, and if Chiara worshipped him just as he asked, she replied that the Devil demanded that she, Chiara, worship him, which she did, throwing herself to the ground on her knees before him, saying that she had done everything to achieve her object of perpetrating a malefice on Lady Margherita. Asked if the Devil returned to tell her that he had afflicted Lady Margherita and bewitched her, she replied that the Devil told her, Chiara, that he had carried out her orders, and cast a spell over Lady Margherita, and specifically that he had paralyzed her hands and feet.[39]

Thus the session ends: because of the late hour the rest of the interrogation is postponed until the next day.

But the following day, February 10, the moment the vicar asks Chiara to ratify the confession she had made the previous evening, the woman denies everything, asserting "that nothing she had told them was true, and what she had said was all because of the fear of being tortured."[40] The judges, "perceiving that she was still unrepentant," subject her to torture once more. And Chiara, "when she had been raised about four cubits from the floor cried out from the pain," but persists in denying that she had placed a bewitched object outside the door of Margherita Pazzani's house. She admits, however, "that she had conjured devils in the way that is reported in the trial record; and that the Devil had appeared before her in the form of a youth, who required that she worship him, which Chiara did, enjoining the Devil … to go and cast a spell over Lady Margherita Panzana." "Deposed from the torment," and brought to an adjacent chamber, Chiara confirms everything that she had confessed "under torture," adding that "when she implored the Devil, who had appeared before her when she conjured him, to come and heal the Lady Margherita as had been promised, then the Devil appeared before Chiara and spoke these words to her, 'Worship me and I will have Lady Margherita cured, and I will do you much good.' "[41]

It may seem unnecessary to dwell so minutely on this monotonous succession of confessions extracted by torture and followed by equally punctual retractions. But torture, in reality, only reaffirms in an extreme form the essential characteristics of the witchcraft trial itself. However obvious, it may not be superfluous to recall that a large majority of inquisitors accepted the existence of witchcraft, just as many witches believed what they confessed before the Inquisition. In other words, in the trial we have an encounter between inquisitors and witches, though on different levels, who share a common vision of reality, one which implies the everyday existence of the Devil, the possibility of having relations with him, and so forth. But precisely because of the discrepancies inherent in the encounter, there is always a gap between the beliefs of the defendant and those of the judge, even when the defendant is, as happens more often than is generally supposed, really a witch who does conjure the Devil in her incantations. And the judge, generally in good faith, seeks to overcome this hiatus, even, if necessary, by recourse to torture. That insidious interrogation technique which we have observed at work, a device which tends to draw out of the defendant what the inquisitor already believes is the truth, also serves the same purpose. In various ways judges superimposed predetermined ideas on the witches' confessions. And we must keep these accretions in mind in our attempt to understand the real character of popular witchcraft, in contrast to the "learned" witchcraft of the demonological treatises.[42]

Even in the case of Chiara Signorini there is a transparent attempt on the part of the judge to make her confession coincide with his perception of the truth. Since there is no other recourse, torture is used and the witch confesses, except that she retracts everything the next day and reverts to her original account. The pattern continues in the following interrogation (February 15). Chiara begins by confirming what she has admitted in the two prior sessions "when she had been subjected ... to torture." But then she denies everything, "declaring that all she had said in these two trials had been at the instigation of the Devil, not because it was true."[43] When she was once again tortured, "she repeatedly denied that she had done or said the things to which she had previously confessed." Finally, interrogated by Tommaso Forni "whether the Devil had appeared before her and she had worshipped him, she replied yes";

her prior testimony, embellished, is dredged up again.

Evidently the woman's confessions are due solely to torture; but it would be a mistake not to take them seriously. First of all, clearly, they provide important, even though indirect, evidence about popular beliefs and traditions. Take, for example, the Devil who appears in the form of a youth or a child – not a casual or arbitrary detail since it recurs in all three confessions. Furthermore, if we compare Chiara's statements on the miraculous apparitions of the Madonna to those on the apparitions of the Devil, we note striking similarities. The two accounts are constructed, so to speak, with the same simple elements, even if the end result differs. Let's look at the following passages:

(1) Once, when [Chiara] prayed for Lady Margherita, the Blessed Virgin herself stood before her ... and spoke to her saying, "My daughter, do not worry whether you will be able to cure her.... Keep on praying hard."[44]

(2) When she implored the Devil, who had appeared before her when she conjured him, to come and heal the Lady Margherita ..., the Devil appeared before Chiara and spoke these words to her, "Worship me and I will have Lady Margherita cured, and I will do you much good."[45]

(1) The Virgin did appear before [her], promising vengeance, and, in fact, did avenge her against the many who were injuring her. Standing before [Chiara] afterwards, [Our Lady] spoke these words or similar ones: "I can tell you that I have punished them," and it was stated that Chiara beseeched Our Lady that those afflicted ones could be made well.[46]

(2) And ... the Devil appeared to Chiara in the form of a youth, and asked: "What do you want from me, why do you call me?" To which she replied: "I want you to avenge me against Lady Margherita Pazzani." Later ... when the Devil returned, he told her that he had cast a spell over Lady Margherita. Since, however, Chiara had promised to heal her, she once again invoked demons, and the Devil appeared before her in the aforementioned form and asked: "What do you want from me?" to which Chiara responded, "I want you to cure Lady Margherita, since she promised me what I wanted," and the Devil said, "I am willing, and I will also do much good" or similar words, promising to cure her, as in fact happened.[47]

(1) And the Blessed Virgin asked to be worshipped, which Chiara did, and she worshipped her kissing the ground, and bowing before her.[48]

(2) And [the Devil] replied: "... I want you to worship me," which Chiara did, falling to the ground before him at once and kissing the ground.[49]

In looking at the parallels between these passages, we should keep in mind the way in which the interrogations were conducted: the resemblance between Chiara's two apparitions, the Madonna and the Devil, is ever present in the judge's mind. And by asking the right questions, he attempts to make the two images reflect one and the same thing. Significantly, in the interrogation of February 15 he inquires whether "she had given her body and soul to the Devil and the souls of her children and husband as well." We recall that Chiara had admitted offering her own body and soul to the Virgin and persuading her husband and children to do the same. But this time her reply is not the expected one: "She stated that she gave the Devil her soul and the souls of her children and her husband, but not her body."[50]

Even more significant, however, than the similarities of the specific details in her descriptions, is the essential identity of the two apparitions, which is explainable only if Chiara really believes her own story. The Virgin who appeared to Chiara seems in fact to be identified with the Devil. But what for the vicar was explained by the pact that had always bound the witch to the Devil has a different and deeper meaning for us. Divinity, as Chiara is capable of conceiving it and venerating it, is a deity that intervenes to extricate her from her difficulties, first casting a spell on her superiors, who had chased her away, later healing them so she might be allowed to return to her land. And it does not matter whether it is a heavenly or diabolical being. The convergence of orthodox and diabolical religion in common piety clearly shows how thin the line separating the two could be in the mind of the believer, especially in rural areas where the faith was often mixed with superstitious elements or even pre-Christian residues.[51] In situations of isolation, extreme hardship, and absolute poverty, the invocation of the Devil may have offered the only hope. Chiara Signorini's last confession, which recapitulates and embellishes her earlier ones, is a case in point.

By now it is February 20. Chiara comes forward "spontaneously and of her own accord" to state that she wants to confess "everything that she had ever done in her life in regard to malefice and to diabolical superstition." Here is the court's account of her story:

And first she said that when she had been driven to despair because of her expulsion from the lands of Lady Margherita Pazzani, and made very poor because of it, she called upon the Devil daily and even hourly. Once while she was mowing grass in the field and calling upon the Devil in her despair, a boy appeared before her who looked about twelve years of age; and questioning Chiara why she was in such despair and hearing the reason, he said: "Give yourself to the Devil, because he will help you." Chiara replied that she would give herself to the Devil and do what he wished of her if he avenged her against Lady Margherita Pazzani; and the Devil himself, in the form of the boy, said to Chiara: "I am the Devil whom you call. If you want me to do what you ask of me, worship me"; and Chiara replied, "I am willing to give you my soul after I die, as long as you do what I desire." And the Devil took his leave, according to Chiara, but then returned in the same form about a month later and said to her: "I have carried out your wishes and cast a spell over Lady Margherita Pazzani, making her paralyzed in her hands and feet." To this Chiara replied, "I thank you because you have done well"; and she worshipped him again at the Devil's own request. And then Chiara boasted to many people on several occasions, saying that the Lady Margherita could never be healed unless she herself wanted it (and Chiara stated in her trial that the Devil had promised this). Because of these and similar statements, Lady Margherita's relatives beseeched Chiara to agree to cure her, promising many things in return. And once again they had her come to the home of Lady Margherita, and in a document drawn up by Bernardino Cantù promised to restore her to the aforesaid possession, and to give much else besides, as stated in that document drawn up before witnesses, if she would cure her before Christmas. Chiara, for her part, swore to carry this out for certain, as the document attests. And Chiara stated that after returning to her house, she once again invoked the Devil, who appeared before her and asked: "What is your desire?" To which Chiara replied, "I would like you to heal Lady Margherita Pazzani." And the Devil: "I shall heal her in fifteen days, as long as you will adore me and give me your soul." This Chiara did. Meanwhile, she said, before she [Margherita] was cured by the Devil, Paolo Magnano came to Chiara, to ask in Lady Margherita's name to cure her quickly, because she was so poorly. Chiara told the aforementioned Paolo Magnano, "Go ahead and tell her she is about to have perfect health, and I'll even have her dancing." She could predict this, Chiara said, because of the Devil's assurances. And that is how it turned out, for Lady Margherita began to walk again, Chiara heard tell, just as she had promised. After this, since Lady Margherita did not live up to the promised agreement, Chiara, in greater despair than ever, invoked the Devil, who appeared before her in the person of a small boy in a room in the home of Ludovico Dienna. He asked her, "What do you want of me?" to which Chiara replied, "I beg you to turn back Lady Margherita Pazzani into that state she was in before you cured her, and I will keep the promise I made to you" (meaning the gift of her soul). The

Devil replied to this, "Worship me," and Chiara worshipped him, and, she said, Lady Margherita instantly reverted to her previous affliction, just as the Devil had promised.[52]

With this elaborate account, the picture would now appear to be complete. And yet in two significant particulars, the inquisitor had not succeeded in molding Chiara's confessions to his own ideological and doctrinal frame of reference. First of all, in the long recital from which we have just quoted, there is no mention of the Virgin's miraculous appearances. Now, even if Fra Bartolomeo had few doubts about their diabolical nature, in the absence of an open confession on Chiara's part, they represent a contradictory element within the trial. Second, even if her account describes invocations of the Devil and the offer of her own soul, the crowning act in the witches' saga is conspicuously absent: the sabbat and everything it implies – intercourse with the Devil, profanation of the sacraments, apostasy from the faith and from baptism. When Chiara, in fact, is asked in the session of February 15 "if she went to the sabbat and lay with the Devil and if she had made a gift of some sacrificial animal to him, and abused any sacrament at his request, and if she had denied the faith and baptism," she replies that "she had done none of these things except what she had said earlier."[53]

Nor does the vicar manage to obtain complete satisfaction even on the question of the Madonna's apparitions. When Chiara is asked "whether the Devil appeared before her in prison," she replies at first that the Devil showed himself one morning "in the body of a small boy all dressed in black," who urged her to kill herself, "since she would be burned by the inquisitor anyway." The judge presses on, wanting to know "if the Devil appeared before her in her cell at any other time." Finally, Chiara replies that "in the beginning she heard a certain voice saying to her, 'Be strong, I will see to it that they do you no harm,'" adding that "she thought it was Our Lady" and that "Our Lady appeared many times to her clothed in white vestments."[54] The witch has been vanquished, but even now, her response is not the desired one.

This needs to be stressed, because it limits what has been said about the influence exercised by the judge over the defendant's replies through his technique of interrogation and torture. Such control did exist, and it would be naive to deny its effects; nevertheless, in some cases, this one among them, it does not succeed in forcing the witch to succumb entirely to the inquisitor's will. We might say that her confession ends up constituting a compromise of sorts between herself and the judge. It contains elements introduced by the latter, which we have noted all along, and elements reflecting the local situation, such as the absence of the sabbat, resembling in this the vast majority of Modenese trials in this period. But in the end, the confession escapes the doctrinal constructions of the demonological treatises.

Chiara concludes with an expression of contrition. She asks to be forgiven and declares herself ready to accept whatever penances the judge will impose, and "although before she fell into the hands of the inquisitor, she had repeatedly invoked the Devil to cure the aforementioned women if they promised her what she desired, now, however, she says that she would not summon the Devil for any reason in the world, nor would she perform such crimes."[55] Her remorse, "however slow in coming," saves Chiara Signorini's life. The assembled judges pronounce that, inasmuch "as she is a heretic, idolater, and apostate from the faith … and according to the laws should be burned at the stake … nevertheless since she is penitent, however tardily, she is spared her life," and they decree that she must end her days in prison.[56] On February 24, 1519, they condemn her to "perpetual imprisonment, and as prison they assign to her the entire confines of the hospital Cha de Dio located in the city of Modena, to serve the poor in that hospital."[57] And thus the proceedings against Chiara Signorini come to an end.

As we suggested earlier, the trial seems to confirm, even if in a limited way, the existence of certain problems and links, which if not entirely new, have been treated somewhat generally and superficially up to now. Documents of this kind may be able to shed light on the nature of the relationship, which assumed dramatic form during the trial, between witches and inquisitors, and thereby invite further study of these sources. From this point of view, cases such as that of Chiara Signorini can have exemplary value even in their most unique aspects.

- Nature of the relationship b/t witches & Inquisitors
- Popular piety — convergence of orthodox & diabolical religion
- Limited influence exercised by judges over defendents — cannot completely mold confession to fit doctrinal belief
- Differences b/t popular beliefs & traditions and doctrinal constructions of demonological treatises — popular witchcraft vs. "learned" witchcraft

From Aby Warburg to E. H. Gombrich: A Problem of Method

The appearance in Italian of the writings of Aby Warburg almost simultaneously with a selection of lectures by Fritz Saxl and the more recent book by E. H. Gombrich, works by the two founders of the Warburg Library (later Institute) and by the present director, is no mere coincidence.[1] This concurrent outpouring of publications (to which could be added the two collections of Erwin Panofsky's essays which had appeared a few years earlier)[2] is based on a specific program of cultural *aggiornamento* aimed at providing for the nonspecialist Italian reader an acquaintance with the research interests and methods of Warburg and his school. This is an extremely meritorious plan, but several observations are immediately in order. First of all, the very concept of *aggiornamento*, or updating, has taken on a meaning that suggests the frivolous or superficial. We hurriedly make ourselves more current, and everything else remains the same. Moreover, Warburg's first writings date back to the last decade of the nineteenth century, Saxl's and Panofsky's to over a half century ago. (Gombrich, who, in a certain sense, belongs to the second generation of Warburgians, is different.) None of this, naturally, is of importance for anyone considering the intrinsic value of the methodology of these essays. But "discovering" at this late date the importance of the teachings of Warburg and of his friends and followers, as the latest intellectual fashion, seems at first to be a little ridiculous.

If we are to speak of a "Warburgian method" we must first of all agree on its essential character and clarify to what point and in what way Warburg's work has been carried on by his disciples. It is essential, therefore, as the late Gertrud Bing writes in her beautiful introduction to the Italian translation of Warburg's writings, to rediscover the true physiognomy of the scholar, who, even in his own lifetime, tried to conceal himself behind the image of his one really finished work: the library he established in Hamburg, which Saxl later transported to London at the beginning of the anti-Semitic persecutions, and eventually became the Warburg Institute.[3] Its program – the study of the continuation, interruptions, and survivals of the classical tradition – interests medievalists no less than students of antiquity or of humanism. For confirmation one need only leaf through the annual *Vorträge* of the Warburg Library, the *Journal of the Warburg and Courtauld Institutes*, or the volumes of the respective series of *Studien* and *Studies*. Such initiatives as the *Corpus Platonicum Medii Aevi* speak for themselves. Here, however, we will not be concerned with the activities of the institute, which will be taken for granted.[4] What will occupy us instead is a relatively circumscribed problem of method which was at the heart of Aby Warburg's research and reflections, and which has been revived and variously applied by his followers, namely the use of iconographic evidence as a historical source.

I

In her biographical profile of Fritz Saxl, usefully appended to the present Italian collection, Bing describes the first meeting in 1911 between the young scholar, who had just begun to interest himself in problems of astrology, and Aby Warburg. At first Saxl felt out of place amidst the luxury of Warburg's patrician Hamburg residence. But his enthusiasm grew as the latter discoursed on his research devoted to the transmission of astrological images in late antiquity:

> He [Saxl] realized that he was in the presence of a man whose experience was much deeper and more committed than his own, and his small endeavors in that field now seemed extremely superficial. But when [Saxl] said, "Perhaps I could leave all my materials with you ... you would put them to much better use than I," Warburg's reply was one that he would never forget: "Problems aren't solved by passing them on to others."[5]

This highly charged sense of the bond between Warburg's life and work strikes us the instant we approach the figure of the scholar. Retrospectively, the events in his life fall into place as if they had been predestined. The sudden decision in his youth to travel among the Pueblo Indians of New Mexico – which would appear at first to be merely a digression[6] – brought him into contact with a world of primitive and violent emotions which subsequently influenced his understanding of classical antiquity and the Renaissance.[7] His study of astrology and magic in the fifteenth and sixteenth centuries became dramatically entwined with the mental disorders which afflicted him for many years – as if the effort to master rationally these ambiguous forces, with their ties both to science and to an obscure and demoniacal world, had to exact a tragic price in real life.[8] At the conclusion of Warburg's last work to appear in his lifetime, written during his sickness, "Heidnisch-antike Weissagung in Wort und Bild zu Luthers Zeiten" (1920), he speaks, without overstatement, of "obedience to the problem which drives us, which for me is that of the influence of the ancients" (*Die Erneuerung*, 2:535). The new arrangement Bing chose for the Italian edition of Warburg's works – a chronological rather than topical one, as in the German original – permits the reader to grasp the development of this "obedience," the stubborn pursuit of the problem which beset Warburg from his youth.[9]

It seems certain that an awareness of his own work and its innovative quality came to Warburg only gradually. He read a paper to the International Congress of the History of Art held in Rome in 1912, a somewhat unusual circumstance for this scholar, who tried to avoid worldly and academic honors.[10] Before presenting to the assembled academicians one of the best works of his mature years, "Italienische Kunst und internationale Astrologie in Palazzo Schifanoia zu Ferrara," Warburg sketched a rapid outline of his life's work, beginning with his thesis on a Botticellian subject. In the attempt to respond to the now familiar question, "What was the significance of the influence of the ancient world on the art and civilization of the early Renaissance?" Warburg had focused on the portrayal of bodily movement and of the flowing hair and garments in the figures of the Florentine Quattrocento (influenced in this to some extent by A. Hildebrand's *The Problem of Form in Painting and Sculpture* [New York, 1907]).[11] The discovery that artists in this period invariably patterned themselves, in their depictions of movement, on works of classical antiquity, was further developed in subsequent research. The recurrence of "genuinely ancient superlatives in the language of mime" (*Die Erneuerung*, 2:461) gradually came to be seen by Warburg not merely as a solution to a formal problem, but as evidence of the changed emotional direction of an entire society. Concurrently, the investigation of the significance of this borrowing from antiquity on the part of Renaissance art led Warburg to modify his view of antiquity itself.

This twofold aggrandizement of the initial premise is obvious in his essay "Dürer und die italienische Antike," which appeared in 1905, twelve years after his first essay on Botticelli. Here for the first time the use of the "intensified mimicry" of the ancients became linked with the recurrence of the "formulae of pathos" (*Pathosformeln*), "genuinely ancient formulae of an intensified physical or psychic expression in the Renaissance style, which strives to portray life in motion" (*Die Erneuerung* 2:447). They were applied "wherever there was an intention to snap the bonds imposed by the Middle Ages on expression" in every sense of the term (ibid., p. 449) – though occasionally this effort ended in compromise. The Florentine merchant Francesco Sassetti, drawing up his testament in 1488 on the eve of what was expected to be a dangerous journey, introduces a reference to the goddess Fortuna, "a measure," wrote Warburg, "of the highest tension of energies," as well as a "figurative formulation of the compromise between 'medieval' faith in God and the self-reliance of Renaissance man" (ibid., p. 151).[12] From concrete fact – the representation of clothing and hair in motion – Warburg had journeyed back to the basic characteristics of Renaissance society, which he viewed, as did Burckhardt, as being in radical opposition to the Middle Ages. But the antiquity which passed on to late Quattrocento Florentine society the patrimony of its own stylized emotional formulas was not, for Warburg, the Apollonian antiquity of the classicists, but rather an age steeped in "Dionysian pathos" (ibid., p. 229, and esp. p. 176).

It is not necessary to underscore how deeply this vision of Warburg's was indebted to Nietzsche. Through the notion of *Pathosformeln*, the representations of the myths inherited from antiquity were conceived as "evidence of mental states transformed into images" in which "later generations ... sought out the permanent traces of the most profound emotions in human existence."[13] This followed the interpretation of mimicry and gestures as traces of violent passions experienced in the past, suggested to Warburg by Darwin's *Expression of the Emotions in Men and Animals* (1872).[14] These "formulae of pathos" can be considered, in Bing's view, actual figurative *topoi*. And in this connection it would be useful to explore the relationship between Warburg and E.R. Curtius, who dedicated to Warburg his greatest work, which concentrates precisely on the theme of the transmission of classical rhetorical *topoi* to medieval literature.[15]

I spoke of evidence. It is well known that Warburg used an extremely varied, in fact, eclectic, body of documentation to resolve the problem of the significance of the art of antiquity for Florentine society of the Quattrocento: testaments, mercantile letters, accounts of amorous adventures, tapestries, paintings, both famous and obscure. In Bing's words, Warburg taught that "it is possible to make human voices speak even from documents of seemingly small importance,"[16] varying documents that might have been among the "curiosities" capable of interesting only historians of everyday life. With such a method, Warburg sought to reconstruct the connection between artistic representations and the social experiences, taste, and mentality of a specific society: the Florentine in the second half of the fifteenth century. *[handwritten margin note: Warburg method]*

Bing demonstrates perceptively how Warburg, in this connection, relied in numerous instances on one of Burckhardt's key words, "life" (but, clearly, without any sort of irrational implications).[17] But in another sense Warburg did recognize his debt to the Swiss historian, acknowledging his ambition to continue the latter's work in some way. Warburg noted in his preliminary observations to the essay "Bildniskunst und Florentinisches Bürgertum" that Burckhardt in his "scholarly self-abnegation" had preferred to discuss the problem of Renaissance culture in externally disconnected units. In his *Civilization of the Renaissance* Burckhardt had presented "the psychology of the social being without reference to figurative art," and in the *Cicerone*, as the very subtitle suggested, he had given "a guide to the enjoyment of works of art." Then Warburg introduced his essay as a gloss to Burckhardt's *Beiträgen zur Kunstgeschichte von Italien* (published posthumously in 1898), in which the latter had not disdained "the labor of investigating the individual work of art and its direct place in the context of the epoch so as to interpret the ideal or practical necessities of *real life* as 'causality' " (*Die Erneuerung*, 1:94; my italics).[18] This was a sufficiently explicit project, reiterated by the concluding words of the already cited "Heidnisch-antike Weissagung in Wort und Bild zu Luthers Zeiten," in which Warburg had expressed hope for a "kulturwissenschaftliche Bildgeschichte" (ibid., 2:535).

Eight years earlier he had lamented that the history of art had not yet succeeded "in putting its own material at the disposal of the 'historical psychology of human expression,' which, in truth, has not yet been written" (ibid., 478).[19] This last sentence is lodged in a context in which Warburg stresses the importance of "iconology" as an antidote to the opposite dangers of a facile determinism and of an irrational exaltation of genius.[20] Even so, it cannot be said that Warburg's method spent itself in iconographic analysis, nor that this approach held a special place in his eyes. The range of his interests was broader. As Bing writes, the problems which concerned Warburg were above all "the function of artistic creation in the history of a civilization [and the] variable relation that exists between artistic expression and the spoken language. All the other themes which are considered characteristic of his research, such as his interest in the content of the representations, his fascination for the survival of antiquity, were not so much actual objectives in themselves, as a means of attaining that end."[21]

II

Warburg's work thus appears to us, on the one hand, externally fragmentary and unfinished,[22] on the other, aside from occasional thematic disunity, organically connected to a nucleus of specific problems. These twin characteristics probably reflected two opposed tendencies. As Saxl remarked, "Warburg was a man of a very imaginative and emotional type, in whom, historical imagination, nourished by concrete historical experience, always struggled against an ardent desire for philosophical simplification."[23] In any case, it was tempting to systematize the presuppositions which had inspired Warburg's concrete, specific research (we know that his favorite saying was "God is in the detail"). The attempt was made by one of the scholars who gathered around Warburg and the library he had founded, namely Edgar Wind, in his "Warburgs Begriff der Kulturwissenschaft und seine Bedeutung für die Aesthetik" (1931) and in the introduction to volume 1 of *Kulturwissenschaftliche Bibliographie zum Nachleben der Antike: 1931* (1934), published under the auspices of the Warburg Library.[24] These systematic statements (at one point a *Begriffssystem* of Warburg's is discussed)[25] without doubt misrepresented the issue. Wind, who was younger by a generation, described the significance of Warburg's work in the light of different interests and in a changed cultural climate. Wind's essays should be viewed not as historiographical assessments, or guides to a critically precise reading of Warburg's writings, but as programmatic statements by an authoritative spokesman of the Warburg Library in the years immediately following the death of its founder.

Wind contrasts Warburg's work and the concept of "culture" that underlines it to two well-defined positions: on the one hand, the predispositions, associated with such dissimilar names as Riegl and Wölfflin, who proposed to rupture every connection between the history of art and the history of culture;[26] on the other,

Geistesgeschichte, as understood by Dilthey. In confronting the attempts to establish an "autonomous" history of art, Wind emphasizes the concept of culture as a unified entity which Warburg had drawn from Burckhardt: a "culture" understood almost in an anthropological sense, in which superstitions and manual activities had their place alongside art, literature, philosophy, and science. This unity (*Gesamtheit*) of the various aspects of cultural life – artistic, religious, political – had also played a prominent role both in Dilthey's theoretical essays and in his concrete research. But Wind observed, in the other side of his argument, that in Dilthey this unity is an *a priori* assumption, which runs the risk, therefore, of hypostatizing abstract concepts of the world and of life.

In this emphasis on the concreteness of research, in this polemic against any sort of prefabricated parallelism, Wind had undoubtedly grasped a specific and significant aspect of Warburg's teaching, but it was one which he sought to combine with a philosophy of culture strongly influenced by Ernst Cassirer.[27] The stress on the importance of the symbol, which in Warburg's own work was explicitly linked to a suggestion of F. T. Vischer's, in Wind's formulation seems to be connected instead to Cassirer's great *Philosophie der symbolischen Formen*, which Cassirer had begun partly under the direct stimulus of the material gathered and organized by Warburg.[28]

Along with Wind's attempts to systematize Warburg's theoretical and conceptual assumptions, others, such as Fritz Saxl, focused instead on Warburg's more concrete findings. Saxl's long article "Rinascimento dell'antichità: Studien zu den Arbeiten A. Warburg's" is in fact a systematic exposition, here and there enriched by new data, of Warburg's own works.[29] Their internal unity certainly did not escape Saxl; but he discerned, in addition to a uniform conception and methodology, a profound thematic coherence. According to Saxl, one finds at the core of these writings the man of the early Renaissance, viewed as a "type" (*Typus*), in his polarities and contradictions so well illustrated by Warburg: contradictions between Christianity and paganism, God and Fortune, naturalism "alla franzese" and idealized style in the ancient mode, and so forth. Saxl identified the principal sources of inspiration underlying Warburg's research in the brief yet rich profile which opens the first volume of the Warburg Library *Vorträge*.[30] Three names are mentioned: Burckhardt (on whom Wind had especially dwelt), Nietzsche, and Usener. The first was chosen for his interpretation of the Renaissance and his individualizing concept of historiography; the second for his accentuation of the Dionysian aspect in antiquity; the third for approaching the history of religions in the context of the struggle between East and West, between Alexandria and Athens, between tyranny and liberty.

Though Saxl in these writings limited himself basically to a preliminary appraisal of Warburg's scholarly activity, the brilliant comprehensive essay prepared in collaboration with Erwin Panofsky, "Classical Mythology in Mediaeval Art" (1933), surpassed them in every sense. A product of the already tested and exemplary cooperation between two mutually complementary scholars, this article was retrospectively considered by Panofsky, with a touch of gentle self-irony, one of the first positive fruits of the forced transplanting of German art historians to American soil.[31] The necessity of writing in a language different from one's own, and especially in a language as precise and unequivocal as English, and for a public such as the American, which was not limited to specialists, gave the impetus, Panofsky writes, "to write books on whole masters or whole periods instead of – or besides – writing a dozen specialized articles; and dared to deal with, say, the problem of classical mythology in mediaeval art in its entirety instead of – or besides – investigating only the transformations of Hercules or Venus."[32] But along with the unusual capacity for synthesis and the wealth of documentation in this article, one should also note its conclusions, which explicitly acknowledge once again the debt to Warburg and his methods, almost as if its purpose had been to introduce the one with the other to a learned audience across the Atlantic. The classical heritage, transmitted and distorted by many intermediaries (oriental, among others) in the course of the Middle Ages, is "reborn," finally, in the fifteenth and sixteenth centuries. But what is the meaning of this "renaissance"? Is it one of those revivals, the authors ask, which (harking back to a Burckhardtian theme later developed, particularly by Panofsky) periodically characterized the civilization of Western Europe? Warburg had already observed that the adoption of the *Pathosformeln* of antiquity by Renaissance artists implied a break not only with art, but with the medieval mind as a whole.[33]

Panofsky and Saxl carry this intuitive statement further: the rediscovery of what was ancient, particularly the "forms" of classical antiquity, implies specific awareness of the "intellectual distance between the present and the past," in short, "the discovery of the modern 'historical system,' " a phenomenon Panofsky juxtaposes with the Renaissance discovery of linear perspective, which approaches scientifically the problem of the "distance between the eye and the object."[34] Starting from a problem in art history – the rediscovery of the forms of classical art reconstructed in the specific domain of the representation of the ancient gods – Panofsky and Saxl succeed in posing the general historical problem of the significance of the Renaissance. They see the period as characterized by its discovery of the historical dimension and by its new relationship with classical antiquity, so different from that of the medieval world.[35] This interpretation of the Renaissance has many points in common with one proposed in Italy by Eugenio Garin in a different context (the importance of Florentine civic humanism, its exaltation of the active life, etc.).[36] In any case, it hinges significantly on the Warburgian theme of the *Pathosformeln*, so much more useful as the typology of Renaissance man, to which Saxl had referred, not too appropriately, in the essay mentioned above, "Rinascimento dell'antichità."

III

I have mentioned works by Saxl which took up themes and methods from Aby Warburg's research. Some of the lectures Saxl gave in England to publicize the programs and goals of the Warburg Institute have been translated into Italian and published with a lengthy introduction by Garin in which he attempts to situate historically the activity of scholars, principally those following in Warburg's footsteps, such as Saxl and Panofsky. This search for a historical context, though useful in itself, is preceded by a brief but unconvincing glance at the success of this type of research in Italy.[37] Even less persuasive, because of its extremely diffuse nature, is the connection Garin suggests between the activity of the Warburg circle and the state of European culture at the turn of the century.[38] What characterizes both, according to Garin (echoing Cassirer), is the crisis experienced by general schools of philosophy owing to the specific, concrete research carried out in the individual "humane sciences."[39] Consequently, in outlining "what was most important in the work of Panofsky and Saxl – namely the method and type of research" (it seems a slight exaggeration to say at the same time that "on the whole it had been virtually ignored, at least by the majority") – Garin singles out the following points: philological concreteness and precision; objectivity and the accompanying rejection of theoretical presuppositions and abstract hypothetical generalizations; and interdisciplinary approaches, the shattering of academic compartments, or those simply dictated by tradition. These were considered, along with the many important research interests discovered or pursued in greater depth by these scholars, the essential characteristics of the "Warburg" method which guaranteed its fruitfulness and exemplary quality.

All this is undeniable; but this great scholarly tradition perhaps deserves a somewhat less vague appreciation. The fact that Gertrud Bing, in presenting, or representing, Warburg's work to the Italian public, felt compelled to ask herself what the common threads were in those writings which for almost half a century have claimed descent from Warburg, and even what the "Warburg method" actually is, leads one to suppose that the problem is more complex than it may at first appear.[40] We shall see later that these methodological approaches are anything but obvious. Notwithstanding their undoubted productiveness, they raise a series of difficulties that have been noted and discussed, above all by the members of the Warburg équipe itself. What we should realize about Saxl – whose work Garin considers the most consistent embodiment of the Warburg method, and contrasts a bit superficially with Panofsky, whom he apparently considered more the "philosopher" and theorizer – is his complexity as a scholar.[41] It is quite impossible to reduce Saxl to the rather abstract stereotype of the impeccable philologist, all engrossed in "things" and laboring, without hesitation or regrets, in the task of historical reconstruction.[42] This complexity, which I shall attempt to illustrate in detail, is another indication of the vagueness of the Warburgian method as proposed by Garin.

Let's begin with Saxl's famous essay, "Veritas filia Temporis," which Garin, toward the end of his introduction, pursuing a remark made by Saxl himself, compares to Giovanni Gentile's essay with the same title.[43] Saxl had gently reproved Gentile for having studied the later history of the subject within a purely philosophical context, without regard for its "cultural, religious, and political" implications. Garin repeats this observation and comments, "It was the underlining, not without a trace of irony, of a different way of making – and of conceiving – history."[44] In other words, on the one hand we have the philosopher who sees only ideas, outside the milieu which generates them; on the other, the historian-philologist, who does not superimpose theory over facts, but immerses himself in them, etc. But things are not quite that simple.

Saxl shows how the motto "Veritas filia Temporis," first cited by Aulus Gellius (although the theme was widespread in the classical tradition), had been used from the early decades of the sixteenth century in different contexts, political, moral (with the passing of time the calumny rife in the courts gives way to truth), and religious, even controversialist (time causes true religion to emerge – Protestant or Catholic, depending on who is employing the motto). But what is the purpose, Saxl asks himself, of harking back to a classical myth, and to the motto and images connected to it, in a context that is polemical, if not downright personally vindictive?[45] The response must be searched for in an "essential characteristic of Renaissance mentality." Such men as the printer Marcolino of Forlì – who was the first to utilize a typographic device inspired by the myth of Truth brought into the light by Time, and decorated by the apposite motto – or Aretino, who probably was the creator of that insignia, saw everyday problems *sub specie aeternitatis*. Both appealed to classical metaphors, inasmuch as they considered their own actions to belong to the world of the classical and the universal, which could find full expression only in an ancient myth. Evidently, Saxl was returning, without mentioning them explicitly, to themes and questions central to Warburg's work: what did classical antiquity mean to Renaissance men? Granted, Saxl does not place any emphasis, as Warburg had, on the "Dionysian" aspect of antiquity (the *Pathosformeln* as a proper expression of emotional states strained to the limit). Here the accent is shifted to what we could call for simplicity's sake the "Apollonian" element. Saxl speaks of the transfiguration of the daily element *sub specie aeternitatis*, of "dignity," of universality.[46]

This is not an accidental shift. Saxl emphasized in the opening essay to the series of Warburg Library *Vorträge* cited earlier that Aby Warburg had not written the history of the rebirth of the Apollonian moment – of the freeing of the West from oriental bondage (according to an antithesis derived from Usener). Saxl implied that the importance of the ancient Dionysian element in the Renaissance had been accentuated a little too unilaterally by Warburg (not by chance, I might add).[47] Similarly, even while using the notion of *Pathosformeln* to explain the transmission of the images of antiquity, Saxl tends to systematically purify it of its "Dionysian" and, in the final analysis, historico-religious implications.[48]

In any case, returning to the essay "Veritas filia Temporis," the hidden dependence on Warburgian themes emerges negatively, so to speak, even in the final section in which the philosophers appear, which contains the remark directed at Gentile's article. The reader might expect a study of figurative expressions – if there were such – in Bruno's and later in Bacon's thought; their conclusions had been that the moderns, thanks to greater experience, were closer to the truth of the ancients. ("Recte enim Veritas Temporis filia dicitur, non Authoritatis," Francis Bacon said.)[49] But Saxl observes, almost apologetically: "It is significant that the philosophers' interpretation of the phrase found no appropriate expression in the arts as long as significant artists were themselves engaged upon it. Abstract theories are the last to be illustrated." And with a certain impatience he analyzes an extremely interesting document which he had discovered: an engraving (doubtless stiff and academic from a formal point of view) by "a certain" Bernard Picart, dated 1707, which seems a virtual comment to the passage of Malebranche cited by Gentile in his essay.[50] Time dispels the clouds from the resplendent figure of Truth, whose rays illuminate obliquely the company of ancient philosophers: Plato, Aristotle, and Zeno move from shadow to light, preceded, in fact guided, by Descartes, who advances hand in hand with Philosophy, to the brilliance of Truth. But for Saxl this engraving, so specifically conceived, so lacking in spontaneity, reveals that we are finally at the end of the episode he has reconstructed; and he observes that this is not "the representation of an idea but the illustration of a theory."[51] This is the English translation: I do not know exactly how the German text reads. Perhaps in the original the Platonizing accent of that "idea" set against (abstract) theory was stated with greater subtlety. In any case, the sense is clear. What weighs on Saxl, more than the historical significance of this new representation of ties between Truth and Time, is the need to emphasize that unlike the majority of works analyzed to that day, born in response "to the demands of some specific, genuine human situation," whether political, religious, or whatever, and therefore capable of affecting and involving the viewer, Picart's engraving is "too wise, too impartial, too abstract, remote and knowing."

It would be superficial to conclude that here historico-cultural and aesthetic judgments do not coincide. To be sure, not even the mark of the Forlì printer Marcolino, to mention only one, was considered a great work of art by Saxl. Rather, in this sharp antithesis which Saxl discovers between the "expression" of a human situation and the "illustration" of pure theory can be discerned the barely audible echo of the Warburgian concept of *Pathosformeln*: representations of myths left behind by antiquity "as evidence of mental states transformed into images [in which] later generations ... sought out the permanent traces of the most profound emotions in human existence."[52] But what matters to Saxl above all else is the problem of the ancient myth of Truth revealed by Time: when representations of it take on extraneous, purely illustrative elements, its interest is diminished or at least greatly weakened. And this is subsequently confirmed in the concluding page of his essay. Viewing an English variant of Picart's engraving, wholly resembling it except for the figure of the protagonist – who is no longer Descartes but Newton – Saxl unburdens himself in a curious, moralistic outburst: "a page from the history of human folly ... English parody of Picart's print ... silly enterprise of the English copyist."[53] And indeed, the substitution of Newton for Descartes as the hero of the Truth revealed by Time, even if motivated by a sentiment of national pride, could not be a negligible document for a historian of culture.

Saxl's research thus appears dictated by a motif which had been crucial for Warburg, namely, the significance of classical antiquity, its myths and representations, for Renaissance men. And we have seen how for Warburg this theme was anything but extraneous to allusions by the "philosophers" (Nietzsche, to begin with!). As for Saxl, even his philology can never be said to be destitute of "presuppositions." And it is significant as well as surprising that in delineating the figure of Saxl as a "pure" historian, Garin should have virtually ignored the great and tormented figure of Aby Warburg – to whom Saxl was so deeply and contradictorily linked.[54]

IV

In a passage outlining his program, Warburg held up the example of Burckhardt, appealing for a broader and freer history of art than the traditional academic form – a history of art directed towards *Kulturwissenschaft*. He rejected any sort of artistic interpretation that was "impressionistic" or aestheticizing. Parenthetically, it is precisely this approach that permits persons who are not art historians to speak, even if only marginally and as outsiders, about the activity of these scholars. As C.G. Heise correctly observed, there was a twofold goal to Warburg's research: on the one hand, he wanted to analyze works of art in the light of historical evidence, of whatever type and on whatever level, so as to be able to explain their origins and significance; on the other, art work itself, and figurative representations in general, had to be interpreted as sources in their own right in the task of historical reconstruction.[55] These are two distinct objectives, even if they are, as we shall see ever more clearly, reciprocally connected.

Let me immediately point out that in this approach there was no place for aesthetic appreciation. Warburg's relative indifference to it is confirmed by persons who were close to him and cannot be doubted.[56] His truest interests lay elsewhere. On a general, methodological level, however, it is a different story. Obviously, to explain the allusions concealed in a painting (if they are there), to indicate its connections to a literary text (if they exist), and to investigate (where one can) its patrons, their social standing and if possible even their artistic tastes, contributes to our understanding and further facilitates the precise assessment of a work of art. Benedetto Croce, to take an illustrious example, asserted in connection with a book issuing from the circle of the Warburg Institute, that the discovery of mythological traces in a Renaissance painting is irrelevant as far as aesthetic enjoyment is concerned, since they would consist in any case of "frozen" allegories, of unpoetical or nonpoetical accretions.[57] In saying this he turned his back on a real historical problem for the sake of his definition of allegory. It was his own formulation, instead, which needed to be reexamined and criticized in the light of the historical facts he could not succeed in explaining. Even if this preliminary phase of interpreting and deciphering assists the spectator to assume an appropriate approach to a painting, it is nevertheless not the same as purely aesthetic appreciation. A painting may be important for the historian, as well as for the student of iconography, because it provides evidence of specific cultural relationships, while being negligible from the aesthetic point of view.[58] We shall return to this problem later.

Now let us examine the other objective Warburg set for himself in his research, namely, the comprehension of "a historical situation on the basis of artistic and documentary sources."[59] How attainable is this, and what is the possible relationship between these two types of sources? Arnaldo Momigliano noted rightly that in comparison with the broader range of Warburg's interests and the greater varieties of his approaches, Saxl's work tends to lean toward iconographic analysis, to the point of turning it into a tool of general historical research.[60] In this regard we might limit ourselves to only two of the works now collected in the Italian edition. Saxl's deciphering of the "program" concealed in the cycle of frescoes of the Farnesina has as its object the understanding of a general historical problem, that is, the importance of astrological beliefs in the Cinquecento, concretely exemplified in the person of the great Sienese merchant Agostino Chigi. Similarly, the remarkable solution to the puzzle of the frescoes and decorations in the Borgia Apartment, hinging on the disconcerting figure of the bull, first identified as the animal totem of the Borgia family and then directly with Alexander VI himself, is an unusually eloquent contribution not only to the artistic but also to the religious and political history of the time.[61] In these writings Saxl is applying a vast erudition which ignores compartmentalization of any sort: political history, Egyptology, sixteenth-century mythography are summoned to deal with problems which are always circumscribed and specific, but which, once resolved, lead to a broader context which might also be called cultural history (as long as the term does not evoke a pale and abstract *Geistesgeschichte*).[62] But what occurs when the instrument of iconographic analysis is missing?

We can try to answer on the basis of some of Saxl's writings not included in the Laterza collection, which contains only lectures dealing with Italian subjects. Let us begin with "Holbein and the Reformation," the English translation of a paper first presented in Hamburg in 1925.[63] From the outset Saxl states his purpose with the utmost precision. He is seeking "to approach a historical problem with the means of the history of art," using as sources engravings and paintings, viewed, however, to the greatest possible extent, independently of their qualities as works of art. On the other hand, he is well aware – and this needs to be noted – that rational discourse tends to harden and generalize the subtleties of pictorial language.[64] The historical problem which Saxl sets out to resolve is that of Holbein's piety. A Basel document of 1530 informs us of the painter's hope that Protestantism would clarify certain doubts that he had about the Eucharist.[65] On the other hand, two pre-1526 woodcuts present us with a Holbein who is already a supporter of the Reformation. In both instances the iconographic evidence leaves no doubt: in the first, we see Christ drawing to himself the humble and the poor, while on the opposite side traditional mediators – the pope, monks, such philosophers as Plato and Aristotle – are tumbling into a deep crevice. In the second, the polemic concerning the mediation between man and God offered by the Roman church is presented with similar vigor: in contrast to Leo X, who is surrounded by monks selling indulgences, are three figures immersed in prayer – David, Manasseh, and a poor man in tattered clothing – to whom God in the heavens reveals himself with a solemn gesture. Undoubtedly, these are documents of anti-Roman propaganda. But, Saxl asks himself, do they "reflect the spirit of Luther?" The loss of the captions which had originally accompanied these cuts compels him to undertake an "indirect" approach to the question.[66] He compares Holbein's two works to the celebrated engraving, discussed by Luther, of the monstrous calf in the likeness of a monk. According to Saxl, both engraving and comment testify to a "coarseness" which is totally absent from Holbein's woodcuts, and even contrary to their spirit. Holbein does not depict monsters, but "the clear and regular forms of the organic world ...; he transforms supernatural brilliance into natural light." This suggests that the artist was not a Lutheran, a hypothesis which Saxl sees confirmed by another woodcut, representing the meditating figure of Isaiah and Luther's famous words at the Diet of Worms. Holbein's Isaiah "undoubtedly reflects a new piety," but Erasmian, not Lutheran in form.[67]

However, the method by which Saxl reaches this first conclusion is not wholly convincing. It is always risky to compare a woodcut with a verbal statement: an image is inevitably more ambiguous, open to several interpretations.[68] And its nuances, as Saxl himself cautioned, are not transferable to a rational, articulate plane except at the cost of a certain distortion (even though we are dealing with that particular rationality which defines two different religious positions). On the other hand, a comparison of Holbein's two anti-Roman woodcuts with the engraving representing the calf-monk monster and Luther's comment is not much more helpful.[69] This lampoon, in the tradition of the popular prints of the day which remarked upon marvels and monsters set in an astrological-prophetic key, had been suggested to Luther by a hostile prophecy delivered against him by the astrologer to the Margrave George of Brandenburg, who, in turn, took it from the birth of a freak in 1522 at Waltersdorf, a town near Freiberg.[70] As a matter of fact, we know, thanks to Aby Warburg's own research, that Luther, even while rejecting astrological beliefs, admitted the genuineness of prophecies associated with *monstra* or miraculous portents (*Die Erneuerung*, 2:487-558). And this explains the seriousness with which he composed in an eschatological context his commentary to the engraving. But the need, overlooked by Saxl, to reply to an unfavorable prophecy must have counted for something in Luther's decision to take the field in this propaganda battle. Moreover, why limit the comparison to one, however important, but also in some ways exceptional, piece of evidence, such as this engraving? A parallel examination of Holbein's two woodcuts and, for example, the series *Passional Christi und Antichristi*, which had an accompanying commentary probably inspired by Luther himself and which at least can be considered a typical example of Lutheran propaganda,[71] obviously would have yielded different results. Cranach's *Passional*, on the whole, displays neither "coarseness" nor monstrosities interpreted as portents. To consider these elements typically Lutheran, as Saxl does, seems a bit too facile and hurried, given that here specific psychological traits of the man Luther ("coarseness") are not at issue, but rather, clearly circumscribed religious positions, engaged from a determinate moment on in a specific controversy (Erasmianism, Lutheranism). In conclusion, the comparison between Holbein's two woodcuts and the engraving of the monk-calf proposed by Saxl ends up being a little too absolute to be really convincing.

But the identification of Holbein's religious position as Erasmian is correct, and the assurance with which Saxl interprets these considerably ambiguous pieces of evidence is easily explained. First of all, we have the celebrated Basel copy of the *Praise of Folly* decorated in the margins with pen and ink drawings by the young Holbein.[72] Second, we have the woodcut dated 1522, generally attributed to Holbein, in which Luther is portrayed as a *Hercules Germanicus* – in other words, clothed in a lion's skin and about to cudgel with a club Aristotle, Saint Thomas, Ockham, and others, while a rope hangs from his nose to which the pope is tied. Granted, Saxl admits, this image appears to express, in its "unadorned crudeness," something of the typically Lutheran *atrocitas*. It may "appear" so, but the image and the comment in Latin verses characteristically differ. The latter invites the reader not to a struggle, but simply to interior purification; and it is significant that such a partisan of the Reformation as Ulrich Hugwald, in the course of sending the manifesto to a friend, should brand it with words of fire, calling it an instrument of Erasmian propaganda, supposing that Erasmus himself had been its author.[73]

I have dwelt on Saxl's procedure in his essay because it illustrates in a sense the risks connected with such a method, even when this method is employed by as great a scholar as Saxl. He did not attain the goal he had set for himself: "to approach a historical problem with the means of the history of art." The key to interpretation is not the works of art themselves (even if considered apart from their aesthetic value) but the captions to the *Hercules Germanicus*. These words of commentary, as well as Hugwald's violent reaction to them, make it clear that Holbein's woodcuts are expressions of Erasmianism. In the absence of unambiguous iconographic evidence (since from the iconographic point of view they could be seen as only vaguely anti-Roman), they furnish, at best, confirmation of an interpretation reached by other means; consequently, since they come first in the exposition, the analysis of the figures does not seem very convincing. For Saxl's narrative to be really persuasive, its order would have to be reversed.

The Holbein essay dates from 1925; "Dürer and the Reformation" from 1948, the last year of Saxl's life. And it is noteworthy that at the beginning of the Dürer piece, he should describe the goals of his research in terms virtually identical to his words of twenty years before: woodcuts, propaganda broadsides, and the pamphlets of the Reformation period are not great works of art but furnish us a "mirror" of the attitudes of the day.[74] On the other hand, the captions, the texts which accompany these representations, serve only as "additional evidence." Saxl proposes to apply the same method to the work of a great artist, Dürer. Here, too, we possess that secondary, "additional" documentation consisting of Dürer's journal notes; even in this essay such apparently auxiliary sources in fact play a key role in Saxl's interpretation.

In the years about 1514, Dürer depicts, in a dramatic and restless style, such themes from classical mythology as the abduction of Proserpina, or themes from the Gospels such as Christ's agony on the Mount of Olives. What is Saxl's comment? "We are nearing the crisis in Dürer's life."[75] Somewhat later his style changes, and a Madonna and child dated 1518 reveals a Dürer full of serenity and grace. But Saxl does not pause over this interlude; he dwells, rather, on the engravings from the immediately subsequent period, 1519-21. We know that in 1519 Dürer espoused Lutheran doctrines, and in his letters alluded to the reformer in terms of warm support.[76] Saxl promptly perceives the reflection of this religious turning point in Dürer's work. In an engraving of 1520 the Madonna and child are represented immobile, with a dramatic darkened sky as background: "This change in Dürer's style takes place in the year of his contact with Luther." This is a modest statement which could almost make one think it might have been coincidence rather than a true connection between the two events. But a little later, in describing a drawing from 1521 representing Christ on the Mount of Olives, Saxl becomes more explicit. The scene is a gloomy one, the landscape deserted, and the body of Christ prostrated on the ground forms a cross: "The drawing expresses Dürer's mood: salvation lies in complete submission to faith. The crisis has passed and the drawing has perfect lucidity, fullness and strength."[77]

The object of Saxl's analysis is evident: to free himself from the toils of a purely formalistic "reading," and to consider the individual work of art as a complex and active reaction (obviously *sui generis*) to the events of contemporary history. Perhaps so, but again, quite apart from the results obtained here, Saxl's method is not convincing.[78] It is only too clear that to read these images, whether they are disturbing or peaceful, as alternate episodes in Dürer's religious journey is arbitrary, and is made legitimate only by the presence or absence of other sorts of documents, introduced surreptitiously. When documents do exist, the images are read in a psychological and biographical key; when they do not, or are not persuasive enough, there is a type of "reading" which is more descriptive and less interpretative. Carried to the extreme, there is a risk of oversimplification in this method which Saxl probably would never have admitted: a broken and agitated style translates to religious crisis in progress; a dramatic but vigorous style indicates religious crisis surpassed; and so forth.

The mishaps that can result from such a "physiognomic"[79] reading of artistic documents are clear enough. The historian reads into them *what he has already learned* by other means,[80] or what he believes he knows, and wants to "demonstrate." The latter is not the case with Saxl; but the hazards implicit in this approach are evident just the same. As long as the historian searches for mere factual data in seals, medals, and frescoes, he faces relatively simple problems.[81] But when modern historiography attempts (perhaps influenced by Marc Bloch and his *Métier d'historien*)[82] to wrench "involuntary" evidence of mentalities and states of mind from a reluctant past, the risk of reaching the notorious "circular" argumentation through a "physiognomic" reading of the figurative evidence is thereby multiplied. The more or less conscious basis of this approach, naturally, is the conviction that works of art, in a broad sense, furnish a mine of firsthand information that can explicate, *without intermediaries*, the mentality and emotive life of a distant age (discussed later in this essay).

The question of the inevitable "circularity" of interpretation, both in the humanities and the natural sciences, has been dealt with discerningly and with a certain inclination for the paradoxical by Edgar Wind, in an essay later taken up and carried further by Erwin

Panofsky. Generally speaking, the dialectic inherent in historical documents is such that "the information which one tries to gain with the help of the document ought to be presupposed for its adequate understanding." But it is also true, as Panofsky emphasizes, that this is not a vicious circle, since "every discovery of an unknown historical fact, and every new interpretation of a known one, will either "fit in" with the prevalent general conception, and thereby corroborate and enrich it, or else it will entail a subtle, or even a fundamental change in the prevalent general conception, and thereby throw new light on all that has been known before."[83] But what follows when this interrelationship ceases? The "circularity" then indeed becomes a vicious circle: Holbein's Erasmianism or the stages in Dürer's religious crisis, known through documentary evidence, are presupposed tacitly and thus "demonstrated" by means of analysis of the figurative evidence.[84] Obviously, an investigation of this sort can, and possibly must, use evidence of another type – for example, Hugwald's reactions to the *Hercules Germanicus*, or Dürer's diaries. The problem is to see what in these cases is the relationship between "monuments" and "documents," between the "primary" and "secondary" material.[85]

In conclusion, that ability to ascend from iconographic data to general historical understanding, which is what made great such essays as those on the Farnesina or on the Borgia Apartment, and so many others, is missing when the iconographic data is indifferent or marginal, and stylistic considerations assume primary importance. And in mentioning "style" I am omitting from consideration any sort of problem of aesthetic appreciation. For anyone desiring to consider works of art, and figurative evidence in general, as a *sui generis* historical source, iconographic analysis may often prove to be insufficient. The problem then becomes one of the relationship between iconographic and stylistic data, and of the relevance of the latter for the purpose of general historical research. For several decades these problems were central to the interests of Erwin Panofsky, a scholar who was, as is well known, Saxl's great friend and collaborator.

V

The person and work of Panofsky would require a complex discussion.[86] Here, I shall limit myself to examining briefly, in connection with what has been said thus far, the significance of his distinctions between iconography and iconology. I shall concentrate intentionally on problems where answers are still lacking, rather than on those which he has effectively resolved.

We know that for Aby Warburg iconographic research was but one of the possible approaches to the scholarly questions which concerned him. In some ways, for Warburg, purely iconographic research made no sense. The choice of specific themes – the death of Orpheus, for example – was as important for the reconstruction of the mentality of Quattrocento society as the style adopted. The same concept of *Pathosformeln* – stylistic formulae taken from antiquity, which were imposed, so to speak, by particularly emotive subjects and situations – bound form and content closely together in the process of analysis.

This connection, which in Warburg's writings is never closely scrutinized or called into question, was carried further by Panofsky in debating Wölfflin's claim that purely formal descriptions of figurative works of art can be provided. Building on observations in the preface to *Hercules am Scheidewege* (1930), Panofsky demonstrated in an essay appearing two years later, "Zum Problem der Beschreibung und Inhaltsdeutung von Werken der bildenden Kunst," that even in the most elementary description of a painting, data referring to form and content are inextricably united.[87] In suggesting the impossibility of "purely formal" description, Panofsky was touching upon a subject, namely that of the *ambiguity* of any representation, which we shall encounter, in totally different connections, at the heart of E. H. Gombrich's scholarly interests.[88] But what really concerned Panofsky was something else: finding the theoretical justification for his own iconographic research. For this purpose, he distinguishes, in Grünewald's *Resurrection*, a "pre-iconographic" stratum ("a man who rises up in the air, his hands and feet perforated") referring to pure experiences of the senses; an iconographic stratum referring to specific literary knowledge (in this case the corresponding passages from the Gospels); and another stratum, the highest, defined as a "region of the perception of reality" (*Region des "Wesenssinns"*). Later, implicitly following suggestions made by G. J. Hoogewerff, he will call the third the "iconological" stratum.[89] Panofsky demonstrates convincingly that on each of these levels description presupposes interpretation: even at the most elementary and immediate level, the ability to describe the Christ of Grünewald as "a man half-way suspended" presupposes the recognition of determinate stylistic points of reference. (Conversely, in a medieval

[Handwritten margin notes: "Panofsky / Three levels! / Phenomenal (pre-iconographic) / significance (iconographic) / Perception of reality (iconological)"]

miniature a figure in an empty space might not be in any way an allusion to a violation of the laws of nature.) For the first two strata – the "phenomenal" or pre-iconographic, and that of the significance, or iconographic – the question of interpretation does not cause problems. But it is a different story with regard to the third level, that of the "perception of reality," or the iconological one, which presupposes the first two, and in a certain sense is their fulfillment. Panofsky writes:

> At the basis of artistic production, beyond its phenomenal sense and its sense of significance, there is a final and essential content: the involuntary and unconscious self-revelation of a basic attitude towards the world, which is characteristic, in equal measure, of the creator as individual, of the single epoch, of a single people, of a single cultural community. [Consequently,] the highest duty of interpretation is to penetrate this final stratum of the "essential meaning" [*Wesenssinn*]. The true and proper objective will have been achieved when it succeeds in grasping and drawing attention to the totality of the moments of its emanation (and thus not only the objective and iconographic moment, but also such purely "formal" factors as the distribution of light and shadows, the articulation of surfaces, even the way the brush, the putty knife, or the burin are used) as "documents" of the unitary sense of the conception of the world contained in the work.[90]

With these considerations, Panofsky was summing up the essence of earlier reflections, especially where Wölfflin and Riegl were concerned. Regarding Wölfflin's notions of the history of art as the history of "seeing," and the relative juxtapositions ("plastic" versus "linear," etc.), Panofsky had objected that such antitheses "derive from a necessity of expression: from a will for form [*Gestaltungs-Willen*] which in a certain sense pervades an entire epoch and is founded on an identical fundamental attitude of the spirit, not of the eye."[91] But how was this "will for form" to be understood? Was it, perhaps, something analogous to Riegl's "artistic volition" (*Kunstwollen*)? In taking a position in regard to this latter concept Panofsky clarified (but in some sense complicated) what his own statement implied. The *Kunstwollen* should not be understood to refer to an individual psychological reality. The artist's intentions, when they are known to us, do not explain the work of art, but rather constitute a "phenomenon parallel" to it; nor should artistic volition be applied to the psychology of a given epoch: "Artistic volition cannot be anything except (and not for us, but objectively) what 'lies' in the artistic phenomenon as its ultimate meaning. With this as a starting point, the characteristics of form and content in the work of art can not only be summed up conceptually but can also be explained on the basis of the history of meaning."[92] These words, written in 1920, refer us specifically to the previously mentioned work published in 1932, "Zum Problem der Beschreibung," and to its revision in the preface of *Studies in Iconology* (1939).

This continuity does not mean that there are no changes or innovations. There are even some very important ones. In the preface to the *Studies*, we see a general loosening and simplification of the terminology: along with the term *iconology*, which replaced the interpretation of "meaning of reality," a "history of *cultural symptoms or symbols* in general" emerges, owing to Cassirer's influence, as a framework or "corrective" for the iconological interpretation.[93] Nevertheless, the continuity is extremely significant. During his American period Panofsky ceased to occupy himself with art theory and allowed the dichotomy to lapse between "history of (immanent) meaning" (successively, in 1932, "interpretation of the meaning of reality," and in 1939, "iconology") and the history of art, forcefully affirmed in his 1920 essay "Kunstwollen."[94] Nevertheless, there is no doubt that even in the mature statements and concrete research contained in his Introduction to the *Studies*, there remains a trace of that transcendental philosophy of art which permeates the theoretical writings of the German period.[95]

But what is most interesting is the manner in which Panofsky attempted to accomplish that admittedly grandiose program announced in the essay "Zum Problem der Beschreibung." The first clue is furnished by the essays collected in *Studies in Iconology*, which are prefaced by a comprehensive exposition of the objectives of the iconological method, as distinct from the iconographic. The *Studies* have exercised an enormous influence on the American art world, actually creating a true "iconological" fashion. Criticism raised against this fashion justifiably has cautioned against an arbitrary extension of the iconographic method. (Even in the sixteenth century, paintings were being produced which can be defined as "genre," for which research into meaning or mythological allusions or any other aspect is obviously out of place.) But even these critics have not challenged the validity of the method itself, nor of its strictly iconological implications.[96] But it was Panofsky himself who ended up dedicating himself preeminently to iconographic research, frequently overlooking that unified view of the various aspects of a work of art (iconographic, stylistic, etc.) that should constitute the specific task of the iconologist.

In point of fact, only one of the essays in *Studies in Iconology*, the last, "The Neoplatonic Movement and Michelangelo" (pp. 171-230), combines an analysis of certain fundamental iconographical motifs with an in-depth stylistic examination, which recovers, if I am not mistaken, a number of themes of criticism based only on "visual forms." On both stylistic and iconographic levels, Panofsky discerns a contradiction common to Michelangelo as an individual and to his entire epoch, namely that between classical and religious ideals. Methodologically this is an extremely interesting approach; and yet the reader cannot escape the impression of a lurking artificiality. If *everything* – from the lines of the drawings to the choice of iconographic themes – must express this fundamental contradiction, the scholar might be lured either to involuntarily slant texts (there are a number of rather daring psychoanalytical conjectures concerning Michelangelo's personality),[97] or to discard the documentation that does not square with the predetermined scheme of interpretation. It is significant that, in illustrating the victory of the Christian ideal in Michelangelo's works after 1534, Panofsky should intentionally neglect the bust of Brutus, considering it an exception, since it was "a political document, rather than a manifestation of artistic propensities."[98] But even if this were true, why should the political Michelangelo be less relevant than the religious? This choice seems to be the consequence of an interpretation which was not fully thought out and is, as a result, too one-sided. It should be noted that Panofsky is perfectly well aware of the "subjective and irrational" nature of the iconologist's approach:

> When we wish to get hold of those basic principles which underlie the choice and presentation of motifs, as well as the production and interpretation of images, stories and allegories, and which give meaning even to the formal arrangements and technical procedures employed, we cannot hope to find an individual text which would fit those basic principles as John xiii, 21 ff. fits the iconography of the Last Supper. To grasp these principles we need a mental faculty comparable to that of a faculty which I cannot describe better than by the rather discredited term "synthetic intuition," and which may be better developed in a talented layman than in an erudite scholar.[99]

Panofsky sees the danger lurking in this appeal to intuition and suggests that it be controlled on the basis of "documents bearing witness to the political, poetical, religious, philosophical, and social tendencies of the personality, period, or country under investigation."[100] Evidently, an approach of this type allows us, at least in principle, to avoid the risk, as in Saxl's case, of reading into figurative evidence what has been learned by other means. And yet, it appears that in later decades Panofsky experienced a certain diffidence concerning the iconological method.

An eloquent indication of this (alongside an ever more pronounced inclination for purely iconographic research, recognizable even in some of the more recent studies) is offered by a correction made by Panofsky in reprinting (in 1955) his introductory essay to *Studies in Iconology*. The object of iconology, he had originally written, is represented by those "underlying principles which reveal the basic attitude of a nation, a period, a class, a religious or philosophical persuasion – unconsciously qualified by one personality and condensed into one work." In the reprinting, the word "unconsciously" is omitted.[101] Undoubtedly this is due to Panofsky's reevaluation of the role of rational, conscious "programs" in the artistic life. O. Pächt drew attention to this reappraisal in an important review of Panofsky's *Early Netherlandish Painting*.[102] Pächt obviously acknowledges the importance of iconographic research; but he also laments Panofsky's tendency to abandon the iconological perspective and consider the ideas consciously projected by the artist in his work as a sufficient key for interpretation of the work itself. He recalls that for Panofsky in 1920 (at the time of the essay "Kunstwollen"), the statements, the intentions consciously formulated – the explicit "poetics," we would say – of the artist did not at all explain the work of art, but could be considered only a phenomenon parallel to it, even though of great interest. Pächt's insistence on the "intrinsic, inner meaning" of the work of art, which only an iconological approach would be in a position to grasp, may seem somewhat vague. What is crystal clear and convincing, instead, is his plea for some sort of methodological coordination between iconographic and stylistic comparison. Obviously, iconographic research is extremely important and even essential. But if it pretends to be self-contained and sufficient to interpret the work of art in every sense, stylistic analysis and aesthetic appraisal end up falling into the hands of practitioners of critical impressionism of the most tedious and insipid sort.

VI

We have seen that the difficulty, emerging from the examination of some of Saxl's writings, of using figurative evidence as a historical source beginning with stylistic analysis, is not always surmounted, even with the aid of Panofsky's iconological method. The irrationality of the iconologist's approach (even if exorcised through confrontation with the most varied documentation possible) revives the risk of "circular" argumentation. Here, perhaps, we are touching a basic difficulty in historiographical knowledge. In any case, E. H. Gombrich has furnished us with a radical solution in the course of considering the question of style. He has reached extremely interesting positions, though even these are not wholly free from contradiction.

Gombrich, born in 1909 (19 years after Saxl, 43 after Warburg) and a student of Julius von Schlosser, became a member of the Warburg Institute just before the Nazi invasion of Austria and subsequently became its director. Speaking of the iconological method in a 1945 essay, he alludes, with a certain detachment, "to Warburg and his followers."[103] And, indeed, Gombrich's education and interests differ considerably from those, say, of Saxl, even though we should keep in mind the latter's rapprochement with the Vienna school, Schlosser's collaboration in the *Vorträge* of the Warburg Library, and the presence in the Warburg group of O. Kurz (a student of Schlosser's).[104]

Gombrich's ties to the Vienna school, and in general to Viennese cultural circles, were very close. Even that lively rapport between the interpretation of the art of the past and modern art, which had characterized (not without some distortion)[105] the work of Wickhoff, Riegl, and Dvořák, reappears in the writings of Gombrich, although in a polemical context. We shall presently see how that should be understood. But first an essential characteristic of Gombrich's scholarly work needs to be emphasized, namely, his overwhelmingly theoretical interests. But his theorizing, let there be no doubt, shuns abstract or shadowy pedantry, generalities, and subtleties that are too often ends in themselves.[106] His method is defined at every step with concrete examples and precise, detailed analyses. But, significantly, even his works of history and not just those of art "theory," such as "Botticelli's Mythologies" or "Icones Symbolicae," originate from a theoretical problem – such as the ambiguity of Botticelli's figures, which the spectator seeks to resolve by constructing totally arbitrary "physiognomic" interpretations around them, or the undifferentiated state of symbol and representation in Renaissance and baroque allegories.[107]

The second volume of the *Bibliography of the Survival of the Classics*, published in London in 1938, opens with a review of Warburg's writings by the young Gombrich. In an admirably balanced piece of criticism, Gombrich observes that Warburg's work, despite its significance for methodology, was itself wholly unsystematic. He insists especially on the fact that Warburg, instead of indulging in more or less casual "analogies in the history of ideas" (*geistesgeschichtliche Parallelen*), had combined different scholarly disciplines (history of style, sociology, history of religions and of language) to resolve specific, clearly circumscribed problems by establishing concrete relationships.[108] This was not a new observation. Wind had also dwelt on it briefly during his polemic with Dilthey. With Gombrich, however, the point was rich in implications. In the same volume he also reviews the essay by Panofsky and Saxl, "Classical Mythology in Mediaeval Art," which I discussed earlier. While Gombrich generally praises the research that went into it, he remarks that in some instances one might suspect that the authors had substituted for genetic connections – that is, relations of derivation or dependence which could be reconstructed philologically – simple analogies or "geistesgeschichtliche Parallelen," words which recall the review of Warburg's writings a few pages earlier.

One of these analogies in the "history of ideas" noted by Gombrich was the parallelism (dear to Panofsky, as we saw earlier) between the discovery of linear perspective and the birth of historical consciousness brought about by the new relationship established with antiquity by the Renaissance.[109] This criticism was not totally unfounded and was correct methodologically in rejecting easy parallelisms and historico-cultural analogies. However, it ended up denying the very possibility of building general historical relationships. What kind of documentation is needed, we might ask Gombrich, to establish a connection between the discovery of perspective and the birth of historical consciousness in the age of the Renaissance? Evidence, perhaps, which demonstrated the existence of both phenomena in a single entity – a writing, let us say, by Brunelleschi or Paolo Uccello which mentioned antiquity, *sacrosancta vetustas*, with deliberate "historical" objectivity? Strictly speaking, even evidence of this type could be considered insufficient:

parallelism or *geistesgeschichtlich* analogy remain just that even if they refer to an individual and not to a society. The only really decisive evidence, then, would be of a kind which documented *awareness* of the analogy between the discovery of linear perspective and the birth of a historical dimension in fifteenth-century men themselves. Depending on the case, history ends up either restricting itself to the consideration of individual coincidences without attaining a broader view, or limiting itself to the opinions that men in various ages have had of themselves. Evidently the historian suggests connections, relationships, parallelisms, which are not always *directly* documented, and are only so to the extent to which they refer to phenomena produced in a common economic, social, political, cultural, and mental context – one which functions, say, as the median point of the relationship.[110] It is the existence of fifteenth-century Florentine humanism, with all its specific qualities and implications, that allows the historian in principle to establish a relationship between the discovery of perspective and the birth of historical consciousness in the modern sense of the term. Without this implicit connection with Quattrocento humanistic culture, we would have only a formal analogy, empty of content (distance between the eye and the object – distance between the individual and the events of the past) and therefore of slight importance.

To grasp the limits and significance of Gombrich's criticism, we need to examine an almost contemporaneous essay, "Wertprobleme und mittelalterliche Kunst." In 1963 when Gombrich collected his studies on "art theory" (*kunsttheorie*), he included this 1937 essay, as if to emphasize the internal continuity of his own work over a span of almost thirty years.[111] In this article, which has as its point of departure a work by E. von Garger, Gombrich takes a vigorous stand against a "physiognomic" (*physiognomisch*) interpretation of the non-naturalistic character of medieval art. Just as we are accustomed, he explains, to form immediate judgments on the state of mind, feelings, and condition of a person from his physiognomic aspects and moods, similarly there are scholars who infer, from the constrictions to which medieval artists subjected figures to make them assume specific shapes, analogous "feelings of constraint on the part of the artist in his relation to the world." This would appear to be a more sophisticated manner of interpretation, but in actual fact it resembles an approach which views movement away from realism in art as distancing oneself from the world, and therefore sees the so-called "transcendence" of medieval art as an immediate reflection of the position assumed towards transcendence by the philosophy of the time. What needs to be refuted here, Gombrich states with emphasis, is not the assumption that there was such an attitude in medieval mentality, but the facility, the immediacy of the correlation, which he compares to Taine's sociological generalizations.[112]

Gombrich is arguing against two sets of ideas which are linked but also distinct (although not too clearly here). The first is the concept of the prevailing artistic life in a historical period as the expression of an "hypostatized collective personality" – almost a "super-work of art by a super-artist" – a notion which, according to Gombrich, is a residue of romantic philosophy of history. His second target is the concept of style as an "integrally expressive system."[113] The first point probably echoes theories held by K. R. Popper, the philosopher and epistemologist, to whom Gombrich frequently acknowledged his debt.[114] Popper's antihistoricist polemic, quickly accepted by Gombrich, who in this essay rejects the "historicism (*Historismus*) of art history in an expressionistic key," is repeated often and harshly in later writings directed especially against Riegl and his interpreters, among whom H. Sedlmayr held a prominent place.[115] Reasoning of this kind is undoubtedly justified when it urges a specific analysis of individual works of art, eschewing an easy acceptance of overly facile and general "explanations" which in reality explain nothing; but it also risks throwing the baby out with the bath, of excluding or at least loosening, in its rejection of a superficial historicism, the bonds between artistic phenomena and history. The notion of the "spirit of the times" remains an attempt – even if approximate and mythological – to respond to a concrete problem, that of the connections existing among the various faces of historical reality (though Gombrich's arguments, directed principally against Hegel and his followers, really apply to generalizations of a Diltheyan type).[116]

The same can be said about the second object of Gombrich's critique. He rejects, rightly, interpretations "in an expressionistic key" of the art of the past, which we have seen him condemn in a passage cited earlier. To interpret the impassioned style of certain medieval miniatures (which have been deliberately reassessed aesthetically by some modern critics as examples of "expressionistic" art) as if we were dealing with the cypresses transformed by Van Gogh into a vortex of lines, means submitting to a subjective taste whereby one does not evaluate the individual work of art but reacts instead *directly* to the style which produced it – a style "treated as if it were itself a work of art."[117] This is an antihistorical misrepresentation, which refuses to see the art object in the context of the stylistic conventions of its day. Here Gombrich's arguments have deep roots which, obviously, go well beyond expressionism as a historically determined movement. What is being rejected is the conception of art born in modern times and superimposed on the art of the past as a necessary break with tradition and as a *direct* expression of the artist's individuality, or at least of his subconscious.[118] Proceeding logically along this line, Gombrich has concluded, in opposition to every aesthetic theory of a "romantic" type, that the work of art must not be considered either as a "symptom" or as an "expression" of the artist's personality.[119] It should be seen, rather, as the vehicle of a particular message that can be grasped by the viewer to the extent that he knows the possible alternatives, the linguistic context of the message.[120] Gombrich's acceptance, however cautious, of a specific current in contemporary aesthetics, implies fundamental criticism on his part of some of the premises underlying works that we have been considering here.[121]

What was behind the frequently cited critique of the essay by Panofsky and Saxl? It was Gombrich's refusal to accept a connection of a "physiognomic" or "expressive" type, or, in other words, of the possibility of being able to jump directly from specific formal qualities in Quattrocento paintings, such as the discovery of perspective, to the general ethos of that society, or of single groups in that society, in regard to reality – the birth of historical consciousness in a modern sense. Naturally, it also implied the refusal to consider works of art by Brunelleschi, Paolo Uccello, and others as *symptoms*, *expressions* of a determinate general ethos, or world view, if you will. And thus we return to Gombrich's more recent "antiromantic," "anti-impressionistic" positions.[122] It seems clear at this point that they imply a refusal to accept the legitimacy of Panofsky's iconology, but, please note, not of his iconography.

Let us return to Panofsky's essay "The Neoplatonic Movement and Michelangelo." After having analyzed the style of the great artist, and before moving on to an examination of the iconographic documents which clarify the role of Michelangelo's personality, Panofsky writes in a key passage: "All these stylistic principles and technical habits have a more than formal significance: they are symptomatic of the very essence of Michelangelo's personality."[123] And, in fact, for Panofsky, the lines of a drawing by Michelangelo or his chisel marks in stone *express* and are *symptoms* of the artist's profound personality, but they also reveal broad historical antitheses, the classical versus the Christian ideal in the Renaissance, experienced in a unique manner by an exceptional individual. But clearly, deductions such as these are based on a "physiognomic" interpretation of works of art – in the case of Michelangelo's works and the stylistic contrasts that are "more than formal" (of "more than individual" significance) which characterize them, according to Panofsky – and on the related concept of style as the "integrally expressive system" that Gombrich rejects.[124] This opposition is linked to Gombrich's real diffidence towards the use of works of art and generally figurative evidence considered from the stylistic point of view as possible sources in historical research, which, as we have seen, inspired the research of Warburg and his followers.

Speaking, in justifiably sharp terms, of Arnold Hauser's *Social History of Art*, Gombrich cautioned that "to attribute to the *Zeitgeist* of an epoch the physiognomic characteristics we find in its dominant artistic types is the constant danger of *Geistesgeschichte*."[125] In his review, also quite critical, of André Malraux's *Voices of Silence* – entitled, significantly, "André Malraux and the Crisis of Expressionism" – Gombrich noted that for Malraux the protagonists of art history are "those imaginary super-artists we call styles" – styles that, in their turn, "expressed" the spirits of their respective ages thanks to the uncritical belief "that the visual arts provided the shortest route to the mentality of civilizations otherwise inaccessible to us."[126] This caveat is reiterated, together with a related one against the "physiognomic fallacy," in Gombrich's inaugural lecture as Durning-Lawrence Professor of the History of Art at University College, London, in 1957.[127] Historians such as J. Huizinga and E. R. Curtius, Gombrich observed, had put us on guard against this danger. Huizinga, I might add, must have been well aware of it if he confessed that he had been led to write *The Waning of the Middle Ages* "while endeavoring to arrive at a genuine understanding of the art of the brothers Van Eyck and their contemporaries, that is to say, to grasp its meaning by seeing it in connection with the entire life of their times" – except that he then included, thereby embroiling himself in a typically vicious circle, Jan Van Eyck as one of the privileged sources, since he "mirrored the spirit of the times in an exemplary way."[128]

In conclusion, it is easy to understand why, in his inaugural lecture, Gombrich should have cautioned art historians against seeing "the styles of the past merely as an expression of the age, the race, or the class situation." (The juxtaposition of the last two terms is characteristic of the author's ideological premises.) We get the distinct impression that this insistence implies scant interest, or even diffidence, towards research focusing on connections between works of art and the historical situation which produced them. In contrast, Saxl, in a writing which surveyed the historiography of modern art, traced a sort of cultural autobiography from positivistic erudition to Wölfflin and Warburg. Once Wölfflin's lesson had been assimilated, he explains, "the main new problem, at least as I see it, was how to link the history of art with other branches of history, political, literary, religious or philosophical."[129] To be sure, even Gombrich does not fail to observe, in his Hauser review for example, that "there is such a thing as a mental climate, a pervading attitude in periods or societies," because of which art and artists "are bound to be responsive to certain shifts in dominant values." But having made this quite generic admission, he returns to the issue that weighs upon him most: "We know that 'style' in art is really a rather problematic indication of social or intellectual change."[130] After what we have noted thus far, we are obliged to acknowledge the truth in this conclusion. There is no doubt that the terrain into which Gombrich has led us is certainly firmer, but also more barren.

VII

Yet it would appear that iconographic research might offer a means of escape from the risk posed by making too hasty and immediate connections, in both directions, between the historical situation and artistic phenomena. In contrast to stylistic data, iconographic information constitutes an element of unequivocal mediation between a determinate cultural, religious, and political milieu and the work of art. By "unequivocal" I mean objectively controllable. It was certainly not accidental that Warburg, and Saxl to an even greater extent, argued for precisely this kind of research. In the 1957 inaugural lecture that I cited above, Gombrich takes a stand on the subject of iconographic research, with his starting point an article by Arnaldo Momigliano in which the latter, after noting the deep disagreements among scholars over the interpretation of figurative materials, criticizes a book on Philo by E. R. Goodenough for having lapsed into a circular argument in this very matter: "G[oodenough] wants to prove an old thesis on Philo using figurative materials and interprets the figurative materials by presupposing his interpretation of Philo."[131] An example, Gombrich states, of how such circles could be broken was offered by Warburg himself in his famous essay on Francesco Sassetti's testament. Following Warburg's lead one finds links "with dark astrological superstitions or philosophical perplexities" where previously only images of peaceful processions had been seen. The "Warburgian method," brought to perfection by Saxl, consists in this ability to break with and reformulate historical interpretations which had been accepted uncritically, and not in the introduction of works of art into a general historical context.[132] Gombrich continues, not without a trace of irony, to point out that iconology (a term that he uses here and elsewhere as synonymous with iconography)[133] also risks falling into a circular argument of an opposite kind, namely, that of projecting nonexistent platonizing allegories into Renaissance paintings which express only a serene sensuality. At this point – and here Gombrich stresses the problem which weighs upon him most – "if iconology is not to become barren, it will have to come to terms with the ever present problem of style in art."[134]

Gombrich puts us on guard against the dangers lurking in iconographic research without naming any particular work. These risks can be illustrated, however, with Edgar Wind's *Pagan Mysteries in the Renaissance*, a book that appeared after Gombrich's inaugural lecture. Wind's scholarship and his skill in interpretation are well known. So much more significant, then, is the fact that here the "critical distance" between the work of art and the text which is meant to explain it is so often lost.[135]

We know that the difficulty or, if you will, the excessive facility of this iconographic research is caused by the fact that for many fifteenth- and sixteenth-century paintings we can point with absolute certainty to the existence of detailed iconographic "programs," which, however, have rarely been preserved. This forces the modern interpreter to grope his way through a forest of the most disparate classical texts, of their commentators and interpreters – from Proclus to Ficino and beyond – without ever forging a link between text and painting that is actually supported by documentary evidence. It is virtually impossible to establish that the executor of the "program" of a painting had this or that passage or this or that interpretation of a certain myth before him. The sole criterion for judgment is the plausibility and the coherence of the interpretation offered. Obviously, one runs the risk of finding support for one's interpretation in texts and glosses which were unknown or unavailable to the "program" 's executor – a hazard that Wind acknowledges, with a somewhat paradoxical argument,[136] as an unavoidable characteristic of this type of research on Renaissance iconography. But this risk is followed by another even more serious: that of reaching an arbitrary, if apparently coherent, interpretation of the paintings in question. Let's take from Wind's *Pagan Mysteries*, though it is an extreme case, the example of an interpretation based on a misreading of a text. It allows us to see, reflected and accentuated, as in a sort of hall of mirrors, the risks in Wind's approach, and to some extent in the entire method.

The painting under scrutiny is Raphael's fresco representing Apollo and Marsyas in the *Stanza della Segnatura*. What allegorical meaning is concealed behind these figures? To begin with, Wind recalls a famous letter from Pico to Ermolao Barbaro, which, after an allusion to Plato's *Symposium*, announces an antithesis between the terrestrial Marsyas and the heavenly Apollo: the soul must re-enter into itself and hear only the melodies of the latter. From this, Wind passes on to examine Dante's invocation of Apollo (*Paradiso* 1. 13-21), and, in particular, the verses "Entra nel petto mio, e spira tue / Sí come quando Marsia traesti / Dalla vagina delle membra sue." They are interpreted thusly: "Entra nel mio petto e infondimi il tuo spirito *così come facesti a Marsia* allorché strappasti via la pelle che gli copriva le membra" ("And so infuse me with your spirit *as you did Marsyas* when you tore him from the cover of his limbs").[137] Clearly this is an incorrect reading. Dante is certainly not invoking the martyrdom of Marsyas as an obligatory step towards spiritual regeneration, but limits himself to supplicating Apollo for the inspiration to sing sublime melodies like those sung by the god during his contest with Marsyas ("Spira tue / Sí come quando Marsia traesti"). But this incorrect interpretation – "to obtain the 'beloved laurel' of Apollo, the poet must pass through the agony of Marsyas," Wind comments – is immediately "confirmed" by the fact that the fresco of Apollo and Marsyas is located between the *Disputa* and the *Parnassus*, in both of which Dante appears, once among the theologians and once among the poets.[138] For Wind, this is confirmation that the *Apollo and Marsyas* "is an example of poetic theology, representing a mystery of the pagans with which Dante opened the first canto of the *Paradiso*," a mystery which expresses the torment of the human soul imbued by divinity, of its agony in the moment when it attains the supreme ecstasy.[139] But this is an unacceptable explanation. It is based, as we have seen, on a misunderstanding of Dante's verses that is not supported – and this is the point – either by Pico's letter (which alludes to the myth of Marsyas but not to Dante), or by the fifteenth- and sixteenth-century commentaries to the *Commedia* (see, for example, Landino's Neoplatonic version).[140] But the misinterpretation is not accidental: Wind reads his authors so one-sidedly from the perspective of a Florentine Neoplatonist that he introduces, as he does here, Neoplatonic allegories where there are none.[141] This is a somewhat curious way to conceive the historian's *Einfühlung.* In any case, the fact that this Neoplatonic reading of Dante should find in Wind's eyes a corroboration in the twofold presence of the poet in the frescoes of the *Stanza della Segnatura* should put us on guard concerning the level of internal coherence and of correspondence between texts and images required to make iconographic interpretation really acceptable.[142] Otherwise, it becomes an instrument for reading what we wish into figurative evidence (and with so much "proof" besides). In leaving this digression, we are confronted by the "vicious circle" about which Gombrich spoke.

VIII

Gombrich restated the unresolved problem of style in the figurative arts as an antidote to the symptoms of decline in iconography, a type of research that in the past had played such an important role in bringing radical changes to the history of art and to Renaissance historiography in general. He was emphasizing themes that have been dear to him from the beginning of his scholarly activity. They have been collected in a comprehensive work whose subtitle, *A Study in the Psychology of Pictorial Representation*, is more eloquent and less ambiguous than the title proper: *Art and Illusion.* What are the ambiguities? In the preface to the second English edition, Gombrich notes the mistaken assumption on the part of certain readers who viewed the book as a defense of the art of illusion. Such an interpretation must have been derived from obtuseness or animosity, though it was picked up at a more sophisticted level by R. Arnheim in a review that, despite occasional perceptive observations, is superficial and unfocused.[143] Gombrich never even dreamed of proposing that art is synonymous with the ability to create illusions. The very premise of the book – that of the uncertainty, the unintelligibility of the artist's rendering of the sensible world – would be impossible without the advent of nonfigurative art. Gombrich underscores this with great clarity at the end of the volume.[144] We know, on the other hand, that he does not look with favor on these artistic currents,[145] which in part explains Arnheim's criticism. But this is not the point that interests us here.

It is difficult to speak of this splendid book; it would be even more difficult to speak of it with the required competence of the psychologist as well as of the art historian. Moreover, behind the apparent fluency and brilliance of the narrative style (the volume originated as a series of lectures), Gombrich's account is closely reasoned and tightly packed. We shall occupy ourselves here only with certain problems connected to the previous discussion.

With a wealth of examples and shrewd observations Gombrich demonstrates that the artist cannot copy reality *as it is*, or *as he sees it*. He compares this notion, in a striking example not chosen accidentally, to an older theory of language as nomenclature. We recall that Gombrich had attempted to use, in a consciously analogical way, certain formulae in information theory to interpret artistic phenomena. The work of Benjamin Lee Whorf, in particular, has emphasized how "language does not give names to pre-existing things or concepts so much as it articulates the world of our experience." Similarly, for Gombrich, "styles ... differ in the sequence of articulation and in the number of questions they allow the artist to ask; and so complex is the information that reaches us from the visible world that no picture will ever embody it all. That is not due to the subjectivity of vision but to its richness. ... It is not a faithful record of visual experience but the faithful construction of a relational model."[146] In constructing this model, the artist must above all be aware of the medium at his disposal.[147] In addition, as Gombrich successfully demonstrates, the representation of reality would be impossible without recourse to a "schema" – a provisional schema, even a very rudimentary or casual one, which can be successively modified through the process well known to psychologists of trial and error.[148] Striking confirmation of this is offered by, among other things, what Gombrich defines as the "pathology of representation." By this he means errors caused by the intervention of a "schema" discordant with reality (the early nineteenth-century lithograph portrays pointed arches in the portal of Chartres Cathedral because the arches of a Gothic cathedral *must* be pointed). "Schema," then, is one of the key words in the book; it has been observed, however, that the author uses it in different senses, causing the reader some confusion.[149]

In any case, this discovery of the decisive importance of the "schema," this initial conjecture destined to be gradually corrected and modified, finally brings Gombrich to demonstrate the first proposition of his premise: the artist can copy reality only by referring to other paintings (part 1: "The Limits of Likeness"). The second proposition is in some way the reverse of the first: Gombrich demonstrates (part 3: "The Beholder's Share") that the reading of an image is never obvious, inasmuch as the viewer always finds himself facing an ambiguous message – "ambiguity is clearly the key to the whole problem of image reading"[150] – and must choose the correct one from among various interpretations. The most typical inventions (the brush stroke, linear perspective) of "illusionistic" or naturalistic painting, as it also can be called, to be correctly interpreted require an experienced eye capable of testing the image on the basis of actual experience. Here I cannot report Gombrich's arguments on the subject; let us look, rather, at the conclusions:

> It is in these facts that we must see the ultimate reason why representational art has a history, and a history of such length and complexity. To read the artist's picture is to mobilize our memories and our experience of the visible world and to test his image through tentative projections. To read the visible world as art we must do the opposite. We must mobilize our memories and experience of pictures we have seen and test the motif again by projecting them tentatively onto a framed view.[151]

These are the psychological facts that explain that "sufficiently striking" phenomenon of the "stability of styles in art."[152] Gombrich had already given attention to this "stability" in his fine and justly famous *Story of Art*.[153] This emphasis on the importance of artistic conventions and on the value of tradition is the positive reversal (to put it one way) of the polemic against "expressionistic" interpretations in the history of art. In addition, it is intimately linked to the attempt, mentioned above, of applying information theory to the analysis of artistic phenomena. It is not only the "novelty" of a message that is comprehensible solely if connected to a tradition, but its very decoding presupposes the existence of a circumscribed range of choices – otherwise, Gombrich cautions, communication would be impossible.[154] But is it fair to state, as Arnheim does in his review, that this emphasis on the importance of tradition keeps Gombrich from explaining what to him matters most, namely, why art has a history?[155] Is the explanation of the stability of style detrimental to the explanation of the transformation of styles?

Gombrich himself had answered some of Arnheim's objections in advance.[156] But Arnheim is certainly pointing to a real difficulty when he observes that, according to Gombrich, stylistic transformations occur when the artist compares his schema with nature, thereby succeeding in breaking out of the cage of traditional style and attaining a greater or different truth in representation. Not that, as Arnheim supposes, this recalling of "representative truth" is irreconcilable with an emphasis on the importance of the schema furnished by tradition for the purposes of pictorial representation. Gombrich has firmly rejected any relativistic extension of his conclusions to this end and has stressed that even if schema interpose themselves in each representation, it is nonetheless possible to speak of more or less correct representations.[157] But the problem perceived by Arnheim still remains: why in certain historical periods are different schema chosen that imply more or less correct representations of reality? Does this not occur, Arnheim asks, because of changing attitudes toward life and the world? "And is not the history of art the history of these changing conceptions?"[158] The question is unacceptable. It loses sight of precisely the very objects of art history (paintings, statues, buildings), and art history itself is reduced to a generic and fuzzy "history of conceptions of the world." On the other hand, Gombrich's definition of "art history," which Arnheim attacks, is certainly overly limited. After having demonstrated brilliantly how Constable saw the English countryside through Gainsborough's paintings, and the latter, in turn, through the work of Ruysdael and Dutch painters in general, Gombrich then asks: "And where did the Dutch get their vocabulary? The answer to this type of question is precisely what is known as the 'history of art.' All paintings, as Wölfflin said, owe more to other paintings than they owe to direct observation."[159] It seems clear once again that when Gombrich declares that art has a *history*, this means simply that the various artistic manifestations are not unrelated expressions, but links in a tradition.[160] The problem of changing styles remains open.

Before looking at how Gombrich dealt with this question (Arnheim, curiously, fails to take this up in his review), let us briefly take stock of what has been said thus far. We have seen that Gombrich began by rejecting "expressionistic" interpretations of art history that establish *immediate* ("physiognomic" or of other types) or superficial connections between works of art and historical or psychological situations. But he concluded with an extreme position in support of tradition in art history, demonstrating that the pictorial representation of reality is made possible, literally, by the existence of other works of art. And, as a consequence, he suggested that art history's chief, in fact, exclusive, assignment should be the reconstruction of the links and relationships of dependence or opposition that connect individual works of art. To catch the diversity of the two approaches, it should suffice to recall Saxl's statement that the most urgent problem in the history of art was that of relating it "with other branches of history: political, literary, religious, philosophical." Confirmation comes when Gombrich, after having referred to the Warburgian notion of *Pathosformeln*, should affirm:

> [Warburg's] insistence that Quattrocento artists, who had previously been regarded as the champions of pure observation, so frequently took recourse in a borrowed formula made a great impression. Aided by interest in iconographic types, his followers found increasingly that dependence on tradition is the rule even with works of art of the Renaissance and the Baroque that had hitherto been regarded as naturalistic.[161]

Evidently here Gombrich is performing a subtle reinterpretation of the Warburgian tradition to which he transferred its *own* problems, since the scholars who had been most intimately tied to that legacy had left them unanswered, or attempted to resolve them too hurriedly. And Gombrich himself implicitly alluded to this reorientation in his research when, in a moving commemoration of Gertrud Bing, he spoke of the skepticism of the new generations that had grown up in a different academic tradition than the *Kulturwissenschaft* in which Warburg's own interests had matured – a skepticism certainly shared by Gombrich.[162] On the other hand, Bing herself was well aware of new concerns and scholarly directions breaking out within the Warburgian tradition. Introducing her teacher's writings to the Italian public, she called for a return to the sources – that is, Warburg's own works – so that the lack of precision and the genericity in the expression "Warburgian method" might be gauged as it applied to the variety of research interests which had flourished in the institute over the past forty years.

We could conclude at this point that the impact of Gombrich's brilliant scholarship on the Warburgian tradition is ambivalent. On the one hand, it implies a gain, a greater understanding of issues connected with pictorial style thanks to the tools of psychology; on the other, a loss because of the reduced interest in the reciprocal relationships between the various aspects of historical reality and artistic phenomena.[163] This would hardly be a restrictive conclusion – obviously, the only way to keep a scholarly tradition alive is to nourish it with new insights – but it would be superficial. It becomes important to see how Gombrich, within his theoretical perspective, resolves the crucial problem of changing styles.

IX

Art and Illusion has a triple dedication: to Emanuel Loewy, Julius von Schlosser, and Ernst Kris, all of whom Gombrich called his teachers. In collaboration with Kris, a former student of Schlosser's who moved from art history to psychoanalysis, Gombrich published an article in 1937-38 entitled "Principles of Caricature."[164] After pointing out that caricature in a strict sense was born at the end of the Cinquecento in the circle of the Carracci, the authors asked themselves the reason for this relatively late date. They began by discarding as untenable the hypothesis that interpreted this delayed event in the light of increasing manual dexterity on the part of painters and designers. Kris and Gombrich then paused over the correlation suggested by Brauer and Wittkower between the birth of caricature and the contemporaneous emergence of individuality and the sense of the comic. But even this possible explanation had to be rejected, first of all, because the two phenomena are not really coincidental (was the discovery of the individual or the sense of the comic unknown in the Renaissance?), and second, for reasons of a general character. The art historian appeals to literature, the literary scholar has recourse to art, and both invoke philosophy when they cannot explain certain problems within their fields. These interdisciplinary borrowings, despite their fruitfulness, cannot mask the methodological problem of the historical "explanation." Since the historian deals with events that do not repeat themselves, the concept of explanation has to be used cautiously. But caricature is a psychological, as well as a historical, phenomenon and as such fits into a repetitive and describable process.[165] And, in fact, our two authors searched for the explanation of the mechanism of caricature in the area of psychology, and located it, thanks to a famous writing by Freud, in the analogy between caricature and the joke.[166]

Freud

All this is important, first because Gombrich recently hearkened back to this piece by Freud to restate his own interpretation of artistic phenomena,[167] and second because the doubts voiced in that distant essay return in a crucial passage of *Art and Illusion*. The need to "explain" what he defines as "the Greek revolution" – namely, that transition crucial for the history of illusionistic art, from Egyptian to Greek art – compels Gombrich to abandon psychology (just as he had anticipated in his 1957 Inaugural Lecture).[168] At this point his old doubts concerning historical explanation reassail him.[169] Almost reluctantly he introduces a new concept, the concept of "function." It is the different function performed by art in Egypt and Greece that explains the decisive transformation in style. Egypt required a funerary art of a pictorial style capable of representing, not changing events, but, in line with a specific religious conception, typical situations removed from the temporal flux – the "what," not the "how."[170] In Greece, the emergence of a freedom in the recital of myths unknown elsewhere, and the consequent possibility for the artist (Homer comes to mind) to focus his attention on marginal and transitory aspects of reality, on the "how" as well as the "what," sparked a sort of chain reaction that induced sculptors to represent the human body in a new way, not pictographically or schematically.[171]

This concept of "function" brings Gombrich to break the enchanted circle of paintings which resemble other paintings, or which attempt to resolve formal problems that they pose: "The form of a representation," he writes, "cannot be divorced from its purpose and the requirements of the society in which the given visual language gains currency."[172] The great transformations in taste are explained, then, for Gombrich, with the change in "requirements" which never appear to be dictated by merely aesthetic motives. Let us turn to the pages concerning the end of classical art:

> The rise of the new religions from the East challenged this function. Perhaps the inevitable trivialization of the image which was the consequence of spreading skill and joy in jugglery had made the art of "mimesis" vulnerable. In the time of Augustus there are always signs of a reversal of taste toward earlier modes of art and an admiration of the mysterious shapes of the Egyptian tradition. ... [The existing formulae had to adapt] to the new demands of imperial ceremony and divine revelation. In the course of this adaptation, the achievements of Greek illusionism were gradually discarded. The image was no longer asked questions of "how" and "when"; it was reduced to the "what" of impersonal recital. And with the beholder's questioning of the image, the artist's questioning of nature stopped. The schema was not criticized and corrected, and so it followed the natural pull toward the minimum stereotype. ... [In the mosaics of Ravenna] art has again become an instrument, and a change of function results in a change of form.[173]

[margin note: New function dictates certain requirements]

But with the "beholder's questioning of the image," a new notion comes into play, that of the "mental set" – a really crucial term in the book, which the Italian translator renders variously as "messa a fuoco mentale" ("mental focus") and "atteggiamento mentale" ("mental attitude"). The transformation in the "function" of art – for Gombrich, this underlies the transformation of the form – presupposes the emergence, on the one hand, of several "requirements," connected, for example, "to the new demands of imperial ceremony and divine revelation"; on the other, of a different attitude on the part of the beholder. The importance of the concept of "mental set" flows directly from the idea, already expounded, of art as "message," as "communication."

[margin note: Mental set]

> All culture and all communication [Gombrich writes] depend on the interplay between expectations and observation, the waves of fulfillment, disappointment, right guesses, and wrong moves that make up our daily life. ... The experience of art is not exempt from this general rule. A style, like a culture or climate of opinion, sets up a horizon of expectation, a mental set, which registers deviations and modifications with exaggerated sensitivity.[174]

[margin note: Gombrich's sequence Requirements Functions Forms Mental set]

On one occasion Gombrich compared artistic communication to the wireless telegraph.[175] Accepting this analogy, we could extract a sequence of this type from his book: *requirements – functions – form – mental set*. At the transmitting pole we have the "requirements" (not just aesthetic ones, but also political, religious, etc.) made by society "in which that given language of forms is valid"; at the receiving pole, we have the "mental set," which is, according to Gombrich's definition, "the attitudes and expectations which will influence our perceptions and make us ready to see, or hear, one thing rather than another."[176] But clearly these notions, and their reciprocal relationships, pose a series of problems which go well beyond Wölfflin's remark, accepted by Gombrich, "that all paintings owe more to other paintings than to direct observation" and that paintings can be understood neither by psychology, nor by information theory, nor by a history of art that limits itself to tracing borrowings between various painters or schools of art.[177] To be sure, this borrowing and this extraordinary "viscosity" in the artistic tradition are real and important facts – Gombrich has demonstrated this beyond question. But they are incapable of explaining not only the profound transformations occurring within this tradition, but even the communication that exists between an artist and his public.

Gombrich acknowledged this when he alluded to "the virtuoso's control over his medium" and to "that awareness of essentials which makes him cut out all redundancies because he can rely on a public that will play the game and knows how to take a hint." To this he also added: "The social context in which this happens has hardly been investigated. The artist creates his own élite, and the élite its own artists."[178] That this is what happens is clear enough; but how it happens remains somewhat obscure.

The very concept of art as communication presupposed in *Art and Illusion* poses questions that need to be answered in a broader context. History (the relationship between artistic phenomena and the history of politics, religion, society, mentalities, etc.), put out quietly at the door, reenters through the window. To be sure, the rejection of "physiognomic," or at least immediate or superficial connections, should now be taken for granted. However, after reading at the end of the preface written specifically for the Italian translation of *Art and Illusion* the research program prudently outlined by Gombrich, one feels the need to ask if the silence over the use of history is intentional: "In posing new questions over the ties between form and function in art, one should perhaps make new contacts with sociology and anthropology. But this, in large part, remains to the future."[179] Gombrich's most recent works do not answer this question specifically, even though they include a notable essay, "The Early Medici as Patrons of Art: A Survey of Primary Sources," which, significantly, takes up themes, though in a different spirit, that were dear to Warburg.[180] The reader who has followed the extremely original work of this great scholar awaits its further results with curiosity, yes, even with impatience.

The High and the Low: The Theme of Forbidden Knowledge in the Sixteenth and Seventeenth Centuries

The subject of this essay is a vast one: perhaps we would do well to begin with a specific text. In his Epistle to the Romans (11:20), Saint Paul urged Romans who had converted to Christianity not to despise the Jews. Christ's message, he implied, is universal. From this followed the exhortation:

μὴ ὑψηλοφρόνει, ἀλλὰ φοβοῦ

(So do not become proud, but stand in awe.)

In Saint Jerome's Vulgate the corresponding passage reads, "Noli altum sapere, sed time."[1]

The Vulgate often provides a very literal translation, and even in this instance "altum sapere" mirrors rather than actually translates the Greek ὑψηλοφρόνειν.[2] But in the Latin West, beginning in the fourth century, the passage was often misinterpreted: *sapere* was understood not as a verb with moral significance ("to be wise") but as one with intellectual meaning ("to know"); the adverbial expression *altum*, on the other hand, was taken as a noun denoting "that which is high." "Non enim prodest scire," wrote Saint Ambrose, "sed metuere, quod futurum est; scriptum est enim 'Noli alta sapere' " ("It is better to fear future things than to know them; in fact, it has been written, 'Noli alta sapere' ").[3]

Saint Paul's condemnation of moral pride thus became a rebuke of intellectual curiosity. At the beginning of the fifth century Pelagius criticized certain unnamed persons who, misunderstanding the meaning and the context of the passage, maintained that in Romans 11:20 the Apostle intended to prohibit "the study of wisdom" ("sapientiae studium").[4] More than a thousand years later, Erasmus, pursuing a reference left by the humanist Lorenzo Valla,[5] observed that the target of Saint Paul's words had been a moral, not intellectual, vice. In his unfinished dialogue, the *Antibarbari*, Erasmus wrote that "the words do not condemn learning, but attempt to free us from pride in our worldly successes." "Paul," he added, "directed the words 'non altum sapere' at the rich, not the learned." Not surprisingly, in his New Testament translation, Erasmus refused to adopt the Vulgate's ambiguous words and wrote instead, more precisely, "Ne efferaris animo, sed timeas." "What is meant here," he explained, "are neither knowledge, nor stupidity, but arrogance and modesty."[6] We shall return to Erasmus's defense of culture later. It should be noted, however, that despite this lucid interpretation of the text, the Pauline passage continued to be misread.

The analogy between the words of Pelagius and those of Erasmus is worth noting. It would appear that there was a persisting tendency to distort the meaning of this passage. Yet it is difficult to accept this conclusion, since all medieval and Renaissance commentators correctly interpreted "noli altum sapere" as a warning against spiritual pride. But Romans 11:20 was followed by two more or less similar moral exhortations: "I bid every one among you not to think of himself more highly than he ought to think" (Rom. 12:3), and "Do not be haughty, but associate with the lowly" (Rom. 12:16). The key word in all these passages is, in the Greek text,

$$\varphi\rho\text{ove}\tilde{\imath}\nu \ (\mu\grave{\eta} \ \dot{\upsilon}\psi\eta\lambda\text{o}\varphi\rho\acute{\text{o}}\nu\varepsilon\iota, \ \mu\grave{\eta} \ \dot{\upsilon}\pi\varepsilon\rho\varphi\rho\text{ove}\tilde{\imath}\nu, \ \mu\grave{\eta} \ \tau\grave{\alpha} \ \dot{\upsilon}\psi\eta\lambda\grave{\alpha} \ \varphi\rho\text{ovo}\tilde{\upsilon}\nu\tau\varepsilon\zeta),^7$$

which Saint Jerome translated as "sapere" ("noli altum sapere," "non plus sapere quam oportet sapere," "non alta sapientes sed humilibus consentientes"). In the third century, Lactantius had already written that *sapere* meant "to seek the truth."[8] A century later, Ambrose, as we have seen, considered *sapere* synonymous with *scire*, "to know." In the Neolatin languages, significantly, the verbs referring to knowing are *sapere, savoir, saber*, even though in Italian, for example, the difference between *scienza* and *sapienza* preserves to some extent the distinction between the moral and intellectual spheres.[9] It is not surprising, consequently, that the words "non plus sapere quam oportet sapere" (Rom. 12:3) have been interpreted as a warning against the intellectual curiosity of heretics in religious matters. Even such commentators as Smaragdus or Rabanus Maurus, who had correctly translated "noli altum sapere" as the equivalent of "do not be proud," concluded, a few pages later, by establishing a connection between those words and the passage "non plus sapere quam oportet sapere," understood in a cognitive sense.[10] Century after century, the Pauline words "noli altum sapere," taken out of context, were quoted by lay and ecclesiastical authors alike as the obvious text against attempts to overstep the limits of human intelligence, as, for example, in the case which we shall examine momentarily, of the *De imitatione Christi*. At the close of the fifteenth century, Niccolò Malermi, one of the first to translate the Bible into Italian, wrote, "Non volere sapere le chose alte" ("Do not seek to know high things").[11]

So we have a lapse: not an individual lapse but a nearly collective one. To be sure, the slippage of Saint Paul's words from a moral to an intellectual meaning had been aggravated by factors of a linguistic and textual order.[12] But the fact that the words "noli altum sapere" came to be interpreted as a warning against the illicit knowledge of "high things" also implies deeper elements.[13]

The human species tends to represent reality to itself in terms of opposites. The flow of perceptions, in other words, is articulated on the basis of clearly opposed categories: light and dark, hot and cold, high and low.[14] The ancient saying attributed to Heraclitus, according to which reality is a war of opposites, a maxim that Hegel retranslated in terms of his own dialectical conception, can be read in a different and equally anachronistic key. A famous biologist once remarked that this fundamental obsession with polarity has profound biological roots: the human mind might be compared to a computer operating on the basis of a logic of the type yes/no, everything/nothing. Even though modern physics is now sufficiently immune from anthropomorphism to avoid logic of this kind, humans continue to act and think in this way. Reality, for them, as it is reflected by language and consequently by thought, is not a continuum, but a sphere regulated by discrete, substantially antithetical categories.[15]

These categories, obviously, have a cultural or symbolic as well as a biological significance. Anthropologists have begun to analyze their changeable meaning – for example, the opposites right/left.[16] But among these basic distinctions, none is so universal as the opposite high/low. Significantly, we say something is "elevated" or "superior" – or, inversely, "low" or "inferior" – without asking ourselves why those things to which we attribute greater value (goodness, force, etc.) must be placed in a high position. Even primates, it seems, react to the antithesis between high and low. But the cultural importance attributed to it in every known society, at least to the best of my knowledge, is probably tied to a different, specifically human element – an element, in fact, which has exerted a decisive influence in the history of *homo sapiens*.[17] Man's long infancy, the unusual slowness of his physical and intellectual development, probably explains the immediate identification of what is "high" with force, goodness, and so on. To the child, lacking in resources of any kind, the all-powerful adult is the incarnation of every "value."

All this, naturally, is only pure conjecture. Nevertheless, all civilizations have located the source of cosmic power – God – in the heavens.[18] Moreover, the symbolism of height is intimately related, as Indo-European languages still show, to political power. If we now return to that passage in the Vulgate which was our point of departure, we see that the warning against the pretension to know "high things" has been applied to different, but connected, levels of reality. In terms of cosmic reality, it is forbidden to look into the heavens, and in general into the secrets of Nature (*arcana naturae*). Regarding religious reality, it is forbidden to know divine secrets (*arcana Dei*) such as predestination and the dogma of the Trinity. In terms of political reality, it is forbidden to know the secrets of power (*arcana imperii*), or political mysteries. These are different aspects of reality, each of which implies a precise hierarchy – different, but connected among themselves or, more precisely, reciprocally reinforced by way of analogy.

Anthropologists, perhaps more than historians, know the danger of projecting our classifications to distant cultures. But we can proceed confidently in the present case, since the reappearance of the Pauline words "noli altum sapere" in different contexts reflects an implied unifying assumption: the existence of a separate sphere, cosmic, religious, and political, which can be defined as "high" and is forbidden to human knowledge.

The ideological value of this threefold exhortation is obvious. It tended to preserve the existing social and political hierarchy, condemning subversive political thinkers who were attempting to penetrate the mysteries of the state. It also reinforced the authority of the Church (or of churches), rescuing traditional dogmas from the intellectual curiosity of heretics. And it also served – and this was no negligible side effect – to discourage independent thinkers who dared to throw open to discussion the ancient image of the cosmos based on the Aristotelian-Ptolemaic presupposition of a clear-cut opposition between the incorruptible heavens and a corruptible sublunar (i.e., terrestrial) world.

This insistence on the limits of reason would seem to contradict, at first glance, the nineteenth-century image of the Renaissance as an age sharply differentiated from the traditional "medieval" world.

Actually, that image was not so much wrong as it was overly simplified. Here it may be useful to mention the case of Erasmus. The defense of culture implicit in his observation about the true significance of Saint Paul's words "noli altum sapere" consciously distanced itself from the tradition in which he himself had developed. In Thomas à Kempis's famous treatise *De imitatione Christi*, we find the following passage: "Do not take pride in the arts or sciences; rather, fear what has been told to you." Fear (*time*): and the text continues, "*Noli altum sapere*, but confess your ignorance."[19] Once again, we can see the extent to which this passage reveals an entire world view. Shall we call it medieval? Obviously the term is too vague and general. Undoubtedly, the Brethren of the Common Life extolled such monastic virtues as humility against the intellectual pride which they attributed to Scholastics. And yet Erasmus, who in his youth had been a follower of the Brethren, identified himself neither with the tradition of the monastic orders nor with that of the Scholastics. In the *Antibarbari*, in fact, he rejected both as examples of "barbarism." His defense of culture was indebted to a different tradition, the humanistic. Granted, the Reformation disputes between Catholics and Protestants led Erasmus to quote increasingly from an ancient proverb: "Quae supra nos, ea nihil ad nos" ("What is above us, pertains not to us"). He was not returning thereby to the monastic tradition of intellectual humility: the maxim, attributed to Socrates, expressed a completely different viewpoint. With true Socratic irony, Erasmus was alluding ambiguously to the limitations of human knowledge, contrasting the simplicity of Christ's message to the subtle speculations of theologians from both religious camps.[20]

The Socratic motto "Quae supra nos, ea nihil ad nos" is frequently quoted in emblem books.[21] In these collections of sayings and proverbs accompanied by images, which circulated so widely among the cultivated public in sixteenth- and especially seventeenth-century Europe, a large number are tied to the theme of the prohibition of knowing "high things." What connects them is the recurrence of Saint Paul's saying, duly misunderstood, "noli altum sapere." Characteristically mingling Christianity and classical culture, these words came to be used, for example, as slogans for the myths of Prometheus and Icarus. Icarus plunging from the heavens and Prometheus punished for his theft of divine fire (see figs. 1 & 2) were seen as symbols of astrologers, astronomers, heretical theologians, philosophers inclined to audacious thoughts, and unnamed political theorists.[22] In a few instances we can decipher the

In Aſtrologos.

Icare per ſuperos qui raptus & aëra, donec
In mare precipitem cera liquata daret.
Nunc te cera eadem feruensq; reſuſcitat ignis,
Exemplo ut doceas dogmata certa tuo.
Aſtrologus caueat quicquam predicere, preceps
Nam cadet impoſtor dum ſuper aſtra uehit.

1. Andrea Alciati, *Emblematum libellus*, Paris 1535, p. 57.

obscure hints hidden in these books of emblems. One of the most famous, the *Emblemata* of Andrea Alciati, which went through about a hundred editions in various languages, includes an emblem representing Prometheus in chains while an eagle is gnawing at his liver. The accompanying caption is a familiar one: "Quae supra nos, ea nihil ad nos" ("What is above us, pertains not to us"). The verse commentary reads: "Roduntur variis prudentum pectora curis / qui coeli affectant scire deumque vices," which literally means, "The hearts of wise men who aspire to know the changes of heaven and the gods are gnawed by various cares." Alciati's comment reflected a passage from the *De fato*, the treatise on free will and predestination

EMBLEMA CVI.

Quæ supra nos, nihil ad nos.

C Aucasia æternum pendens in rupe Prometheus
    Diripitur sacri præpetis vngue iecur.
Et nollet fecisse hominem figulosq, perosus
    Accensam rapto damnat ab igne facem.
Roduntur varijs prudentum pectora curis,
    Qui cœli affectant scire, deùmq, vices.

2. Andrea Alciati, *Emblemata*, Frankfort a.M. 1567, p. 106.

written a few years earlier by Pietro Pomponazzi, which was circulating at that time in manuscript form. "Prometheus vere est philosophus," Pomponazzi had written, "qui, dum vult scire Dei arcana, perpetuis curis et cogitationibus roditur" ("In truth, Prometheus is a philosopher who, seeking to probe the secrets of God, is perpetually gnawed by cares and worry"). Pomponazzi's heroic image of himself was transformed in Alciati's emblems into angry invective.[23]

Emblem books, since they were based on images, easily crossed linguistic frontiers, even when they were not written in an international language such as Latin. Their circulation all over

IN ASTROLOGOS.

Icare per superos qui raptus & aëra donec
In mare precipitem cera liquata daret.
Nunc te cera eadem feruensq; resuscitat ignis,
Exemplo ut doceas dogmata certa tuo.
Astrologus caueat quicquam predicere preceps,
Nam cadet impostor dum super astra uehit.

3. Andrea Alciati, *Emblematum liber*, Augsburg 1531, unnumbered folios (xliv).

Europe overcame confessional as well as national boundaries. In fact, they generally recalled a deeper and more diffuse cultural level, one based on subconscious or only partially conscious presuppositions, such as, for example, the idea of the analogy between cosmic, religious, and political hierarchies – the analogy to which the prohibition "noli altum sapere" referred.

At a certain point, however, the traditional limits imposed on human knowledge were overthrown. It suffices to recall the tremendous developments in astronomy from the beginning of the seventeenth century onwards. To be sure, Galileo and Kepler did not hesitate to gaze into the heavens, using new instruments such as the telescope. The *arcana naturae*, the secrets of nature, began to be revealed. What were the repercussions of these scientific discoveries on the old prohibitions against knowledge of the *arcana Dei* and the *arcana imperii*, the secrets of God and the secrets of power? Recent scholarship has highlighted the importance of certain intellectual or religious attitudes – those of the Puritans, for example – in scientific progress. Here I shall attempt, however briefly, to take a different approach.

In John Donne's *Ignatius His Conclave*, Loyola asks Copernicus, "Hath your raising up of the earth into heaven brought men to that confidence, that they build new towers or threaten God againe? Or do they out of this motion of the earth conclude that there is no hell, or deny the punishment of sin?"[24] These, according to one of the most perceptive minds of that age, were two of the likely effects of the "new science": blasphemous intellectual pride or the rejection of the powerful cohesive social force of religion. For the moment, we shall put the first aside and consider the second.

I do not think the notion of drawing subversive analogies from "the new science" to religious and political questions was limited to learned circles. Costantino Saccardino, the leader of an unsuccessful popular conspiracy against the papal government who was hanged in Bologna as an atheist in 1622,[25] had said: "Baboons those who believe in it [hell] … princes want you to believe, so that they can have things their own way, but … finally the whole dovecote has opened its eyes."[26] In these very years, groups of French and Italian intellectuals known as *libertins érudits* were maintaining that religion was a lie, although a useful one. Without it, the masses would have gone astray, and society would have collapsed.[27] A man like Saccardino – a professional jester and a follower of Paracelsian medicine – explicitly overturned this aristocratic doctrine. It was his optimistic hope that the attitude of the common people had changed. They no longer looked passively on the deeds of kings or politicians as on a world stage: they had begun to pierce the secrets of power, even the most hidden one of all, the political uses of religion.

"Out of this motion of the earth," Donne had asked, "do they conclude that there is no hell, or deny the punishment of sin?" This also was precisely Saccardino's conclusion. Naturally, there is no evidence that he knew about the Copernican system. But we can ask if his consciousness of living in a new age in which traditional beliefs were breaking up ("finally the whole dovecote has opened its eyes") was wholly independent of developments in the scientific world.

To the best of my knowledge, Saccardino's case is quite exceptional. Moreover, a lower-class revolution, such as the one to which he aspired, obviously was doomed to failure in seventeenth-century Europe. An analogy from the "new science" of nature to the science of society, to succeed, had to relate, as Hobbes had seen, to such powerful existing realities as absolute states. Significantly, an analogy of this kind was called "atheistic" – a vague term which could be applied to political as well as religious questions. This is further proof of the profound interrelationship existing among the three levels of knowledge: the cosmic, the religious, and the political. And it is useful to recall here the invective of Simplicius in Galileo's *Dialogue on the Great World Systems*: "This way of philosophizing tends to subvert all natural philosophy, and to disorder and set in confusion heaven and earth and the whole universe."[28] This dread of the subversive implications of the new heliocentric system, ascribed by Galileo to the followers of the old Aristotelian cosmology, was not a mere rhetorical exaggeration. We find it echoed, in fact, a few years later by Descartes in his *Discourse on Method*: "I cannot in any way approve of those turbulent and unrestful spirits who, being called neither by birth nor fortune to the management of public affairs, never fail to have always in their minds some new reform. And if I thought that in this treatise there was contained the smallest justification for this folly, I should be very sorry to allow it to be published."[29] This cautious statement helps to clarify further Descartes's decision not to publish his treatise *Le Monde* after Galileo's condemnation by the Church of Rome. He was well aware of the political implications of the new science, even if he was far from sharing them.

Catholic censure of the heliocentric system has been judged, depending on the circumstances, an act of blind intolerance or of stubborn pedantry. And yet we cannot exclude the possibility that it was also inspired by an obscure fear of the religious and political implications of the new cosmology.[30] In the mid-seventeenth century, an Italian Jesuit, Cardinal Sforza Pallavicino, adopted a more flexible attitude towards scientific progress. He too alluded to the ancient analogy between the *arcana naturae* and the *arcana imperii*, the secrets of nature and the secrets of political power, but clearly opposed one to the other. It was possible to foretell the behavior of nature because natural laws were few, simple, and inviolable. But to predict the behavior of kings and princes was as reckless as attempting to foretell the inscrutable will of God.[31] In the same spirit, the nobleman Virgilio Malvezzi, who was related to Sforza Pallavicino, wrote that "whoever adduces God as the reason to explain natural events is a poor philosopher, and he who does not adduce Him to explain political events is a poor Christian."[32] Thus, on the one hand, we have the realm of science, open to all in principle, even artisans and peasants, since, as Pallavicino observed, natural philosophy "extends to the shops and the countryside" and does not exist only "in books and in the academies." On the other hand, we have the realm of politics, forbidden to "private citizens" attempting to penetrate the secrets of power. Thus, the neat balance between the predictability of nature and the unpredictability of politics introduced the very theme around which the entire discussion turned: the need to keep the common people from participating in political decisions. At the same time, however, the subtle distinction drawn by Sforza Pallavicino showed a realistic understanding of the nature of scientific progress, in spite of his warning to those who did not observe "the confines of human knowledge."[33]

This trespassing of the ancient limits was duly recorded in emblem book collections. In the seventeenth century, Icarus and Prometheus became the symbols of a powerful intellectual thrust towards discovery. A distinct reversal of values caused "audacity," "curiosity,"[34] and "intellectual pride" – vices traditionally associated with these myths – to be considered as so many virtues. It had been foreseen by John Donne: "Hath your raising up of the earth into heaven brought men to that confidence, that they build new towers or threaten God againe?" Icarus and Prometheus too – like the Titans or the builders of the Tower of Babel – had been vanquished; but theirs had been a glorious defeat. In fact, in an emblem book dating from the end of the seventeenth century, Prometheus is no longer represented as a vanquished God chained to the mountain. His hand, in the act of grazing the sun, is accompanied by the lofty caption "Nil mortalibus arduum" (see fig. 4) – "Nothing is too difficult for mortals."[35] Even the fall of Icarus no longer matched the new attitudes: he appears in another emblem collection as a winged youth, swimming tranquilly in the air (see fig. 5). The motto "Nil linquere inausum" ("Dare anything") was accompanied by a comment that juxtaposed the flight of Icarus to Columbus's discovery of a new world.[36] The Jesuit Daniello Bartoli, on the other hand, had observed that without the daring of Columbus, which he compared to that of Icarus, Europe would have "neither spices nor mines ... not

4. Marcello Marciano, *Pompe funebri*, Naples 1666, detail of figure facing p. 102.

even knowledge of that half-world, America."[37] The notions of "risk" and "novelty" were now being seen as positive values – appropriate, in fact, to a society ever more dependent on commerce. A new culture was being born, one based on new social values.

If we return now to the Pauline words "noli altum sapere," it will have become clear why they no longer seemed acceptable in this period. Actually, we can trace, almost step by step, the process by which this venerable saying was ultimately rejected. At the beginning of the seventeenth century in a frequently reprinted emblem book by

5. Anselmus de Boodt, *Symbola varia*, Amsterdam 1686, p. 292.

a young Dutch lawyer, Florentius Schoonhovius, we rediscover the ancient exhortation "noli altum sapere" in a somewhat modified form: "Altum sapere periculosum" ("It is dangerous to know high things") (see fig. 6). Here too the reference is to Icarus. A long discourse by Schoonhovius identified the emblem's intended target: inordinately curious theologians disputing over such divine secrets as predestination, free will, the fall of Adam. They would have done better, he exclaimed, to set aside these abstruse and useless discussions, and content themselves with the Bible! Our prosperous country, he continued, would not risk being dragged down to ruin by religious discord.[38]

Schoonhovius was alluding to the burning problem of religious controversy which in 1618 had reached a crisis level in the Dutch republic. The partisans of the rigid Calvinist doctrine of predestination were meeting a growing opposition on the part of the more moderate Arminians. These theological discussions had serious political implications, since the latter, who were in a minority, championed religious toleration. Consequently, they backed Oldenbarnevelt and other opponents of the political authority of the

Altum fapere periculofum.

EMBLEMA III.

Icarus & Phaëton nimium dum magna capeffunt
Occidit hic flammis, ille peremptus aquis:
Mens infirma hominum cœli perrumpere clauftra
Cum ftudet; in tenebras præcipitata ruit.

6. Florentius Schoonhovius, *Emblemata*, Gouda 1618, p. 9.

Calvinist ministers.[39] A synod was convoked at Dordrecht to resolve the entire affair. Schoonhovius decided to publish his emblem collection at that precise moment in an appeal for religious peace.

The fall of Icarus as a symbol of overly inquisitive theologians and the motto "noli altum sapere" circulated widely among these Dutch religious groups. The brother-in-law of the consul of Haarlem wrote a letter in February 1618 which harshly condemned those foolish theologians who, like Icarus, had failed miserably for having dared to soar too high towards forbidden goals. A few years earlier the great classical philologist Isaac Casaubon, writing to a leading figure among the Arminians, Hugo Grotius, observed that it would have been in the interest of all Christianity, and of the Arminians in particular, if some constraints had been applied to those meddlesome theologians who were seeking (and here he is obviously echoing the Epistle to the Romans, 12:3) to know more than they ought, "sapientes supra id quod oportet sapere."[40]

Thus Schoonhovius's emblem was striking an already familiar chord. Its context, however, was in a certain sense new. If we look at the first page of his book, we see immediately facing the beginning of

7. Florentius Schoonhovius, *Emblemata*, Gouda 1618, unnumbered folios (xii).

the text, a portrait of the young author encircled by the words "Sapere aude" (fig. 7). Three emblems follow immediately: "Nosce te ipsum" ("Know thyself"); "Sapiens supra fortunam" ("The wise man cannot be defeated by fortune"); and, as we have already seen, "Altum sapere periculosum" ("It is dangerous to know high things"). The series dealt with the subject of knowledge, with obvious Stoic undercurrents. The meaning of the first caption, however, clearly differed from the last, "Altum sapere periculosum."

"Sapere aude" is taken from Horace's Epistle to Lollius.[41] The literal meaning is "dare to be wise." Horace addresses these words to a fool who is waiting for the water to dry up before daring to cross a stream. Originally, the passage was linked to the idea of common sense, not to knowledge. But it is easy to perceive that Horace's words assumed a different meaning in Schoonhovius's emblem collection. Here too *sapere* had slid from a moral to an intellectual sphere, influenced by the next motto, "Altum sapere periculosum."[42] The result was a sort of unstable compromise: "It is dangerous to know high things," but "dare to know."

To comprehend fully the significance of the last exhortation we need to remember that European intellectuals in this period increasingly felt that they were part of a cosmopolitan *respublica literatorum*, a republic of intellectuals.[43] Solidarity with other intellectuals outweighed their respective religious or political commitments. We might say that the search for truth was becoming a sort of religion, in itself a political responsibility. But this insistence on the spirit of research was not for everyone. "Hic vero libertas aliqua inquirendi, aut etiam dissentiendi doctis omnino concedenda est" ("We must grant a certain freedom to search, and even to disagree, especially to intellectuals"), wrote the Arminian Conrad Vorstius, professor of theology at Leiden, to Casaubon, "otherwise we might appear to be obstructing the slow march of truth."[44] Freedom of inquiry had to be granted especially – or was it only? – to a specific social group: intellectuals. A new image of intellectuals was emerging, one that, for better or worse, is still with us.

"Altum sapere periculosum": the search for truth can have dangerous social implications, as the case of Holland showed. The Arminians were vanquished at the Synod of Dordrecht. A year later, in 1619, the theological victory won by Calvinist orthodoxy was followed by political victory. Oldenbarneveldt was executed; many Arminians, or Remonstrants as they were called, escaped to exile, particularly to France. Schoonhovius, probably disillusioned by religious strife among his companions in the faith, abandoned Calvinism and converted to Catholicism. Incidentally, he would write no other emblem books. But the words of Horace in their new meaning, "sapere aude" ("dare to know"), continued to circulate. Pierre Gassendi, who was in contact with the *libertins érudits* and with the Arminian exiles in Paris, adopted the phrase as his personal slogan.[45]

A book appeared in Holland at the beginning of the eighteenth century. Its title page was decorated with a vignette representing a man in the act of climbing a mountain (fig. 8). A cornucopia can be seen on the peak, framed by clouds. A winged god holding a scythe – Time – holds the man's hand and helps him to ascend. The motto

8. Anton van Leeuwenhoek, *Epistolae ad Societatem Regiam Anglicam*, Leiden 1719, title page.

reads, "Dum audes, ardua vinces" ("If you will dare, you will conquer difficulties"). The emblem cleverly alludes to three different sayings, combining them into one: "Veritas filia Temporis" ("Truth is the daughter of Time"); "Altum sapere" (because *ardua* also means "high things"); and "Sapere aude." In effect, there is Time, there is height, there is audacity ("Dum audes ...," "If you will dare ..."), but where is "sapere"? We need only to look at the title of the book: *Epistolae ad Societatem Regiam Anglicam* (Letters to the English Royal Society) by Anton van Leeuwenhoek, the great Dutch biologist who was the first scientist to use a microscope.[46] The significance of the vignette could be translated: the time has come; the secrets of nature are no longer hidden from us; the intellectual daring of scientists will lay the gifts of nature at our feet.

The shaky balance between "do not know high things" and "dare to know" had been shattered. The eighteenth-century history of this exhortation to overcome the ancient barriers to knowledge has already been sketched by others.[47] It is indeed significant that Horace's motto was considered the very embodiment of Enlightenment values. "Was ist Aufklärung?", What is Enlightenment? Kant asked at the end of the century. His answer was: "*Sapere aude!*" – even if, in his turn, and from a different point of view, he emphasized the limits of human knowledge. But this is another story.

Titian, Ovid, and Sixteenth-Century Codes for Erotic Illustration

One of the characters in Terence's *The Eunuch*, the young Chaerea, disguised as a eunuch, slips into the house where the young woman he loves dwells. (The scene has already taken place off stage: Chaerea is describing it to his brother.) The girl is preparing herself for the bath. The eyes of both fall upon a picture of the meeting of Jove and Danae hanging on the wall: "The subject was the story of Jove's sending down a shower of gold into Danae's bosom." The youth exults at the thought that soon he would be imitating the greatest of the gods, he "whose thunder shakes the highest realms of heaven," by seducing the maiden: "Was I a mere manikin, not to imitate him? Imitate I would, and like nothing better."[1]

This passage was cited frequently by Saint Augustine to demonstrate the evil effects of lascivious pictures. Through him it passed into the debate over images that burst out in the Catholic church in the sixteenth century. The theologian Johannes Molanus cited Terence's verses and Augustine's indignant comment in a chapter entitled "In Pictures One Should Beware of Anything that Provokes Lust," in his treatise *De picturis et imaginibus sacris* (1570). Almost thirty years earlier, the Dominican controversialist Ambrogio Catarino Politi had done the same in his *De cultu imaginum* (1542), but with different intent: to demonstrate by way of analogy the efficacy of sacred images through the reaction of the young Chaerea to the representation of the love of Jove and Danae.[2]

The passage from *The Eunuch* and its sixteenth-century success pose, implicitly and succinctly, a series of closely linked problems, some familiar to us. Here, I shall try to list them.

1. I will begin with the most general: how does an erotic image function? The answer (it has been said) varies depending on whether the sexual act is or is not represented directly. In the first case, the beholder identifies himself with the figures performing the act. (It should be observed that the audience to which the erotic pictures are directed is exclusively masculine,

77

for obvious historical reasons: what is being suggested thus is an identification with the male protagonist.) In the second, the beholder sees in the depicted figures (generally nude women, for the reason just stated) the partners in an imaginary sexual relationship. In both cases, the role of the spectator is essentially that of a *voyeur*.[3] But there are also intermediate variants on this theme. In the portrayals of love between Jove and Danae the sexual act is indeed represented, but in a symbolic way (Jove appears in the form of a shower of gold): this allows young Chaerea to substitute himself mentally for Jove in Danae's bed, and at the same time to identify himself with the god himself. The voyeurism of the beholder acquires a narcissistic charge: through coitus Chaerea – an ordinary man, a man of no consequence, a "manikin" – becomes the equal of the great Jove, who makes the heavens tremble with his thunder.

2. The psychological process that I have described takes on different forms depending on the relationship established between the reality in which the viewer participates and the reality portrayed in the erotic image. This relationship is conditioned by the codes – cultural and stylistic – in which the image is formulated. The two realities may be either homogeneous or heterogeneous; in the latter case there may be a *tendency* towards the base (the comic or vulgar) or towards the more refined (the tragic or the sublime).[4] We know only the cultural, not the stylistic, code of the painting mentioned by Terence (even though we can surmise it with a certain approximation).[5] The effect in any case was a turning upward: by means of an exalted code such as the mythological, Chaerea could aspire to identify himself with the mighty Jove.

3. The question of the level (high, medium, low) of the codes employed in erotic representations shifts the discussion from the beholder to the work itself. What is an erotic image? In a strict sense, it is one which proposes deliberately to excite the viewer sexually.[6] The painting seen by Chaerea was presumably such a one (the scene takes place in the house of the courtesan Taide). But the purpose behind the image is frequently difficult to decipher. A broader definition should thus include also those images that, beyond their author's intentions, end up assuming, perhaps over a period of time, an erotic charge in the eyes of the public.

During the sixteenth century, the question of erotic images, that is, whether they were intended as such or not, increasingly preoccupied Catholic authorities, as the previously mentioned writings of Politi and Molanus attest. Two different but closely connected phenomena (in a certain sense the first was only an aspect of the second) contributed to this concern: on the one hand, a determination to exert as broad a control as possible over sexual life; on the other, an awareness that images could serve in the campaign to reestablish sundered or weakened links with the faithful, although in some cases it was actually a matter of forging connections that had never existed. These goals were only in part a reaction to the Protestant polemic against sacred images. Even more decisive was the growing awareness of the important function of pictorial representations, *idiotarum libri*, in propaganda efforts directed towards masses, who were overwhelmingly illiterate. Indicative is the recurrent appeal to positions that had been expressed by Gregory the Great.[7] Even if elements in this campaign differed greatly from those of the past and were occurring in an environment in which the spread of printing had greatly altered the relationship with the written word and images, comparisons could be made with attempts to proselytize barbarians made in the High Middle Ages.

In the eyes of such a clear-headed theologian as Politi, the common denominator between erotic and sacred images was *efficacy*. The former stimulated sexual appetite, the latter, religious sentiment. They were directed, however, to different audiences, at least in some respects. In sixteenth-century Italy we can distinguish, schematically, two iconic circuits (let us call them that): one, public, widespread, and socially undifferentiated, and the other, private, circumscribed, and socially elevated. The first contained statues, frescoes, canvases, and panels of large dimensions – objects exhibited in churches and public places, accessible to all. The latter consisted of the above, as well as paintings and panels of small dimensions, gems, and medals preserved in the homes of an elite of lords, prelates, nobles, and, in some cases, merchants. To be sure, this is a simplistic distinction, warped, moreover, by the growing diffusion of printing: it suffices to mention the widespread circulation of sacred images in commonplace settings.[8] Nevertheless, the identification of two iconic circuits, one public, the other private, seems useful, at least in a preliminary evaluation, for the question of erotic images that interests us here.

The only intentionally erotic images admitted to the public sphere were in fact the "immoral images" exhibited, as Gillio wrote, "in brothels and taverns."[9] Unfortunately, we do not know the iconography which inspired them, or the stylistic currents to which they were related. We have more information, instead, on the unintentionally erotic images, especially those of a sacred character: the case reported by Vasari of the pious women troubled by a painting of Saint Sebastian by Bartolomeo[10] was probably not so unusual. The Counter-Reformation campaign against the nude had as its chief goal a sweeping removal of images that possessed even a slight erotic potential. This led to the decision to discourage such scriptural subjects as the drunkenness of Noah, David and Bathsheba, Susanne and the Elders.[11]

Intentionally erotic images, inaccessible to the masses with the exception mentioned, could be found in great numbers in the private iconic circuit of the elite. In the overwhelming majority of cases they were couched in a culturally and stylistically elevated code, the mythological, whether they represented ancient images or images expressly painted or carved by contemporary artists. Sixteenth-century erotic fantasy discovered in classical mythology a ready-made treasury of themes and forms able to be instantly comprehended by such an international clientele as the patrons of Titian's "poems." Even a current more closely tied to genre painting, Venetian courtesan portraiture, frequently disguised itself under a thin mythological veil.[12]

In the course of the sixteenth century, ecclesiastical attacks on even representations of this type grew in intensity. In his *Disputatio … de cultu et adoratione imaginum* (1552), Politi accused prelates who possessed depictions of mythological subjects, whether ancient or modern, of downright idolatry. He was unmoved by the excuses of "corrupt" men who alleged that they collected and preserved these pictures "not for the purpose of revering or adoring them, but for the enjoyment of the spectacles and in memory of the ancients, as a demonstration of the skill of the artist." These churchmen were told that they would have done better if they had destined for the poor the money they poured into works of this kind. Gregory the Great had proceeded very differently when he had the pagan idols destroyed: and to think that Platina felt he had to exculpate him by denying the fact! But, to be sure, a man drunk on pagan culture, as Platina was, could not but revere these things, Politi observed, that through spiritual eyes are not held in esteem. Images of false gods, in fact, lead not only to idolatry but also to lust in the beholder who gazes on "the naked limbs of Venus or Diana ... and the salacious gestures of Satyrs, and the shameful and drunken furies of Bacchus and the Bacchantes."[13]

However vague and allusive, Politi's polemic cannot help but call attention to Titian's paintings on mythological themes, which included, alongside the bacchanals, the Venuses, the Dianas, also the "Danae" painted in Rome and then copied many times,[14] obviously to satisfy specific orders placed by the artist's highly placed clients. Thanks to the condemnation by Augustine, the scene of love between Jove and Danae, as we have seen, came to be considered in the sixteenth century the very prototype of the image created to excite the beholder sexually.

But is it correct to say that these mythological paintings of Titian's are "intentionally erotic"? In recent decades various scholars, influenced by Panofsky's iconological approach, have replied in the negative, discerning in them a number of symbols and arcane allegories of a philosophical character. Panofsky's posthumous book on Titian has given the most authoritative support possible to this position.[15] The following pages are intended to reopen the discussion, especially in regard to certain assumptions implicit in iconological studies devoted to Titian.

First of all, we cannot ignore that contemporaries viewed Titian's mythological "poems" as explicitly erotic paintings. And the artist himself would have agreed. Titian's letter to Philip II has been frequently cited. After recalling the "Danae where one could see everything from the front," he promised to send another "poem," one of "Venus and Adonis," in which it would be possible to view, "just to vary things," "the other side."[16] But we should also look at what Ludovico Dolce, a friend and great admirer of Titian's, wrote to Alessandro Contarini about this second painting:

> The Venus has her back turned, not for any artistic deficiency but to demonstrate double the art. Because in turning her face towards Adonis, straining with both her arms to retain him, and half-seated on a soft fabric of peacock-blue, she demonstrates in every way certain sweet and lively sentiments, and such that they cannot be seen except in her; the miraculous shrewdness of that divine spirit [Titian] is also revealed that in her intimate parts we recognize the creases on the flesh caused by her seated position. Why, it can in truth be said that every stroke of the brush is one of those strokes that nature executes with its own hand..... I swear to you, sir, that there is no man so keen in sight or judgment, that seeing

does not believe her alive; nor anyone made so cold by the years, or so hardened in his being, who does not feel a warming, a softening, a stirring of the blood in his veins. It is a real marvel; that if a marble statue could by the stimuli of its beauty so penetrate to the marrow of a young man, that he stained himself, then, what must she do who is of flesh, who is beauty personified and appears to be breathing?[17]

As we see, aesthetic evaluation in terms of realism imperceptibly surpasses the appreciation, which is exceedingly explicit, of the painting's capacity to stimulate erotically. This may explain why this letter has been generally ignored in the literature on Titian and why a renowned scholar even felt he should quote it only in a censored form.[18]

One might object, however, that this evidence does not exclude the possibility of a second layer of meaning in the image, containing the symbols and learned allusions dear to iconologists. But can the existence of this secondary stratum be demonstrated? In the case of the mythological "poems" painted by Titian in his late maturity, the answer is no. The conflicting interpretations recently offered over the *Abduction of Europa* are a good example. M. L. Shapiro has identified the textual "source" of that painting not in Ovid, as had always been thought, but in a Horatian ode (*Carmina* 3.27). This led to the attempt to read a complicated set of Stoic symbols into the painting. The seemingly wildly erotic image of Europa being dragged off by the bull was actually thought to conceal a more complex message: the depiction of surrender to passion condemned by the Stoics. The fish and the dolphins swimming alongside Europa, the cupids who escort her, were embodiments, in fact, of the passions of the soul: fear, joy, desire, pain. The monstrous fish is the symbol of fear, the dolphin of joy, first because Moschus in his poem *Europa* speaks of "joyous" leaps by dolphins, second because Titian's dolphin is of a silvery color and Horace, in another ode, declares "the silver house laughs" ("ridet *argento* domus"); one of the flying cupids symbolizes desire, and the other pain, as his distraught expression demonstrates "rather fittingly," together with "the rather angular outline of his form that should be compared with the soft roundness of both *Joy* and *Desire*."[19]

Fortunately, arguments of this kind have been promptly rejected. Another scholar, D. Stone, Jr., has shown beyond the shadow of a doubt that the "source" for the *Abduction of Europa* is neither Ovid nor Horace, but rather an Alexandrian romance that Titian may have read in F. A. Coccio's vernacular version.[20] From the imaginary painting minutely described by Achille Tazio, Titian took, in particular, Europa's position on the bull: "The young woman was seated on his back, but not the way a man sits on a horse, but side-saddle, with both feet dangling on the right and with the left hand clasping one of the horns." (The iconographic oddity of this pose did not escape Panofsky, *Problems in Titian*, p. 166.) It is possible, then, to identify a text behind the painting, one that in this case was followed scrupulously. But it is a purely descriptive text, lacking in symbolic, Stoic, or Neoplatonic overtones. To Shapiro's typically iconological question, "Is the Stoic program there to veil the pagan nudity?"[21] we can reply negatively, because the presence of a "program" tied to Stoicism cannot be demonstrated. There remains Europa's nudity: veiled or, better, exalted by the "brilliant white robe" of which Achille Tazio's vernacular version speaks and which Titian did not fail to reproduce in his painting. How far can we go with a conclusion of this sort, which in the particular case of the *Abduction of Europa* appears unquestionable?

Not Ovid, then, but a vernacular translation of an Alexandrian romance. And yet we know that Titian found in Ovid the inspiration for most of his mythological "poems," for those paintings, in other words, which in the eyes of contemporaries had, as we have seen, an essentially erotic character. Panofsky has spoken of an exceptionally deep attachment for Ovid on Titian's part – an Ovid read and scrutinized to the last detail of the text.[22] But of the text – or of the translation?

According to Panofsky, Titian "felt free to use all kinds of visual models, ancient or modern, while yet, on the whole, remaining independent of the specific tradition which flourished all around him in countless illustrated editions, translations and paraphrases of the *Metamorphoses*." In several cases, in fact, Titian would not have hesitated to detach himself from this tradition and return directly to Ovid's original text. But Panofsky's amply illustrated thesis is, actually, untenable. In refutation, it can be demonstrated that (1) Titian did not know Latin; (2) he read the *Metamorphoses* only in translations; (3) his innovations with respect to the iconographic tradition should be traced to the vernacular versions, and not to the Ovidian text. If all this is true, he was not a humanistic painter, as has often been maintained, but one tied closely to the contemporary vernacular culture of the *poligrafi*.[23]

The first point, naturally, is decisive. It is customary to juxtapose

[handwritten margin note: Titian– tied closely to vernacular culture]

Titian's paintings, especially his mythological works, with the writings of Latin, and even Greek, authors from which they were thought to derive: in speaking of the *Abduction of Europa*, not only Ovid or Horace, but Moschus. This suggests two possibilities: either Titian was capable of reading these texts directly, or he had a scholar translate them for him. The existence of a "program" developed for him by a humanist at the court of Ferrara is demonstrated by that group of paintings completed in the 1520s for Alfonso d'Este.[24] The first conjecture has been accepted without qualms in regard to the mythological works of Titian's maturity. But there is a piece of evidence, once again from Ludovico Dolce, which proves conclusively that Titian could not read Latin (not to mention Greek). We find it in Dolce's dedication "to M. Titiano, painter and gentleman [*cavaliere*]," dated Padua, October 10, 1538, introducing a collection of texts which included two vernacular translations by Dolce – the sixth satire of Juvenal and Catullus's epithalamium for the marriage of Peleus and Teti – in addition to an original work by Dolce (*Dialogo in cui si parla di che qualità si dee tor moglie, et del modo, che si ha a tenere*).[25] The dedication dealt with the traditional theme of comparing the arts – in the present instance, literature and painting:

> Juvenal, excellent master Titian, Juvenal, keenest champion and battler against the iniquity of his day, among his beautiful satires, left one in which exhorting a friend to flee from the bonds of his wife, penned such a noble and perfect picture of the luxuries and vices of women, that he, without doubt, can win over the miracle of your divine genius. Images, emanating from perfection of the art, such as is only truly yours, so much resemble reality, that by adding the spirit to them, nature would seem superfluous: and yet, life is lacking. But in the picture to which I refer, one sees not only the similitude of that truth and that life, but the very truth and the very life. Having taken and put together from this such an example as I discern and have been able to accomplish, I now send it to you so that, unable to decipher your own, you may observe in mine whether good writers know how to sketch with their pens the secrets of the soul as well as good painters can with their brushes what is revealed to the eye; or, instead, if they, together with you who are the most worthy, remain surpassed by far.

An explanation is called for to comprehend fully the gist of Dolce's friendly challenge. In translating Catullus's epithalamium he departed somewhat from the Latin text and furnished, instead, a vivacious description (the first in our possession) of the *Bacchus and Ariadne* that Titian had painted fifteen years earlier, taking his inspiration from, among other sources, that very Catullan text (see the Appendix to this essay). By these means, Dolce was attempting to reaffirm the superiority of the pen over the brush. But this does not concern us here. What counts, instead, is the clear statement that Titian was unable to understand a text by a Latin author without the assistance of a vernacular version.

It is unnecessary to insist on the importance of this point, first of all because sixteenth-century translations, as we know, were anything but faithful renderings. Usually they were reworkings, often abridged or expanded. Let us take an example.

Panofsky had already noted that there existed in classical antiquity a dispersed and fragmentary textual interpretation that corresponded to the pictorial success of the myth of Danae, which certainly does not commence with Titian, although he gave it a powerful impetus.[26] Even allusions by Ovid, that mythographer par excellence, are brief and incidental. What can have been the source of the inspiration for Titian's paintings: equally fleeting notices in Horace, the *scholia* made to Apollonius Rhodios's *Argonautica*, or, instead, Fulgentius "metaforalis" and the medieval mythographic tradition?

Typically, these questions have never been asked in an explicit way. The answer to them seemed obvious (even if it was not). In reality, Titian had available a text that was neither fragmentary nor obscure: the *Methamorphosi cioè transmutationi tradotte dal latino diligentemente in volgar verso ... per Nicolò di Agustini*, many times reprinted (1522, 1533, 1537, 1538, etc.). The "diligence" vaunted in the title had not kept the translator from making substantial additions to the text in certain places. Four verses, tersely allusive in Ovid (*Metamorphoses*, 4.607-10), had grown to three stanzas. First, the Ovidian text: "There was one only, Acrisius, the son of Abas, sprung from the same stock, who forbade the entrance of Bacchus within the walls of his city, Argos, who violently opposed the god, and did not admit that he was the son of Jove. Nor did he admit that Perseus was son of Jove, whom Danae had conceived of a golden shower" (Loeb Classical Library trans.). And now the vernacular expansion:

> The reason why Acrisius scorned
> Bacchus, was because he had told him
> that the daring Perseus whom he loved so much
> was not the son of Jove, the perfect god,
> as was true, and thus hated him.
> And this begetting had the result

> that king Acrisius begat a daughter,
> Danae by name, beautiful beyond belief.
>
> The father, who beheld her to be so charming,
> fearing for her virginity,
> kept her locked in a tower,
> with great care and much dignity;
> so that Jove, who knew this,
> one day put aside his divinity
> and descended on her tower
> to perform his usual amorous feats.
>
> Then through an opening which he saw in the roof,
> he quickly changed himself into a shower of gold
> and through it descended onto her bed
> so quietly that no one took notice.
> And then, to achieve the ultimate pleasure,
> he mounted her, and disclosed
> that he was Jove, and lay with her
> and impregnated her with Perseus.[27]

That Titian should have used this convenient vernacular version, rather than consult classical or medieval texts with the assistance of some humanist or other, is a plausible hypothesis, even if unproven. But it becomes certainty when we discover that the translations (including Nicolò degli Agostini's) contain not only those variants from the accepted iconographic tradition ascribed by Panofsky to a careful reading of Ovid's text, but actually the cues for certain departures from it that previously were attributed to Titian's poetic license.

Let us begin with the last case, which, in a certain sense, is the most telling for my thesis. In the course of analyzing one of the "poems" painted by Titian for Philip II, *Diana Surprised in the Bath by Actaeon*, Panofsky remarked that, from the viewpoint of composition, the work "is not significantly indebted to any previous illustration of the Actaeon myth": it was an iconography created "almost ex nihilo."[28] The newest element, if one disregards such details as the red curtain and the presence of a negress among the nymphs in Diana's court, is "the unexpected presence of an architectural setting: a curious combination of a rusticated pier with a dilapidated Gothic vault, the only Gothic vault in Titian's oeuvre."[29] Panofsky conjectures that it must have been Ovid's text which suggested this singular architectonic setting to a sixteenth-century reader such as Titian, by means of the allusion to nature imitating art:

> There was a vale in that region, thick
> grown with pine and cypress with their
> sharp needles. 'Twas called Gargaphie,
> the sacred haunt of high-girt Diana.
> In its most secret nook there was a
> well-shaded grotto, wrought by no
> artist's hand. But nature by her own
> cunning had imitated art; for she
> had shaped a native arch of the living
> rock and soft tufa. A sparkling spring
> with its slender stream babbled on
> one side and widened into a pool girt
> with grassy banks.
>
> *(Metamorphoses* 3.155-63; Loeb trans.)

But we can see how much closer to Titian's pictorial version is the vernacular translation, duly expanded in respect to the original, by Giovanni Andrea dell'Anguillara, and published in Venice in 1555, four years before the completion of the *Actaeon*:

> Said Gargaphie is that noble place
> over which the goddess exercised sylvan care:
> it is not a grotto produced by art,
> but rather nature has well imitated art.
> A natural arch divides that cavern,
> which is placed in the center of the natural walls;
> all of a delicate tufa is the cavern made,
> front and sides, as well as interior vault.
>
> There is dripping everywhere around the cave,
> and a clear fountain on the right-hand side,
> where below in the guise of a vessel
> nature had excavated that tufa.
> One drop follows another only intermittently,
> nor is the dripping continuous,
> but because of the many drops fallen, a stream rises,
> filling that vase, and then overflows and spills over.
>
> In the cavern the heavens, which composed nature,
> by drops and frost divided and broken,
> has a thousand varied and capricious forms,
> that reveal they were made by a skilled artificer.
> Limp, ovate and spongy pyramids
> hang down, and with their drops cause an aqueduct;

it has such an arrangement, that a chisel
could not have made it more pleasing, or beautiful.[30]

Titian could not but have been struck by the translator's insistence
on the extraordinary natural architecture of the grotto. The artist took
from Anguillara's verses not only the idea of the natural "vessel"
brimming over with water, but also, doubtless, the idea of characteriz-
ing that architecture as Gothic. "A thousand varied and capricious
forms," "limp, ovate, and spongy pyramids": consider the anonymous
author (sometimes thought to be Raphael) of the report on Roman
architecture sent to Leo X in 1515 who stated that the painted arches
of the Gothic style were born "from trees not yet cut" "whose branches
had been bent back, and bound together"; or Vasari, who defined
Gothic architecture as "a malediction of tiny tabernacles piled on each
other, with so many pyramids and points and leaves, that it seems
impossible that they can stand, not to mention support anything."[31]

But Anguillara's vernacular version is decisive for the genesis of
the *Actaeon* in both a negative and positive sense, because of the
elements suppressed, as well as those added to the Latin text.
Cavalcaselle had already correctly noted that the setting for *Diana
and Actaeon* indeed is a wood, "but not of cypresses or of pines," as
Ovid had written.[32] Now, it is precisely the reference to pines and
cypresses that is lacking in the translation.

Lastly, we have the case of *Perseus and Andromeda*, for which
Panofsky's demonstration of dependence upon the Latin text seems
to be more compelling. Three features in the painting do not have
precedents in earlier pictorial representations of the Andromeda
myth: (1) the coral branches on the bank, mentioned by Ovid at the
end of the episode; (2) the position of Perseus descending from the
heavens head-first (*praeceps*, the text states); (3) the sword of Perseus,
which is curved rather than straight, here too conforming precisely
to the words of Ovid: "girt on his hooked sword," "buried his sword
clear down to the curved hook," "he smites with his hooked sword"
(*Metamorphoses* 4.666, 720, 727; Loeb trans.).[33]

Now let us look at the vernacular version by Nicolò degli Agostini. It
not only translates the passage on the origins of coral, but highlights
it with an apposite subtitle, *De Coralli*. The term *praeceps* is rendered
exactly: "and he took leave of her with lowered head." As for the
curved weapon brandished by Perseus, it is mentioned no less than
six times, and there is an actual embellishment with respect to the

9. Titian, *Perseus and Andromeda*, London, Wallace Collection.

original: "he seized again his scythelike sword," "he gripped his scythelike sword," "and he repeatedly wounded her with his scythelike sword," "and with his scythelike sword he struck her a blow," "and then with his scythelike sword he turned towards the beast."[34] And there is more. At least in this one case Titian was inspired, not only by the text of the translation, but also by the illustrations that accompanied it (even if they lacked the detail of the hooked sword). It suffices to compare the painting in the Wallace collection with the depiction of *Perseus and Andromeda* in the 1538 Venetian imprint (see figs. 9 and 10). The composition is identical. (Note that in the first edition of Agostini's version, also printed in Venice, Perseus descends from the sky at Andromeda's right rather than the left.) From the very start, however, as emerges from the X-ray photographs published by Gould, Titian attempted to alter Andromeda's position, painting her with her arms raised behind her head, rather than bound behind her back.[35] He came to a definitive solution – one arm raised, the other lowered – only later.[36]

Thus, Titian's indebtedness to Ovid passes through a vernacular version also in the case of *Perseus and Andromeda*. But what sort of translation was it?

10. *Perseus and Andromeda*, in Ovid, *Le Metamorphosi ... tradotte ... per Nicolò di Agustini*, Venice 1538, folio 43v.

11. *Perseus and Andromeda*, in Ovid, *Metamorphoseos vulgare*, Venice 1501, folio xxxiiiir.

Agostini's rendition of the *Metamorphoses* in ottava rima holds a pivotal place between the medieval translations and the genuinely sixteenth-century versions by Dolce and Anguillara. This can be demonstrated by taking a rapid journey back into time.

Agostini's verse version, interwoven with prose allegories, first appeared in print in 1522. The same year concludes the publishing history of a previous translation which was many times reprinted beginning in 1497. A comparison of these two vernacular texts demonstrates that (*a*) both contain a series of identical prose allegories; (*b*) the illustrations accompanying both are basically identical, even if those in the older version are considerably less crude in workmanship; (*c*) the text of the older version, in prose, is the basis of Agostini's in *ottava rima*. But who was the author of the prose version? The proemium, dated March 20, 1370, informs us that the work had been "composed, translated, and allegorized" by Giovanni Bonsignori of Città di Castello.[37] Both Bonsignori's allegories and translation are based in large part on the allegorization and paraphrase of the *Metamorphoses* by Giovanni del Virgilio, the Bolognese teacher who was a contemporary of Dante.[38] A small detail introduced by del Virgilio in his Ovidian paraphrase permits us to recapitulate swiftly the textual transmission just outlined. Separating himself from the preceding tradition, Giovanni del Virgilio states that Jove "when he spotted *an opening,* turned himself into liquid gold and fell like a shower on Danae's womb" ("cum videret *unum foramen* ibi convertit se in aurum liquefactum et pluit in gremium Danaes"). Bonsignori translates this as "Then *through an opening,* turning himself into gold, he descended and rained upon Danae's bed" ("Per *uno forame* convertendose in oro se distese et piove sopra lo lecto de Danae"). Agostini's verse rendition reads: "Then *through an opening* which he saw in the roof, he quickly changed himself into a shower of gold and through it descended onto her bed" ("Poi *per una fessura* che nel tetto / vide, cangiossi in pioggia d'oro presto / e per quella discese sul suo letto."[39] This signifies that the vernacular version of the *Metamorphoses* read by Titian had passed through two, perhaps three, intermediaries (Giovanni del Virgilio, Giovanni Bonsignori, Niccolò degli Agostini?). Similarly, the source for the composition of the *Perseus and Andromeda* can be traced back to the illustrations included either with Agostini's (fig. 10) or Bonsignori's (fig. 11) translations. (It should be noted that in the first work a cloth is draped chastely around Andromeda's hips, and Perseus's weapon is a sort of scimitar; the position of the two personages, however, is inverted with respect to the painting.)

It is well known that Titian freely borrowed the most varied figurative materials. Contemporary paintings, ancient statues, and even, as in this case, more or less crude illustrations taken from Ovid translations ended up being reshaped and fused in a language that was his alone. We are also well aware that the stimuli for this extraordinary inventiveness could be literary as well as figurative. But the present demonstration that Titian used only vernacular texts provides us with a picture of his education and culture that differs considerably from the customary one.

But what does all this have to do with my original question concerning erotic representations in the sixteenth century? To answer we need to return to my earlier contrast between the two iconic circuits, the public and the private: the first, broad and socially undifferentiated; the second, restricted and socially of high rank. As I cautioned, it is a schematic distinction, one that would soon be disturbed by the advent of printing. Thanks to this invention, a public whose contours are still a little blurred but which included, at any rate, elements from the lower classes (artisans and even peasants) came into contact not only with the printed page but with the images that frequently accompanied it. The existence of relatively inexpensive, often illustrated books suddenly expanded, in both a quantitative and qualitative sense, the patrimony of words and images available to these social groups. The presumably enormous repercussions of this phenomenon are beginning to be investigated only now.[40]

As for the question under examination here, we can only guess at the enrichment of the erotic imagination provoked by such images as the nude Andromeda used to illustrate vernacular versions of the *Metamorphoses*. This statement may sound paradoxical, perhaps, since these pictorial representations frequently were rudimentary and clumsy. And yet they were capable of stimulating the imagination of a Titian. The erotic charge of these illustrations, sometimes drawn by unskilled hands, is confirmed by a marginal piece of evidence, but not one to be ignored. The nudes which adorn the sixteenth-century books preserved in our libraries – even fortuitous nudes, such as Truth and Fortune in printers' marks – often have come down to us disfigured by the pen-and-ink erasures of now distant readers. By blotting out or disguising the feminine or masculine sexual attributes of these figures, this public was giving vent to an impulse of the mind (or was it of the body?) that was perhaps ephemeral, but that demonstrated just the same that these images had not left it indifferent. Counter-Reformation zealotry one will say. And perhaps it was. But what lies behind this trite expression that we cannot seem to do without?

A survey, unfortunately still in its initial stages, of manuals for confessors and penitents printed in Italy between the end of the fifteenth and the close of the sixteenth century yields a preliminary, not unexpected result. Up to 1540, roughly, avarice is the sin discussed at greatest length, by far; lust follows. About this date that process of control and thoroughgoing repression of sexual life that we are accustomed to attribute, as far as Catholic countries are concerned, to the Counter-Reformation began to take hold. Why did tensions typical of a society in which commerce played such an important (even if not prevalent) role become secondary to those connected with the sexual life? And why, more or less around this time, did similar forms of control spring up even in Protestant countries, foremost in Calvin's Geneva?[41] In a final analysis, all this probably can be explained by the demographic strains emerging in European society,[42] even when the control exercised by the authorities, whether lay or ecclesiastical, took different forms depending on the political and religious situations.

But the study of confessionals suggests another, less obvious motive for reflection. The minute analyses of the sin of lust concentrate on the senses of touch and sound well into the sixteenth century. Sight is hardly mentioned. The social occasions that abet the transgression of the commandment "Do not fornicate" are principally dancing and singing. To make "cantiones vel sonetos … lascivia turpia et inhonesta ad provocandum" is a mortal sin, wrote Bartolomeo Caimi in his confessional.[43] He did not warn against immoral images, simply because their diffusion must have been minimal or nil, except among the upper classes. Only later in the century did sight emerge slowly as a prominent erotic sense, immediately after touch. In the still unwritten history of the senses, due weight will have to be given to this eroticization of sight in respect to hearing, tied to such specific historical circumstances as the diffusion of the printing press and the increased circulation of images.[44]

Nude Dianas and Venuses, nymphs and bacchantes, even if to a limited degree, now fell under the gaze of a public much larger than the prelates and nobles so scathingly condemned by Politi about mid-century. More time had to pass before erotic representations would replace the culturally elevated mythological canon with that middling one, whether realistic or comic, of genre painting. Meanwhile, that refined and complex world of pagan divinities recreated by humanists was being translated by the illustrators of printed books into frequently humble and rudimentary forms – except when that process took an opposed direction, as in the case of Titian's *Andromeda*. But the circular journey traveled by erotic images in the sixteenth century remains to be explored. Indeed, not only Philip II in his private chamber, but many anonymous readers of the vernacular *Metamorphoses* must have projected, as with Terence's

Chaerea, their own most intimate fantasies into the amorous deeds of the ancient gods.

Appendix

The literary "sources" for *Bacchus and Ariadne* have been summarized by Panofsky, *Problems in Titian*, pp. 141-43. I reproduce below verses 252-67 of Catullus's *carmen* 64 (Loeb Classical Library trans.), followed by Dolce's vernacular version.

> In another part of the tapestry youthful Bacchus was wandering with the rout of Satyrs and the Nysaborn Sileni, seeking thee, Ariadna, and fired with thy love; ... who then, busy here and there, were raging with frenzied mind, while "Evoe!" they cried tumultuously, "Evoe!" shaking their heads.
>
> Some of them were waving thyrsi with shrouded points, some tossing about the limbs of a mangled steer, some girding themselves with writhing serpents: some bearing in solemn procession dark mysteries enclosed in caskets, mysteries which the profane desire in vain to hear. Others beat timbrels with uplifted hands, or raised clear clashings with cymbals of rounded bronze: many blew horns with harsh-sounding drone, and the barbarian pipe shrilled with dreadful din.
>
> Such were the figures that richly adorned the tapestry which embraced and shrouded with its folds the royal couch.

And now Dolce's version (*Paraphrasi nella sesta satira di Giuvenale ... Dialogo in cui si parla di che qualità si dee tor moglie ... lo epithalamio di Catullo nelle nozze di Peleo e di Theti* [Venice, 1538], fols. P *r-v*):

> In another part of the rich work, Bacchus could be seen, his blond locks crowned and adorned with grapes and flowers. Silenus, flushed and swollen with wine, followed on an ass. And he was closely surrounded by a dense chorus of satyrs and *sileni*, all of them giving praise in their own way, making drunken gestures and in a craze calling out to Bacchus with joyful voice and swaying heads. Others held spears quavering in their hands that were adorned with the leaves and stems of that vine which he holds sacred, which concealed the horrid spike. Others still were brandishing and swinging about with both hands the bloody remains of a steer hacked into many parts; others draped writhing serpents around their necks and chests; another group celebrated in empty baskets as was their custom sacrifices to Bacchus, sacrifices which one who is not an adept of their sacred lore seeks in vain to hear. Still others made cymbals sound, striking with hard woods, or produced softer tones with slender reeds. Many, blowing hard into a winding horn, filled the surrounding sky with raucous voices. And swelling up both cheeks made the horn

sound from afar with a dreadful noise. Nor for any other reason had that ever blond and youthful god stirred than to be espoused with you, and raise you to eternal glory, enflamed and consumed by your beauty, O unhappy woman. Thus adorned and embellished with these figures, the rich drapery made a proud covering for the superb marriage bed.

The reference to the "flushed and swollen" Silenus, not mentioned by Catullus (but present in Bacchus's procession described by Ovid, *Ars Amandi* 1.541 ff.), suffices to demonstrate that Dolce here, rather than translating, was attempting to give a literary equivalent to Titian's painting.

Titian - elevated socially & esteemed but wasn't a humanist - no knowledge of Latin

Breakdown b/t learned & popular culture

cultural amphibians

❧ Clues: Roots of an Evidential Paradigm

God is in the detail.   *A. Warburg*

An object which speaks of the loss, of the destruction, of the disappearance of objects. It does not speak of itself. It speaks of others. Will it also include them?   *J. Johns*

In the following pages an attempt will be made to show the silent emergence of an epistemological model (a paradigm, if you prefer)[1] towards the end of the nineteenth century, in the humanities. Sufficient attention has not been paid to this paradigm, though it is very much operative in spite of never having become explicit theory. Such a study may help us to break out of the fruitless opposition between "rationalism" and "irrationalism."

I

A series of articles on Italian painting appeared in the *Zeitschrift für bildende Kunst* between 1874 and 1876. They were signed by an unknown Russian scholar, Ivan Lermolieff, and translated into German by an equally obscure Johannes Schwarze. The new method of the attribution of old masters proposed by the articles provoked conflicting reactions and lively discussions among art historians. The author then shed the twin masks, revealing himself to be the Italian Giovanni Morelli (a surname for which Schwarze is the equivalent and Lermolieff very nearly its anagram). Art historians today still speak of a "Morellian method."[2]

Of what did this method consist? Museums, Morelli stated, are full of paintings with inexact attributions. But it is difficult to trace every piece to its real creator: we are frequently dealing with unsigned works which may have been touched up or are in a deteriorated condition. In these circumstances it is essential to be able to distinguish originals from copies. Yet, to accomplish this, Morelli insisted, we should not depend, as was so often the case, on the most

96

conspicuous characteristics of a painting, which are the easiest to imitate: eyes raised towards the heavens in the figures of Perugino, Leonardo's smiles, and so on. We should examine, instead, the most trivial details that would have been influenced least by the mannerisms of the artist's school: earlobes, fingernails, shapes of fingers and of toes. Morelli identified and faithfully catalogued by this method the shape of the ear in figures by Botticelli, Cosmé Tura, and others, traits that were present in the originals but not in copies. He ended up proposing many new attributions for works hanging in the principal European museums. Some of the new identifications were sensational: in a reclining nude in Dresden which had passed as a copy by Sassoferrato of a lost painting by Titian, Morelli identified one of the very few authentic works by Giorgione.

In spite of these results, Morelli's method was heavily criticized, in part, perhaps, because of the almost arrogant certainty with which he applied it. In time, it came to be judged mechanical, crudely positivistic, and fell into disrepute.[3] Still, many scholars who aligned themselves against it may have continued unobtrusively to use it in making their attributions. It is to Edgar Wind that we owe renewed interest in Morelli's writings. Wind viewed them as typical examples of the modern attitude to art, an attitude leading to the appreciation of details rather than of the work in general. Morelli represented a carrying to extremes of the cult devoted to artistic spontaneity whose ideas he had absorbed in his youth through contact with Romantic circles in Berlin.[4] Wind's interpretation is not very convincing, since Morelli was not concerned with aesthetic problems (a fact which was later held against him), but with problems of a preliminary philological order.[5] Actually, the implications of Morelli's method were of a different sort, and much more complex. We shall see how Wind himself was a hair's breadth from discovering them.

"Morelli's books," Wind writes, "look different from those of any other writer on art; they are sprinkled with illustrations of fingers and ears, careful records of the characteristic trifles by which an artist gives himself away, as a criminal might be spotted by a fingerprint ... any art gallery studied by Morelli begins to resemble a rogue's gallery."[6] This analogy was developed brilliantly by Enrico Castelnuovo, who compared Morelli's presumptive method to the one ascribed, almost contemporaneously, to Sherlock Holmes by his creator, Arthur Conan Doyle.[7] The art connoisseur resembles the detective who discovers the perpetrator of a crime (or the artist behind a painting) on the basis of evidence that is imperceptible to most people. There are countless examples of Holmes's shrewdness in discovering clues by means of footprints, cigarette ashes, and the like. But to be convinced of just how accurate Castelnuovo's analogy is we need only to glance at "The Cardboard Box" (1892), in which Sherlock Holmes literally "morellizes." The case begins, in fact, with two severed ears sent through the mails to an innocent maiden lady. And here is the expert at work: "Holmes paused, and I [Watson] was surprised, on glancing round, to see that he was staring with singular intentness at the lady's profile. Surprise and satisfaction were both for an instant to be read upon his eager face, though when she glanced round to find out the cause of his silence he had become as demure as ever."[8] Later, Holmes explains to Watson (and to the reader) the course of his lightning mental process:

> As a medical man, you are aware, Watson, that there is no part of the body which varies so much as the human ear. Each ear is as a rule quite distinctive, and differs from all other ones. In last year's *Anthropological Journal* you will find two short monographs from my pen upon the subject. I had, therefore, examined the ears in the box with the eyes of an expert, and had carefully noted their anatomical peculiarities. Imagine my surprise then, when, on looking at Miss Cushing, I perceived that her ear corresponded exactly with the female ear which I had just inspected. The matter was entirely beyond coincidence. There was the same shortening of the pinna, the same broad curve of the upper lobe, the same convolution of the inner cartilage. In all essentials it was the same ear. Of course, I at once saw the enormous importance of the observation. It was evident that the victim was a blood relation, and probably a very close one.[9]

We shall see, shortly, the implications of this parallel.[10] But first it may be well to look at another of Wind's valuable intuitions: "To some of Morelli's critics it has seemed odd that personality should be found where personal effort is weakest. But on this point modern psychology would certainly support Morelli: our inadvertent little gestures reveal our character far more authentically than any formal posture that we may carefully prepare."[11] "Our inadvertent little gestures ...": for the phrase "modern psychology" we can forthwith substitute the name of Freud. What Wind wrote about Morelli has, in fact, drawn the attention of scholars to a long-neglected passage in Freud's famous essay "The Moses of Michelangelo" (1914).[12] Freud began the second section by writing:

Long before I had any opportunity of hearing about psycho-analysis, I learnt that a Russian art-connoisseur, Ivan Lermolieff, had caused a revolution in the art galleries of Europe by questioning the authorship of many pictures, showing how to distinguish copies from originals with certainty, and constructing hypothetical artists for those works of art whose former supposed authorship had been discredited. He achieved this by insisting that attention should be diverted from the general impression and main features of a picture, and he laid stress on the significance of minor details, of things like the drawing of the finger-nails, of the lobe of an ear, of aureoles and such unconsidered trifles which the copyist neglects to imitate and yet which every artist executes in his own characteristic way. I was then greatly interested to learn that the Russian pseudonym concealed the identity of an Italian physician called Morelli, who died in 1891 with the rank of Senator of the Kingdom of Italy. It seems to me that his method of inquiry is closely related to the technique of psycho-analysis. It, too, is accustomed to divine secret and concealed things from unconsidered or unnoticed details, from the rubbish heap, as it were, of our observations.[13]

The essay on the *Moses* of Michelangelo originally appeared anonymously: Freud claimed it as his own only when he included it among his collected works. It has been supposed that Morelli's inclination to suppress his own identity as an author, concealing it under pseudonyms, may have ended up affecting even Freud; and various more or less acceptable theories have been offered on the significance of this coincidence.[14] What is certain is that Freud, under the veil of anonymity, acknowledged in a manner that was both explicit and reticent, the considerable intellectual influence exercised by Morelli upon him at a stage long before the discovery of psychoanalysis. To reduce this influence, as some have attempted to do, to merely the essay on Michelangelo's *Moses*, or in general terms to those essays dealing with art history,[15] unduly limits the scope of Freud's own words: "It seems to me that [Morelli's] method of inquiry is closely related to the technique of psycho-analysis." Instead, the entire statement by Freud from which I have just quoted assures Giovanni Morelli a special place in the early development of psychoanalysis. It is, in fact, a documented connection, not a hypothetical one, as is often the case with Freud's "antecedents" or "precursors"; moreover, the encounter with Morelli's writings occurred, as I have said, in Freud's "preanalytic" phase. We are dealing with an element, then, that contributed directly to the crystallization of psychoanalysis, and not (as in the case of the piece on the dream of J. Popper "Lynkeus" mentioned in the reprintings of the *Traumdeutung*)[16] with a coincidence noted subsequently, after the discovery had been made.

Before asking what Freud might have gained by reading Morelli, we should try to pinpoint the time of this occurrence, or perhaps we should say the times, since Freud speaks of two separate encounters: "Long before I had any opportunity of hearing about psycho-analysis, I learnt that a Russian art-connoisseur, Ivan Lermolieff ..."; "I was then greatly interested to learn that the Russian pseudonym concealed the identity of an Italian physician called Morelli...."

We can only guess at the date of the first statement. As a *terminus ante quem* we can suggest 1895 (the year Freud and Breuer's *Studies on Hysteria* were published) or 1896 (when Freud used the term *psychoanalysis* for the first time).[17] The *terminus post quem* is 1883. In December of that year Freud mentioned in a long letter to his fiancée his "discovery of art" during a visit to the Dresden Museum. He had not been interested in art previously, but now, he wrote, "I sloughed off my barbarism and began to admire."[18] It is difficult to imagine that Freud could have been interested in the writings of an unknown art historian before this date; it is perfectly plausible, instead, that he should have begun to read them not long after the letter to his fiancée about the Dresden gallery, since Morelli's first volume of collected essays (Leipzig, 1880) dealt with works by Italian masters in the Munich, Dresden, and Berlin museums.[19]

Freud's second encounter with the writings of Morelli probably can be dated with greater precision. Ivan Lermolieff's real name was made public for the first time on the title page of the English translation of his collected articles mentioned above, which appeared in 1883; in later editions and in the translations after 1891 (the date of Morelli's death) both his name and the pseudonym always appear.[20] We cannot exclude the possibility that one of these volumes, sooner or later, fell into Freud's hands; but he may have learned of Ivan Lermolieff's identity by pure chance in September 1898, rummaging in a Milanese bookshop. Freud's library, now in London, contains a copy of Giovanni Morelli (Ivan Lermolieff), *Della Pittura italiana: Studii storico critici – Le Gallerie Borghese e Doria Pamphili in Roma* (Milan, 1897). The date of purchase is inscribed on the title page: Milan, September 14.[21] Freud's only visit to Milan took place in the fall of 1898.[22] At that particular time, moreover, Morelli's book would have interested Freud for still another reason. For several months he had been occupying himself with memory lapses: a little earlier, in Dalmatia, he had tried in vain to recall the name of the artist responsible for the Orvieto frescoes (an episode which he later studied in *Psychopathology of Everyday Life*). Morelli's book actually mentioned the painter (Luca Signorelli) as well as the other artists who had popped into Freud's memory (Botticelli, G. A. Boltraffio) as possibilities.[23]

But what could a reading of Morelli's essays have meant to the young Freud, still far from psychoanalysis? Freud himself tells us: it was the idea of a method of interpretation based on discarded information, on marginal data, considered in some way significant. By this method, details usually considered of little importance, even trivial or "minor," provided the key for approaching higher aspects of the human spirit: "My adversaries," Morelli wrote ironically (just the sort of irony that would have delighted Freud), "like to consider me a person who is unable to discern the spiritual meaning in a work of art and for this reason gives special importance to external matters, the shape of a hand, of an ear, and even, *horribile dictu*, to such an unpleasant subject as fingernails."[24] Morelli could have claimed as his own that Vergilian motto so dear to Freud which he used as the epigraph for *The Interpretation of Dreams*: "Flectere si nequeo Superos, Archeronta movebo" ("If Heaven I can not bend, then Hell I will arouse").[25] Moreover, to Morelli, these marginal facts were revealing because they constituted the instances when the control of the artist, who was tied to a cultural tradition, relaxed and yielded to purely individual touches "which escaped without his being aware of it."[26] What is so remarkable, even more than the allusion to the unconscious,[27] not exceptional for the period, is the identification of the essence of artistic individuality with elements outside conscious control.

I have traced parallels between the methods of Morelli, Holmes, and Freud. I have already spoken of the connections between Morelli-Holmes and Morelli-Freud. The striking similarity between the methods of Holmes and Freud has been discussed by Steven Marcus.[28] Freud himself revealed his interest in the adventures of Sherlock Holmes to a patient, the "wolf-man." But in the spring of 1913 to a colleague, Theodor Reik, who had compared the psychoanalytic method to that of Holmes, Freud spoke with admiration of the techniques attributed to Morelli. In each case, infinitesimal traces permit the comprehension of a deeper, otherwise unattainable reality: traces – more precisely, symptoms (in the case of Freud), clues (in the case of Sherlock Holmes), pictorial marks (in the case of Morelli).[29]

How does one explain this threefold analogy? At first glance the solution would seem very simple. Freud was a physician; Morelli had a medical degree; Conan Doyle had practiced medicine before turning to literature. In each of these cases the model of medical semiotics is evident: that discipline which permits the diagnosis of diseases inaccessible to direct observation based on superficial symptoms, sometimes thought to be irrelevant in the eyes of the layman – Dr. Watson, for example. It is worth noting, incidentally, that the duo Holmes-Watson, the perceptive detective and the obtuse physician, represents the splitting of a single real person, one of the young Conan Doyle's professors, renowned for his extraordinary diagnostic abilities.[30] But these are not simply biographical coincidences. Towards the end of the nineteenth century – more precisely in the decade 1870-80 – a presumptive paradigm began to assert itself in the humane sciences that was based specifically on semiotics. Its roots, however, were much older.

II

Man has been a hunter for thousands of years. In the course of countless chases he learned to reconstruct the shapes and movements of his invisible prey from tracks on the ground, broken branches, excrement, tufts of hair, entangled feathers, stagnating odors. He learned to sniff out, record, interpret, and classify such infinitesimal traces as trails of spittle. He learned how to execute complex mental operations with lightning speed, in the depth of a forest or in a prairie with its hidden dangers.

This rich storehouse of knowledge has been passed down by hunters over the generations. In the absence of verbal documentation to supplement rock paintings and artifacts, we can turn to folklore, which transmits an echo, though dim and distorted, of the knowledge accumulated by those remote hunters. An oriental fable that circulated among Kirghiz, Tartars, Jews, Turks, and others relates the story of three brothers who meet a man who has lost a camel or, in variant versions, a horse.[31] They describe it for him without hesitation: it is white, blinded in one eye, and carries two goat-skins on its back, one full of wine, the other of oil. Then they have seen it? No, they have not. So they are accused of stealing and brought to trial. For the brothers, this is a moment of triumph: they demonstrate in a flash how, by means of myriad small clues, they could reconstruct the appearance of an animal on which they have never laid eyes.

Obviously, the three brothers are repositories of some sort of venatic lore, even if they are not necessarily hunters. This knowledge is characterized by the ability to construct from apparently insignificant experimental data a complex reality that could not be experienced directly. Also, the data is always arranged by the observer in such a way as to produce a narrative sequence, which could be expressed most simply as "someone passed this way." Perhaps the actual idea of narration (as distinct from charms, exorcisms, or invocation)[32] may have originated in a hunting society, relating the experience of deciphering tracks. This obviously undemonstrable hypothesis nevertheless seems to be reinforced by the fact that the rhetorical figures on which the language of venatic deduction still rests today – the part in relation to the whole, the effect in relation to the cause – are traceable to the narrative axis of metonymy, with the rigorous exclusion of metaphor.[33] The hunter would have been the first "to tell a story" because he alone was able to read, in the silent, nearly imperceptible tracks left by his prey, a coherent sequence of events.

"To decipher" or "to read" animal tracks are metaphors. We have tried, however, to take them literally, as the verbal condensation of a historical process which brought us, perhaps over a long span of time, to the invention of writing. The same sort of connection has been articulated, in the guise of an aetiological myth, by Chinese tradition, which attributes the invention of writing to a high official who had observed bird tracks on the sandy banks of a river.[34] On the other hand, if we abandon the realm of myths and hypotheses for that of documented history, we are struck by the undeniable analogies between the venatic model just discussed and the paradigm implicit in the Mesopotamian divination texts, which began to be composed in the third millenium B.C.[35] Both presuppose the minute investigation of even trifling matters, to discover the traces of events that could not be directly experienced by the observer. Excrement, tracks, hairs, feathers, in one case; animals' innards, drops of oil on the water, heavenly bodies, involuntary movements of the body, in the other. Granted that the second series, as opposed to the first, was virtually limitless in the sense that practically everything was grist for the work of the Mesopotamian diviners. But the principal difference between them is something else: divination looked to the future and the interpretation of venatic clues to the past (perhaps a past only instants old). And yet there were great similarities in the learning process between the two; the intellectual operations involved – analyses, comparisons, classifications – were formally identical. Only formally, to be sure; the social context was totally different. It has been noted, in particular, how profoundly the invention of writing shaped Mesopotamian divination.[36] In fact, among other royal prerogatives, the power to communicate with their subjects by means of messages was attributed to the gods – messages written in the heavens, in human bodies, everywhere – which the divines had the task of deciphering (a notion destined to issue in that ageless image of the "book of nature"). And the identification of soothsaying with the deciphering of divine characters inscribed in reality was reinforced by the pictorial features of cuneiform writing: like divination, it too designated one thing through another.[37]

Even a footprint indicates an animal's passing. In respect to the concreteness of the print, of a mark materially understood, the pictogram already represents an incalculable step forward on the road towards intellectual abstraction. But the abstract capacities presupposed by the introduction of pictographic writing are, in turn, of small consequence next to those required for the transfer to phonetic writing. Actually, pictographic and phonetic elements continued to coexist in cuneiform writing, just as in Mesopotamian divination literature the increasing tendency to generalize deductively did not cancel out the fundamental ability to infer causes from their effects.[38] This explains both the way in which technical terms taken from a legal vocabulary infiltrated the Mesopotamian language of divination, and the presence of passages dealing with medical physiognomy and semiotics in divination treatises.[39]

Thus, we have returned to semiotics. We find it included in a constellation of disciplines (although the term is obviously anachronistic) which have a common feature. It might be tempting to juxtapose two pseudosciences, divination and physiognomics, with sciences such as law and medicine, ascribing the disparity in such a comparison to the spatial and temporal distance of the societies under discussion. But this would be a superficial conclusion. Something did indeed link these different methods of seeking knowledge in ancient Mesopotamia (if we exclude divination by inspiration, which was based on experiences of an ecstatic type):[40] it was an attitude oriented towards the analysis of specific cases which could be reconstructed only through traces, symptoms, and clues. Mesopotamian legal texts themselves did not consist of collections of laws or ordinances but of discussions of concrete examples.[41] Consequently, we can speak of a presumptive or divinatory paradigm, directed, depending on the forms of knowledge, towards the past, present, or future. For the future, there was divination in a strict sense; for the past, the present, and the future, there was medical semiotics in its twofold aspect, diagnostic and prognostic; for the past, there was jurisprudence. But behind this presumptive or divinatory paradigm we perceive what may be the oldest act in the intellectual history of the human race: the hunter squatting on the ground, studying the tracks of his quarry.

What I have been saying explains how a diagnosis of cranial trauma reached on the basis of bilateral squint could turn up in a Mesopotamian treatise on divination.[42] More generally, it explains historically how an array of disciplines could emerge which centered on the deciphering of signs of various kinds, from symptoms to writing. Passing from Mesopotamia to Greece this constellation changed profoundly, following the birth of such new disciplines as historiography and philology, and a new social and epistemological autonomy in medicine and other ancient disciplines. The body, language, and human history for the first time were exposed to objective examination, which on principle excluded divine intervention. We are still today the heirs of this decisive turning-point in the culture of the *polis*. It may be less obvious that in this transformation, a paradigm definable as semiotic or presumptive played a primary role.[43] It is especially evident in the case of Hippocratic medicine, where the definition of its chosen method depended on the explicit notion of symptom (*semeion*). The Hippocratic school maintained that only by attentively observing and recording all symptoms in great detail could one develop precise "histories" of individual diseases; disease, in itself, was out of reach. This emphasis on the presumptive nature of medicine was probably inspired by the contrast, pointed out by the Pythagorean physician Alcmeon, between the immediacy of divine knowledge and the speculative nature of human perception.[44] A conjectural paradigm operating on diverse levels found its implicit justification in the denial that reality is transparent. Physicians, historians, politicians, potters, carpenters, sailors, hunters, fishermen, women: for the Greeks these were only some of the groups dealing in that vast world of conjectural knowledge. Its borders – governed, significantly, by the goddess Metis, Jove's first wife, who personified divination by aqueous means – were marked by such terms as "conjecture" and "speculate" (*tekmor, tekmairesthai*). But as I have stated, this paradigm remained implicit – suppressed by the prestigious (and socially higher) model of knowledge developed by Plato.[45]

The defensive tone of certain passages in the Hippocratic corpus[46] indicates that as early as the fifth century B.C., the polemic against the uncertainties of medicine, destined to last into our own day, had already begun. This continuum is explained by the fact that relations between doctor and patient, characterized by the latter's inability to verify the knowledge and authority professed by the former, have not changed much since the time of Hippocrates. But the terms of the controversy, together with the profound transformation experienced by the idea of "rigor" and "science," have changed in the course of almost two and a half millennia. Obviously, the decisive point is constituted by the appearance of a scientific paradigm based on Galileian physics, but one which turned out to be more durable than it. Even if modern physics cannot call itself "Galileian" (although it has not rejected Galileo), his epistemological and even symbolic significance for science in general has remained intact.[47]

It should be clear by now that the group of disciplines which we have called evidential and conjectural (medicine included) are totally unrelated to the scientific criteria that can be claimed for the Galileian paradigm. In fact, they are highly qualitative disciplines, in which the object is the study of individual cases, situations, and documents, precisely *because they are individual*, and for this reason get results that have an unsuppressible speculative margin: just think of the importance of conjecture (the term itself originates in divination)[48] in medicine or in philology, and in divining. Galileian science, which could have taken as its own the Scholastic motto *Individuum est ineffabile* ("We cannot speak about what is individual"), is endowed with totally different characteristics. Mathematics and the empirical method implied, respectively, quantification and the repetition of phenomena, while the individualizing perspective by definition excluded the latter and admitted the former only as mere instrument. All this explains why history never became a Galileian science. It was during the seventeenth century, in fact, that the grafting of antiquarian methods to historiography indirectly revealed the remote conjectural origins of the latter, hidden for centuries.

This original feature has not changed despite the ever-closer links between history and the social sciences. History has stayed a social science *sui generis*, forever tied to the concrete. Even if the historian is sometimes obliged to refer back, explicitly or implicitly, to a sequence of comparable phenomena, the cognitive strategy, as well as the codes by which he expresses himself, remain intrinsically individualizing (although the individual case may be a social group or an entire society). In this respect the historian is like the physician who uses nosographical tables to analyze the specific sickness in a patient. As with the physician's, historical knowledge is indirect, presumptive, conjectural.[49]

But our hypothesis is too orderly. In the realm of conjectural disciplines, one – philology, or more precisely, textual criticism – has from its very emergence presented certain atypical characteristics.

Its objective, in fact, took shape through a process of drastic selection of the pertinent characteristics, later to be reduced even further. This internal curtailing of the discipline was expressed by two decisive historical milestones: the inventions of writing and of printing. Textual *Textual* criticism originated as a consequence of the first (when the decision was *Criticism* taken to transcribe the Homeric poems) and became well established after the second (when the earliest, often hurriedly produced editions of the classics were replaced by more reliable ones).[50] At first, all the elements tied to orality and gesture and later even those tied to the physical characteristics of writing were thought to be irrelevant to the text. This twofold process resulted in a progressive dematerialization of the text, which was gradually purified at every point of reference related to the senses; even though a material element is required for a text's survival, the text itself is not identified by that element.[51] All this seems obvious today, but actually it isn't at all. One need only think of the crucial function played by intonation in oral literature, or by calligraphy in Chinese poetry, to realize that the concept of text I have just mentioned is tied to an extremely significant cultural choice. That this selection was not determined by the mere substitution of mechanical for manual means of reproduction is demonstrated by the well-known example of China, where the invention of printing did not break the link between literary text and calligraphy. We shall see shortly how the problem of pictorial "texts" historically has been expressed in radically different terms.

The abstract notion of text explains why textual criticism, even while retaining to a large extent its divinatory qualities, had the potential to develop in a rigorously scientific direction, as in fact occurred in the course of the nineteenth century.[52] The radical conception of considering only the portions of a text which could be reproduced (first manually and later, after Gutenberg, mechanically) meant that, even while dealing with individual cases,[53] one avoided the principal pitfall of the humane sciences: quality. Significantly, Galileo turned to philology in the very moment that he was founding modern natural science through an equally drastic reduction. The traditional medieval juxtaposition of world and book was based on evidence that both were immediately decipherable, while Galileo, instead, stressed that "philosophy ... written in this great book which is always open before our eyes (I call it the universe) ... cannot be understood if we do not first learn the language and the characters in which it is written," namely, "triangles, circles and other geometrical figures."[54] For the natural philosopher as for the philologist, the text is a profound, invisible entity to be reconstructed independently of material data: "figures, numbers and movements, but not smell, nor tastes, nor sounds, *which I do not believe are anything more than names outside the living animal.*"[55]

With these words Galileo set natural science on the anti-anthropocentric and anti-anthropomorphic direction which it would never again abandon. A gap had opened in that world of knowledge, one destined to enlarge with the passing of time. And, to be sure, there could be no greater contrast than between the Galileian physicist professionally deaf to sounds and insensitive to tastes and odors, and his contemporary, the physician, who hazarded diagnoses by placing his ear on wheezy chests or by sniffing at feces and tasting urine.

The Sienese Giulio Mancini, the personal physician of Urban VIII, was one of these men. There is no evidence that he knew Galileo personally, but it is quite likely that the two met because they belonged to the same Roman circles (from papal court to Academy of the Lincei) and knew many of the same people (from Federico Cesi to Giovanni Ciampoli and Giovanni Faber).[56] Nicio Eritreo (Gian Vittorio Rossi), in an extremely lively sketch, outlined Mancini's atheism, his extraordinary diagnostic abilities (described in terms drawn from the language of divination), and his willingness to extort from his patients paintings about which he was "intelligentissimus."[57] Mancini had, in fact, written a work entitled *Alcune considerationi appartenenti alla pittura come di diletto di un gentilhuomo nobile e come introduttione a quello si deve dire*, which circulated widely in manuscript form but did not actually appear in print until a little over three decades ago.[58] As the title indicates, the book had not been written for painters but for gentlemanly dilettantes – those *virtuosi* who were flocking in ever greater numbers to the exhibitions of ancient and modern paintings being held yearly at the Pantheon on the nineteenth of March.[59] Without this artistic market, Mancini might never have written what was probably the newest element in his *Considerazioni*, the part devoted to the "recognition of painting" – to the methodology, in other words, for identifying fakes, distinguishing originals from copies, and so on.[60] The first attempt to establish connoisseurship (as it would come to be called a century later) can be traced back, then, to this physician celebrated for his lightning diagnoses, a man who, confronted by a patient, could divine with a rapid glance "what would be the outcome of the sickness" ("quem exitum morbus ille esset habiturus").[61] At this point it may be permissible to see in this fusion of the clinician's and connoisseur's eye something more than a simple coincidence.

Before looking more closely at some of Mancini's arguments, we should note a premise shared by him, the "noble gentleman" to whom the *Considerazioni* were addressed, and ourselves. The premise is an unstated one because it has been held (wrongly) to be self-evident: namely, that between a canvas by Raphael and a copy (be it a painting, an engraving, or, today, a photograph) a difference exists that is impossible to eliminate. The commercial implications of this assumption that a painting is by definition unique and impossible to reproduce are obvious.[62] They are connected to the appearance of the connoisseur as a social figure. But the premise springs from a cultural selection which is anything but predictable, as demonstrated by the fact that it is not applicable to written texts. The presumed eternal characteristics of painting and literature do not enter into this. We have already mentioned the historical developments through which the notion of written text became purified of traits not considered pertinent. This refinement has not – yet – taken place in the case of painting. To our eyes, manuscript copies or printed editions of the *Orlando Furioso* can reproduce the text as Ariosto wanted it; copies of a portrait by Raphael, never.[63]

The different status accorded to copies in painting and in literature explains why Mancini, as connoisseur, could not use the methods of textual criticism, even while establishing a general analogy between the acts of painting and writing.[64] And with this analogy as a starting point, he was obliged to look for help to other budding disciplines.

The first goal that Mancini set for himself concerned the dating of paintings. In pursuing it, he stated that it was essential to have "a certain practice learning about the variety of paintings and their periods, just as antiquarians and librarians know letters, from which they deduce the epoch of the writing."[65] The allusion to knowledge of letters has to refer to methods worked out in those very years by Leone Allacci, Vatican librarian, for the dating of Greek and Latin manuscripts – methods that would be further developed a half century later by the founder of paleography, Mabillon.[66] But, Mancini continued, "in addition to the properties common to the century," there also exist "properties that belong to the individual," as "we see these distinctive characteristics in writers." So the analogy between painting and writing, first proposed on a macroscopic scale ("ages," "century"), was subsequently restated on a microscopic, individual level. In this sphere

Allaci's protopaleographical methods did not work. These very years, however, saw an isolated effort to analyze individual scripts from an unusual vantage point. The physician Mancini, citing Hippocrates, observed that it might be possible to move from "functions" to "impressions" of the soul, which in turn are rooted in the "properties" of individual bodies: "through which and with which supposition I believe certain fine minds in this century of ours have written down and attempted to establish a rule for discerning the intellect and intelligence of others in the handwriting of one man or another."

The Bolognese physician, Camillo Baldi, must have been one of these "fine minds." His *Trattato come da una lettera missiva si conoscano la natura e qualità dello scrittore* contained a chapter, the sixth, which can be considered the oldest European text on handwriting. It was entitled "What Meaning Can Be Read into the Representation of the Character," where "character" designated "the figure and the drawing of the letter as it is executed by pen on paper."[67] But in spite of his initial enthusiasm, Mancini lost interest in the stated purpose of the new graphology and the reconstruction of writers' personalities accomplished by going from their written "characters" (i.e., letters) to their psychological "character" (a synonymy which takes us back to a single, remote disciplinary matrix). Mancini paused, instead, on the initial premise of the new discipline: individual handwritings differed and were impossible to imitate. By identifying equally inimitable elements in painting he might have been able to achieve his object, namely the development of a method which would permit the separation of originals from fakes, works by great masters from copies or the productions of their followers. All this explains his exhortation to determine whether

> one can discern in paintings the master's boldness, especially in those parts which of necessity are done deliberately and cannot easily be imitated, as is the case especially with hair, beards, and eyes. Ringlets in the hair can only be imitated with difficulty, and it becomes apparent in the copy; and if the copyist does not want to imitate them, then they will lack the master's perfection. And these features in a painting are like strokes and flourishes in handwriting, which require the master's boldness and resolution. The same can be said about bold strokes of brilliance which the artist executes with masterful touches impossible to imitate, as in the folds of clothing and reflected light, which depend more on the artist's fantasy than on the actual reality of the object.[68]

So we can see that the parallel between acts of writing and painting previously discussed by Mancini in various contexts is reexamined in this passage from a new and unprecedented point of view (with the exception of a passage by Filarete which Mancini may not have known).[69] The analogy is emphasized by the use of such technical terms recurring in contemporary handwriting treatises as "boldness," "strokes," "flourishes."[70] This is also the origin of the insistence on "speed": in an increasingly bureaucratic age, the characteristic guaranteeing success for a chancery cursive on the copyist's market was, besides elegance, the swiftness of the *ductus*.[71] In general, the importance Mancini attributed to decorative elements testifies to the serious attention he was paying to the salient features of Italian handwriting models prevailing from the late sixteenth to the early seventeenth centuries.[72] The study of written "characters" revealed that the identification of a master's hand should be looked for in the parts of a painting executed most rapidly, and thus potentially freed from the representation of reality (tangles of hair, cloth "which depend more on the artist's fantasy than on the actual reality of the object"). We shall return to the riches buried in these statements – riches that neither Mancini nor his contemporaries were able to bring to the surface.

"Characters." This word reappears in its proper or analogical sense about 1620, in writings by the founder of modern physics on the one hand, and in the works of the originators of paleography, graphology, and connoisseurship, on the other. To be sure, only a metaphorical relationship existed between the disembodied "characters" read by Galileo in the book of nature through the eyes of the brain,[73] and those materially deciphered by Allacci, Baldi, or Mancini on paper and parchment, canvas, or tablets. But the identity of terms brings up once again the heterogeneity of the disciplines which I have juxtaposed. Their scientific value, in the Galileian sense of the term, decreased abruptly as one passed from the universal "properties" of geometry to "properties common to the century" in writing and then to the "individual properties" of paintings – or even calligraphy.

This descending scale confirms that the real obstacle to the application of the Galileian paradigm was the centrality (or the lack of it) of the individual element in the single disciplines. The more that individual traits were considered pertinent, the more the possibility of attaining exact scientific knowledge diminished. Of course, the preliminary decision to neglect individual features did not in itself guarantee that physico-mathematical methods could be applied, and without them there could be no talk of adopting the Galileian paradigm in a strict sense. But at least in that case it was excluded without more ado.

At this juncture two roads were open: either sacrifice knowledge of the individual element for generalizations (more or less scientific, more or less capable of being formulated in mathematical terms) or attempt to develop, even if tentatively, a different paradigm, founded on scientific knowledge of the individual ... but a body of knowledge yet to be defined. The first course was taken by the natural sciences, and only much later by the so-called humane sciences. The reason for this is clear. The tendency to obliterate the individual traits of an object is directly proportional to the emotional distance of the observer. In his *Trattato di Architettura* Filarete declared that it was impossible to create two perfectly identical buildings, just as Tartars' "snouts are made alike, or indeed Ethiopians are all black, and yet if you examine them closely have differences alongside the similarities." He did admit, however, that "many animals do resemble one another, such as flies, ants, worms, frogs and many fish so that members of the species cannot be told apart one from the other."[74] In the eyes of a European architect, even the slight differences between two edifices (European) were significant, those between two Tartars or Ethiopians were negligible, and those between two worms or two ants, actually nonexistent. A Tartar architect, an Ethiopian ignorant of architecture, or an ant would have suggested different hierarchies. Individualizing knowledge is always anthropocentric, ethnocentric, and so on. Of course, even animals, minerals, or plants could be viewed from an individualizing perspective – that of divination, for instance[75] – especially in cases clearly outside the norm. Teratology, as we know, was an important component of divining. But in the early decades of the seventeenth century even the indirect influence of a model such as the Galileian tended to subordinate the study of anomalous phenomena, such as divination, to investigation of the norm, to furthering the general knowledge of nature. In April 1625 a two-headed calf was born in the outskirts of Rome. The naturalists in the Academy of the Lincei became interested in the case. It was the topic of conversations in the Vatican gardens of the Belvedere between Giovanni Faber, the academy's secretary, Ciampoli (both, as we have seen, close to Galileo), Mancini, Cardinal Agostino Vegio, and Urban VIII. The first question they asked was the following: Was the bicephalous calf one or two animals? For physicians it is the brain that distinguishes the individual; for Aristotelians, it is the heart.[76] In Faber's account we can probably detect an echo of the participation of Mancini (the only medical man present at the discussions). So, in spite of his astrological interests,[77] he analyzed the specific characteristics of the monstrous birth, not for the purpose of foretelling the future but, rather, to achieve a more precise definition of the normal individual, who, as a representative of a species, could reasonably be considered a repeatable phenomenon. With the same attention which he was accustomed to dedicate to paintings, Mancini pored over the anatomy of the two-headed calf. But the analogy with his activity as connoisseur ended here. In a sense, he personified the linking of the divinatory paradigm (Mancini the diagnostician and connoisseur) and the generalizing paradigm (Mancini the anatomist and naturalist) yoked together, but each of different origin. Despite appearances, the precise description of the autopsy performed on the calf, recorded by Faber, and the detailed engravings of the animal's internal organs which accompanied it[78] were not intended to reveal the "individual properties" of the object as such, but to reach beyond them to "the common properties" of the species (which in this case were natural rather than historical). The naturalistic tradition going back to Aristotle was thereby revived and sharpened. Sight, symbolized by the sharp-eyed lynx on the shield of Federico Cesi's academy, became the privileged function of those disciplines excluded from the suprasensorial eye of mathematics.[79]

The humane sciences (as we would call them today) were at least ostensibly represented among these disciplines, primarily for their tenacious anthropocentrism, expressed with such naïveté in the quotation from Filarete. And yet there were attempts to introduce the mathematical method even in the study of what was most human.[80] Understandably, the first and most successful, carried out by the political arithmeticians, assumed as its subject human events that were most affected by biology: birth, procreation, and death. This drastic reductionism permitted rigorous inquiry, and at the same time served the requirement for information in the areas of the military or finance of absolute states, oriented as they were, and given the scale of their operations, in an exclusively quantitative direction. But the indifference to qualitative matters of those who used the new science of statistics did not entirely cause it to break its ties with that circle of disciplines which we have dubbed conjectural. The calculation of probability, as the title of Bernoulli's classic work, *Ars conjectandi*, tells us, was an attempt to give a mathematically exact formulation to problems which had also confronted divination in a radically different form.[81]

But the humane sciences as a whole remained firmly anchored to the qualitative, though not without some uneasiness, especially in the case of medicine. In spite of advances, its methods seemed doubtful, its results questionable. A work such as Cabanis's *The Certainty of Medicine*, published towards the end of the eighteenth century, recognized this lack of accuracy, even as it strove to acknowledge a scientific character of its own in medicine.[82] There seemed to be basically two reasons for this "uncertainty." First, it was not enough to catalogue individual diseases so that they would fit into an orderly scheme: in every individual a disease assumed different characteristics. Second, knowledge of diseases remained indirect and conjectural: by definition, the living body was beyond reach. To be sure, the cadaver was dissectable: but how could one's steps be traced from it, already impaired by death, to the characteristics of the living individual?[83] In the face of this twofold difficulty it was inevitably recognized that the efficacy of medical procedures was not subject to proof. In conclusion, the inability of medicine to achieve the exactness of the natural sciences stemmed from the impossibility to quantify, except with purely auxiliary functions. And the impossibility of quantifying was due to the unavoidable presence of what was qualitative, of the individual; and the presence of the individual was indebted to the fact that the human eye is more sensitive to differences (even marginal ones) between human beings than those between rocks or leaves. The future epistemological essence of the humane sciences was already being formulated in these discussions on the "uncertainty" of medicine.

An understandable impatience can be read between the lines of Cabanis's book. In spite of the more or less justifiable objections which could be directed against medicine on the methodological plane, it remained fully recognized as a science from the point of view of society. But in this period not all forms of conjectural knowledge benefited from similar prestige. Some, such as connoisseurship, which was relatively recent, occupied an ambiguous position on the periphery of the recognized disciplines. Others, more closely tied to daily life, actually remained outside. The ability to identify a defective horse by the condition of his hocks, an impending storm by sudden changes in the wind, a hostile intention in a sudden change of expression, was certainly not to be learned from a farrier's manual or meteorological or psychological treatises. Knowledge of this sort in each instance was richer than any written codification; it was learned not from books but from the living voice, from gestures and glances;

it was based on subtleties impossible to formalize, which often could not even be translated into words; it constituted the patrimony, partly unitary, partly diversified, of men and women from all social classes. These insights were bound by a subtle relationship: they had all originated in concrete experience. The force behind this knowledge resided in this concreteness, but so did its limitation – the inability to make use of the powerful and terrible weapon of abstraction.[84]

Written culture had for a considerable period of time attempted to give a precise verbal formulation for this body of local knowledge that was without origin, memory, or history.[85] By and large, the results were dull and impoverished. Just think of the abyss separating the schematic rigidity of the physiognomy treatises from the flexible and rigorous insight of a lover or a horse trader or a card shark. Only in the case of medicine, perhaps, had the written codification of conjectural knowledge resulted in real enrichment (although the history of the relationship between learned and popular medicine remains to be written). In the course of the eighteenth century the situation changed. An out-and-out cultural offensive by the bourgeoisie appropriated for itself much of the knowledge, conjectural and nonconjectural alike, of artisans and peasants, codifying it and thereby intensifying a gigantic process of acculturation begun earlier (obviously in a different guise) by the Counter-Reformation. The *Encyclopédie*, naturally, is the symbol and chief instrument in this offensive. However, even minor (but revealing) episodes need to be studied, such as the case of the Roman bricklayer who proved to a presumably stupefied Johann Joachim Winckelmann that the "tiny, flat stone" between the fingers of a statue discovered at Porto d'Anzio was actually "the stopper of an ampulla."[86]

The systematic gathering of these "small insights," as Winckelmann calls them on another occasion,[87] nourished, between the waning eighteenth and early nineteenth centuries, the new formulations of ancient lore – from cooking to hydrology and veterinary medicine. For an increasingly large number of readers, access to specific experiences was mediated by means of the printed page. The novel actually provided the bourgeoisie with both a substitute for and reformulation of initiation rites – that is, for access to experience in general.[88] And thanks precisely to the literature of imagination, the conjectural paradigm enjoyed new and unexpected success in this period.

I mentioned earlier, in connection with the probable venatic origin of the conjectural paradigm, the oriental fable of the three brothers who described an animal they had never seen by interpreting a series of clues. The story first appeared in the West in the collection of Giovanni Sercambi.[89] It reappeared as the centerpiece of a much larger anthology of stories, presented as translations from Persian into Italian by a certain Cristoforo the Armenian, published in Venice in the mid-sixteenth century with the title *Peregrinaggio di tre giovani figliuoli del re Serendippo*. In this version the book was reprinted and translated several times – first into German and then, in the course of the eighteenth century, riding that wave of interest for things oriental, into the principal European languages.[90] The story of the sons of King Serendippo enjoyed such great success that it led Horace Walpole in 1754 to coin the neologism *serendipity* to designate the "making [of] discoveries, by accidents and sagacity, of things which they were not in quest of."[91] A few years earlier Voltaire, in chapter 3 of *Zadig*, had revised the first novella in the *Peregrinaggio*, which he had read in the French translation. In Voltaire's version the camel of the original had become transformed into a bitch and a horse, which Zadig succeeded in describing minutely by deciphering their tracks on the ground. After he was accused of theft and conducted before the judges, Zadig exculpated himself by recounting out loud the mental process which had enabled him to sketch the portrait of two animals he had never seen: "I saw on the sand the tracks of an animal, and I easily judged that they were those of a little dog. Long, shallow furrows imprinted on little rises in the sand between the tracks of the paws informed me that it was a bitch whose dugs were hanging down, and that therefore she had had puppies a few days before."[92] These lines, and those which followed, were the embryo of the mystery novel. They inspired Poe, Gaboriau, and Conan Doyle – the first two directly, the third perhaps indirectly.[93]

The reasons for the extraordinary success of the detective story are well known. I shall discuss some of them below. I can observe straightaway, however, that the genre was based on a model of learning that was both very ancient and modern. I have already talked about its distant roots in antiquity. As for its modernity, it will suffice to cite the page on which Georges Cuvier extolled the methods and successes of the new science of paleontology:

Today, anyone who sees only the print of a cloven hoof might conclude that the animal that had left it behind was a ruminator, and this conclusion is as certain as any in physics and in ethics. This footprint alone, then, provides the observer with information about the teeth, the jawbone, the vertebrae, each leg bone, the thighs, shoulders and pelvis of the animal which had just passed: it is a more certain proof than all Zadig's tracks.[94]

A more precise sign, perhaps, but one that was also closely allied. The name "Zadig" had taken on such symbolic value that in 1880 Thomas Huxley, on a lecture tour to publicize Darwin's discoveries, defined as "Zadig's method" that procedure which combined history, archaeology, geology, physical astronomy, and paleontology: namely, the ability to forecast retrospectively. Disciplines such as these, profoundly diachronic, could not avoid turning to the conjectural or divinatory paradigm (and Huxley spoke explicitly of divination directed toward the past),[95] discarding the Galileian model. When causes cannot be reproduced, there is nothing to do but to deduce them from their effects.

III

We could compare the threads of this research to the threads in a carpet. We are at a point where we see them arranged in a tight, homogeneous weave. The consistency of the design is verifiable by casting an eye over the carpet in various directions. Vertically, we would have a sequence of the type Serendippo-Zadig-Poe-Gaboriau-Conan Doyle. Horizontally, we find at the beginning of the eighteenth century a certain Monsieur J.-B. Dubos listing, one after another in decreasing order of unreliability, medicine, connoisseurship, and the identification of scripts.[96] Diagonally, even, jumping from one historical context to another – over the shoulder of Monsieur Lecoq feverishly crossing an "expanse of earth, covered with snow," dotted with the tracks of criminals, comparing it to "an immense white page upon which people we are in search of have written, not only their movements and their goings and comings, but their secret thoughts, the hopes and anxieties that agitated them,"[97] we shall see emerging authors of physiognomy treatises, Babylonian soothsayers deciphering messages composed by the gods on rocks or in the heavens, and Neolithic hunters.

The carpet is the paradigm that, as I went along, I have called, depending on the context, venatic, divinatory, conjectural, or semiotic. These, clearly, are not synonymous adjectives, but nonetheless refer to a common epistemological model, expressed through various disciplines that are frequently linked by borrowed methods or key terms. Then, between the eighteenth and nineteenth centuries, with the emergence of the "humane sciences," the constellation of conjectural disciplines changed profoundly: new stars were born and quickly fell, such as phrenology, or experienced great success, as did paleontology.[98] But it is medicine, above all others, which assumes a preeminent position, thanks to its prestige epistemologically and socially. All the "humane sciences" attempt to relate themselves to it, explicitly or implicitly. But to which side of medicine? In mid-nineteenth century we see choices emerging: the anatomical model on the one hand, the semiotic on the other. The metaphor "anatomy of society," employed even by Marx in a crucial passage,[99] expresses the admiration for systematic knowledge in an age which had witnessed the collapse of the last great system, the Hegelian. But in spite of Marxism's great success, the humane sciences increasingly ended up accepting (with one notable exception, as we shall see) the conjectural paradigm of semiotics. And here we return to the trio Morelli, Freud, and Conan Doyle with which we began.

Thus far I have spoken of a conjectural paradigm and its synonyms in a broad sense. It is now the moment to dismember it. It is one thing to analyze footprints, stars, feces, sputum, corneas, pulsations, snow-covered fields, or cigarette ashes; it is quite another to examine handwriting or paintings or conversation. There is a basic difference between nature, inanimate or living, and culture – certainly greater than the infinitely more superficial and mutable differences that exist between individual disciplines. Morelli set out to identify, within a culturally conditioned system of signs such as the pictorial, those which appeared to be involuntary, as is the case with symptoms (and the majority of clues). And in these involuntary signs, in the "material trifles" – a calligrapher might call them "flourishes" – comparable to "favorite words and phrases" which "most people introduce into their speaking and writing unintentionally, often without realizing it," Morelli recognized the surest clue to an artist's identity.[100] He was thus resurrecting (indirectly perhaps)[101] and further developing methodological principles which had been formulated much earlier by his predecessor, Giulio Mancini. It was no accident that these principles should finally reach maturity after so long a time. In this very period there had emerged an ever more visible trend consisting of closer control of society by the state, employing a conception of the individual which also was based on small and involuntary traits.

Every society feels the need to distinguish its essential elements; but the way this need is approached varies with time and place.[102] There is the name first of all: but the more complicated a society, the more a name is inadequate to circumscribe an individual's identity unambiguously. In Greco-Roman Egypt, for example, a person standing before a notary for the purpose of contracting matrimony or concluding a commercial transaction was required to have a short physical description recorded next to his name, including mention of any scars or other particular marks.[103] The chances of error or fraudulent substitution of persons remained high just the same. In contrast, a signature at the bottom of contracts offered many advantages: at the end of the eighteenth century, the abbot Lanzi, in a passage from his *Storia pittorica* devoted to the methods of connoisseurship, stated that the inimitability of individual hand-writing had been intended by nature "to safeguard" "civil [i.e., bourgeois] society."[104] Certainly signatures could be falsified, and illiterates were excluded from this form of control. But in spite of these drawbacks, century after century, European societies did not feel the need for more secure and practical methods for determining identity – not even when the birth of large factories, the geographical and social mobility that came with them, and the rapid rise of cities radically altered the terms of the problem. And yet even under conditions such as these, to cover one's tracks and reemerge with a new identity was child's play – and not only in large urban centers the size of London and Paris. But it was not until the closing decades of the nineteenth century that new and competing systems of identification began to be proposed from various quarters. The need erupted from contemporary events connected with the struggle between the classes: the birth of an international association of workers, the repression of working-class movements after the Commune, changes in the perception of crime.

The emergence of new capitalist methods of production – in England from circa 1720 on,[105] and in the rest of Europe almost a century later, with the advent of the Napoleonic code – spawned legislation, tied to a new bourgeois concept of property, which increased the number of punishable crimes and the gravity of the penalties. This criminalization of the class struggle was accompanied by the creation of a penal system based on long detention.[106] But prisons produce criminals. The number of recidivists in France, constantly on the rise after 1870, had reached a percentage by the end of the century equal to half of indicted criminals.[107] The problem of identifying these backsliders constituted the more or less conscious bridgehead for the comprehensive program of social control which followed.

For the proper identification of recidivists it was necessary to prove (*a*) that an individual had been condemned previously and (*b*) that he was the same person as the one who had already been thus sentenced.[108] The first point was resolved by the creation of police files. The second presented more serious difficulties. The old punishments which stamped a person forever through branding or mutilation had been abolished. The fleur-de-lis burned into Milady's shoulder permitted D'Artagnan to recognize her as a convicted poisoner – while two escapees, Edmond Dantés and Jean Valjean, succeeded in reappearing in society under false, respectable names (these examples should suffice to demonstrate how great an impression the figure of the relapsed criminal exercised on the nineteenth-century imagination).[109] Bourgeois respectability demanded signs of recognition that were just as indelible, if less sanguinary and degrading, as those of the *ancien régime*.

The idea of an enormous criminal photographic archive was rejected at first because it posed unsolvable problems of classification: how was one to isolate distinct features in the continuum of an image?[110] The quantification route seemed simpler and more precise. In 1879, Alphonse Bertillon, an employee in the Paris prefecture, began to employ an anthropometric method (which he explained in various articles and memoranda)[111] based on minute bodily measurements recorded on a personal file. Clearly, an error of just a few millimeters created the possibility of judicial error. But the principal defect in Bertillon's anthropometric method was its purely negative quality. It permitted the exclusion, at the moment of identification, of individuals not corresponding to the data, but not the positive verification that two identical series of data referred to a single individual.[112] The unavoidably elusive nature of the individual, chased out through the door by means of quantification, was reentering by the window. Thus, Bertillon proposed to integrate the anthropometric method with the so-called "spoken portrait," namely the verbal, analytical description of the separate entities (nose, eyes, ears, etc.), the sum total of which should have restored the image of the individual – thereby permitting the process of identification. The pages filled with ears exhibited by Bertillon cannot help but recall the illustrations in Morelli's own works appearing at about this time.[113] There may not have been a direct influence: however, it is striking to see that Bertillon, in the course of his activity as expert graphologist, used as clues revealing falsification the peculiarities or "idioms" of the original which the counterfeiter seldom succeeded in reproducing, but might substitute with his own.[114]

As may be supposed, Bertillon's method was incredibly complex. I have already alluded to the problem posed by measurements. The "spoken portrait" complicated matters still more. How was one to distinguish, in the description, a humped-curved nose from a curved-humped one? How did one classify the nuances of blue-green eyes?

It was F. Galton who suggested, beginning with his paper published in 1888, which he subsequently revised and improved, a method of identification that simplified both the collecting of data as well as its classification.[115] The new technique was based on fingerprinting. But Galton honestly acknowledged that, both theoretically and practically, he had been preceded in this by others.

The scientific analysis of fingerprints had been begun in 1823 by the founder of histology, J. E. Purkynê, in his *Commentatio de examine physiologico organi visus et systematis cutanei*.[116] He identified and described nine basic types of papillary lines, simultaneously claiming, however, that there are no two individuals with identical fingerprints. The practical applications to which the discovery could be put were ignored, although its philosophical implications were discussed in a chapter entitled "De cognitione organismi individualis in genere."[117] Knowledge of the individual, Purkynê stated, is crucial in the practice of medicine, beginning with diagnosis: symptoms reveal themselves differently in individuals and thus must be treated in different ways. Thus, some modern scholars, whom he does not name, have defined medicine as the "art of individualizing" ("artem individualisandi," "die Kunst des Individualisirens"). But the foundations of this art rest on the physiology of the individual. Here, Purkynê, who had studied philosophy in Prague as a young man, was rediscovering the deepest current in the thought of Leibniz. Each person, "ens omnimodo determinatum," has an individuality recognizable even in its most imperceptible and infinitesimal characteristics. Neither the facts of a particular case nor external influences suffice to explain it. It is necessary to posit the existence of an internal norm or "typus" which maintains the variety of organisms within the limits of each species. Awareness of this "norm," Purkynê declared prophetically, "would reveal the hidden knowledge of individual nature." The error of physiognomics had been to confront the variety of individuals from the viewpoint of preconceived opinions and hasty conjectures: consequently, it had been impossible up to this point to establish physiognomics on a scientific, descriptive basis. Abandoning the reading of hands to the "vain science" of palmistry, Purkynê focused his attention on a much less visible fact, and he discovered the secret mark of individuality in the lines imprinted on the tips of the fingers.

Let us leave Europe for a moment and pass on to Asia. In contrast to their European colleagues, and completely independently of them, Chinese and Japanese soothsayers had become interested in the not-so-obvious markings on the surface of the hand. The custom, verified for China, and especially Bengal, of pressing a fingertip blackened with pitch or ink on letters and documents[118] probably had behind it a series of factors of a divinatory nature. Anyone accustomed to deciphering mysterious writings in the veins of wood or rock, or in the tracks left by birds or in drawings impressed on turtle shells,[119] could have easily accepted as writing the lines imprinted by a dirty fingertip on any sort of surface. In 1860 Sir William Herschel, chief administrator in the Hooghly district of Bengal, noticed that this custom was widespread among the local population, appreciated its possible utility, and decided to put it to work for the benefit of the British government. (He was not interested in the theoretical aspects of the question; he did not know of Purkynê's Latin treatise, which had lain unread for half a century.) As Galton observed retrospectively, there was a real need for an efficient method of identification in the British colonies, and not in India alone: natives were illiterate, quarrelsome, cunning, deceitful, and, in the eyes of a European, indistinguishable. Herschel announced in an 1880 issue of *Nature* that after seventeen years of testing, fingerprinting had been officially introduced in the Hooghly district and had now been in force for three years with excellent results.[120] Imperial officials had appropriated the conjectural knowledge of the Bengalese and turned it against them.

Galton took Herschel's article as the point of departure for systematically rethinking and examining the entire question. The confluence of three very different elements made his investigation possible: the discovery made by Purkynê, a pure scientist; concrete knowledge, linked to the daily practice of the people of Bengal; and the political and administrative good sense of Sir William Herschel, a faithful servant of Her Britannic Majesty. Galton paid homage to the first and to the third. He also attempted to distinguish racial peculiarities in the fingertips, but without success; he declared, however, that he would pursue the research on Indian tribes in the hope of discovering there "a more monkey-like pattern."[121]

Galton, in addition to making a decisive contribution to fingerprint analysis, had also foreseen its practical implications. In a very short time the method was introduced in England, and from there little by little spread throughout the world (France was one of the last countries to accept it). In this way, every human being – Galton observed proudly, applying to himself praise pronounced for Bertillon by an official in the French Ministry of the Interior – acquired an identity, an individuality which could be relied upon with lasting certainty.[122]

And so, what had been until recently, in the eyes of British administrators, an indistinct mass of Bengalese "snouts" (to use Filarete's disparaging term) became at one stroke individuals, each one distinguished by a specific biological mark. This prodigious extension of the concept of individuality was in fact occurring by means of the State, its bureaucracy and police. Thanks to the fingerprint, even the least inhabitant of the poorest village of Asia or Europe was now identifiable and controllable.

But the same conjectural paradigm employed to develop ever more subtle and capillary forms of control can become a device to dissolve the ideological clouds which increasingly obscure such a complex social structure as fully developed capitalism. Though pretensions to systematic knowledge may appear more and more far-fetched, the idea of totality does not necessarily need to be abandoned. On the contrary, the existence of a deeply rooted relationship that explains superficial phenomena is confirmed the very moment it is stated that direct knowledge of such a connection is not possible. Though reality may seem to be opaque, there are privileged zones – signs, clues – which allow us to penetrate it.

This idea, which is the crux of the conjectural or semiotic paradigm, has made progress in the most varied cognitive circles and has deeply influenced the humane sciences. Minute paleographical details have been adopted as traits permitting the reconstruction of cultural exchanges and transformations – with explicit allusions to Morelli which sealed the debt Mancini had incurred with Allacci almost three centuries earlier. The depiction of flowing vestments in Florentine Quattrocento painters, the neologisms of Rabelais, the cure of scrofula patients by the kings of France and England, are only a few examples of how slender clues have been adopted from time to time as indications of more general phenomena: the world view of a social class, a single writer, or an entire society.[123] A discipline such as psychoanalysis came into being, as we have seen, around the hypothesis that apparently negligible details could reveal profound phenomena of great importance. The decline of systematic thought has been followed by the success of aphoristic reasoning – from Nietzsche to Adorno. The very term *aphoristic* is in itself revealing. (It is a clue, a symptom, a lead: there is no getting away from the paradigm.) *Aphorisms* was, in fact, the title of a famous work by Hippocrates. In the seventeenth century, collections of political aphorisms began to appear.[124] Aphoristic literature is, by definition, an attempt to formulate evaluations of man and society on the basis of symptoms and clues: a man and a society that are sick, *in crisis*. And even *crisis* is a medical, Hippocratic term.[125] It can easily be demonstrated that one of the greatest novels of our century, Proust's *Recherche*, was constructed according to a scientific conjectural paradigm.[126]

But can we actually call a conjectural paradigm scientific? The quantitative and antianthropocentric orientation of natural sciences from Galileo on forced an unpleasant dilemma on the humane sciences: either assume a lax scientific system in order to attain noteworthy results, or assume a meticulous, scientific one to achieve results of scant significance. Only linguistics has succeeded, during the course of the present century, in escaping the quandary, subsequently posing as a more or less finished model for other disciplines.

The question arises, however, whether exactness of this type is attainable or even desirable for forms of knowledge most linked to daily experience – or, more precisely, to all those situations in which the unique and indispensable nature of the data is decisive to the persons involved. It was once said that falling in love is the act of overvaluing the marginal differences which exist between one woman and another (or between one man and another). But this can also be said about works of art or about horses.[127] In such situations the flexible rigor (pardon the oxymoron) of the conjectural paradigm seems impossible to suppress. These are essentially mute forms of knowledge in the sense that their precepts do not lend themselves to being either formalized or spoken. No one learns to be a connoisseur or diagnostician by restricting himself to practicing only preexistent rules. In knowledge of this type imponderable elements come into play: instinct, insight, intuition. I have scrupulously refrained up to now from bandying about this dangerous term, *intuition*. But if we really insist on using it, as synonymous with the lightning recapitulation of rational processes, we shall have to distinguish a *low* from a *high* form of intuition.

Ancient Arabic physiognomics was rooted on *firâsa*, a complex notion which, in general, designated the ability to pass, on the basis of clues, directly from the known to the unknown.[128] The term came from the vocabulary of the *sufi* and designated mystical intuitions as well as forms of discernment and wisdom that were attributed to the sons of the king of Serendipity.[129] In this second meaning *firâsa* was none other than the instrument of conjectural knowledge.[130]

This "low intuition" is based on the senses (though it skirts them) and as such has nothing to do with the suprasensible intuition of the various nineteenth- and twentieth-century irrationalisms. It can be found throughout the entire world, with no limits of geography, history, ethnicity, sex, or class – and thus, it is far removed from higher forms of knowledge which are the privileged property of an elite few. It is the property of the Bengalese, their knowledge having been expropriated by Sir William Herschel; of hunters; of sailors; of women. It binds the human animal closely to other animal species.

Look at the signs – draw inferences – can't be directly studied – construct a story

Notice things that others might not recognize the significance of

Look at indirect evidence

Distinction b/t physical artifacts & texts

Intuitive method coupled w/connoisurship
↳ How can anything ever be falsified? –
multiple interpretations – how do you decide who's right & who's wrong?

🧶 Germanic Mythology and Nazism: Thoughts on an Old Book by Georges Dumézil

A reevaluation of the so-called culture of the right has been under way for a number of years now. In the process, the absurd elimination of a number of old problems considered incompatible with the dogmatism of the left has been replaced by an attitude that indiscriminately dredges up, with few subtleties, a variety of problems and solutions. This confusion between questions and answers is not always involuntary, nor innocent. But the rejection of solutions does not necessarily mean that the problems are nonexistent or irrelevant. Even racism, to take an extreme example, is *one* answer (scientifically unfounded and with a monstrous practical outcome) to a very real question related to the connection between biology and culture. Similar distinctions are imposed even on the historian of human societies. To this day, in some quarters, research into extended cultural continuities is not only suspect, but inherently unacceptable because it has been controlled for so long (with a few significant exceptions) by scholars more or less tied to the culture of the right.

The case of Georges Dumézil illustrates the complexity of the question beautifully. His work is important, of great breadth and has stood up well for more than half a century.

On a number of occasions, Dumézil has pointed to 1938 as a year marking a crucial break in his intellectual development. In the books and essays on comparative Indo-European mythology written before that date, he recognizes signs of struggle in research seeking to find the right road. The caesura, profound and irreversible, followed from the encounter some years earlier with Marcel Granet, the great Sinologist.[1]

One of the first fruits was *Mythes et dieux des Germains* (Paris, 1939); in the introduction Dumézil openly acknowledges his debt to Marcel Mauss and Granet. A second, radically revised edition, entitled *Les dieux des Germains* (Paris, 1959), appeared twenty years later. In his introduction, Dumézil justified the new work by pointing to the hurried and premature character of the 1939 book, as well as to the scholarly progress of the intervening years.[2] Self-criticism and constant revision are, after all, typical features of Dumézil's method. It is significant, nevertheless, that in the preface to the second edition he should reiterate the break constituted by the year 1938: *Mythes et dieux des Germains* was in fact proclaimed as a work of the author's full maturity.

In a recent perceptive article, Arnaldo Momigliano observed, "It is almost certain that, from the beginning, an element of political discord separated Dumézil from his Durkheimian teachers." He adduces as evidence both the dedication of Dumézil's first book, *Le festin d'immortalité*, to Pierre Gaxotte (Maurras's secretary, later close to the Vichy government), and the book *Mythes et dieux des Germains*, about which Momigliano states: "It reveals clear traces of sympathy for Nazi culture."[3] The message here is clear, although specific passages of *Mythes et dieux* are not cited. Then too, the book has not only been out of print for quite some time, but is difficult to locate, even in the better libraries.[4] It may be an opportune moment, then, to examine this work.

Before beginning, I should mention briefly two reviews published in 1940, a year after the book's appearance. After glancing at the historical and philological aspects of Dumézil's research, both reviewers dwell on statements made by Dumézil about recent German history. In the *Deutsche Literaturzeitung*, S. Gutenbrunner assessed in basically favorable terms comparisons made with the "spiritual patrimony" (*Gedankengut*) of National Socialism. He observed that "even if the German reader sees things differently than Dumézil, the book can be viewed as a recognition of the unity enduring between the Germanic and German spirits."[5] On the French side much warmer praise appeared in the pages of the *Revue historique*, addressed not just to *Mythes et dieux des Germains* as a whole, but also specifically to the passages of contemporary relevance:

> It is not one of the lesser items of interest in the work of M. Dumézil that he was able to indicate, with great discretion, and a strong sense of nuances, how that astonishing and formidable Germany that we see today rising up before our very eyes, is the extension of certain tendencies, mythically warlike and mystically juvenile, which were already revealed, in the same group, by the evolution of traditions received from the most ancient Indo-European past.[6]

The author of the review was Marc Bloch.

These words were written by a great historian, a Jew, a man who, a few years later, would pay with his own life for his active participation in the anti-Nazi resistance. Bloch must have prepared this piece after the war had begun: the fascicle of the *Revue historique* dated April-June 1940 appeared after France had signed the armistice. In that tragic moment in his own life and his country's, described in the pages of an *Etrange défaite*, Bloch saw in Dumézil's book, not just the "clear traces of sympathy for Nazi culture" seen by Momigliano, but an enlightening and critical contribution on Hitler's Germany. There is a dilemma here that calls for a close reading of the text.

Dumézil took stock of his own research in the closing pages of *Mythes et dieux des Germains*. There is an element in Germanic mythology – militaristic evolution – that distinguishes that mythology from other Indo-European forms. This tendency is recognizable in the martial as well as royal and priestly characteristics assumed by the figure of Odin. The fact that "bearskin warriors" (*berserkir*), followers of Odin mentioned in the Icelandic sagas, have traits resembling not only the "masked societies" of the *Gandharva* Indian type, linked to a sovereign divinity such as Varuna, but also to "warrior societies" such as the Indian *Marut*, associated with a martial divinity like Indra, would seem to indicate "an apparently unfathomable prehistoric confusion." In terms of the tripartite Indo-European ideology discovered and described by Dumézil, dating from this period, it is possible to speak of the prevalence of the second (warrior) function at the expense of the first (sovereign). The "militarization" of mythology in a prehistoric age was considered to have ensured the rebirth of Germanic myths during the nineteenth century. In other cultures, Dumézil observes, the evocation of ancestral beliefs remained an artificial, rhetorical phenomenon. In Germany instead, for the past century and a half, the " 'beautiful Germanic legends' have been not only repopularized, but also *remythisées*: they have become myths, in a strict sense, because they justify, sustain, and provoke individual and collective behavior which possesses all the characteristics of the sacred." Dumézil, naturally, feels obliged to cite Wagner:

> Wagnerian names, the Wagnerian mystique, inspired the German combattants of 1914-18, more in the hours of sacrifice and defeat than in the hours of victory.... The Third Reich has not been obliged to create its basic myths; on the contrary, it is Germanic mythology, revived in the nineteenth century, which gave its form, its spirit, its institutions to a Germany rendered miraculously pliable by unprecedented misfortunes;

perhaps it is because he had first suffered in trenches haunted by the spirit of Siegfried that Adolf Hitler could conceive, forge, and practice a sovereignty that no German overlord has known since the fabulous reign of Odin. The "neo-pagan" propaganda of the new Germany is certainly an interesting phenomenon for the historian of religions: but it is voluntary, in some degree, artificial. Much more intriguing, in any case, is the spontaneity by which the German masses and their chiefs, after eliminating foreign elements, naturally allowed their actions and reactions to flow into social and mystical patterns. The resemblance of these to the most ancient Germanic organizations and mythologies may not always have been apparent to them.... It is this sort of preestablished congruence between past and present, more than the instances of conscious imitation of the past, that constitutes the originality of the current German experience.[7]

In a preceding chapter, the sixth, dedicated to "Les Guerriers-Fauves" ("The Savage Warriors"), Dumézil had illustrated one of these cases of "spontaneous congruence between past and present." In the berserkir, the groups of youthful warriors recorded in the Icelandic sagas, he recognized the successors of the Harii described by Tacitus, not to mention the *Einherjar*, the counterparts in real life of the mythical legions of warriors who were followers of Odin. "The berserkir, in effect," Dumézil wrote, "are the 'young'; they assume in the life of Germanic societies this function of fantasy, of tumult and of violence which is no less necessary for the collective equilibrium than the conservative function (order, tradition, respect for taboos) assumed by mature men and, eventually, the old." These traditions associated with the ancient "male societies" gave rise to two divergent developments: on the one hand, they became bastardized in the winter masquerades diffused in Germanic folklore; on the other, their persistence transformed the original warlike frenzy into a "regulated force, tending toward a sort of chivalry." Dumézil concludes: "The preceding considerations may explain some of the more recent German social phenomena: the development and success of the paramilitary brigades, the *dura virtus* and the privileges of the Assault Units, the particular kinds of policing that uniformed youth have sometimes been tempted to practice."[8]

A reader coming upon these pages today is seized by uneasiness difficult to describe. Such an expression as "particular kinds of policing" to describe the activities of Nazi military and paramilitary bodies is highly euphemistic. But in the case of Dumézil back in

1939, should we speak of euphemisms or scholarly objectivity? In the passages I have just cited, mention of the men and institutions of the Third Reich is not accompanied by explicit judgments. There are no words of criticism or of condemnation, but praise or enthusiasm are equally lacking. At first glance, the tone seems consciously sober and neutral. To be sure, when Dumézil directs his attention to the distant past, the discussion occasionally edges from a descriptive to a normative plane. An example of this is his reference to the integration "necessary to the collective equilibrium" between the functions of violence and tumult exercised by youth, and the maintenance of order entrusted to the elders. But through the "preestablished congruence between past and present" the reader was being implicitly invited to seek the embodiment of this ideal of social equilibrium in the contemporary situation. If such paramilitary groups as the SA were portrayed as the heirs of the youthful warrior groups of Germanic mythology, what represented the equalizing, conservative element working for order? The Nazi party, perhaps, and its Führer, so much more powerful, as Dumézil recognized, than the old Germanic chiefs?

The invitation to ask questions like these came from the author himself: at the conclusion of his book he observed that in addition to the correspondences between present and past that he had brought to light, "the reader will certainly have noted many others."[9] Now, notoriously, continuity between Germanic mythology and the political, military, and cultural impulses of the Third Reich was one of the cardinal points of Nazi propaganda. Hitler's regime drew a powerful element of ideological legitimacy from this repeatedly flaunted continuity. In at least one instance Dumézil actually suggested themes capable of being exploited as propaganda. In "Census iners" ('Frozen Wealth'), the final chapter of *Mythes et dieux des Germains*, devoted to the attitude towards wealth in ancient Germanic civilization, Dumézil quoted a passage from Saxo Grammaticus which focused on the contrast between King Roericus, who was rich but cowardly, and his conqueror, the proud King Rolvo. According to Saxo, Roericus was "rich in resources but poor in the way he used them: his worth came less from his probity than from his usury" ('praestans opibus habituque fruendi / pauper erat, probitate minus quam fenore pollens'). But the *Census iners* accumulated over many years was of no avail: Rolvo dethrones him and distributes the booty among his companions in arms. In publishing a few passages from this *texte capital* of Saxo's, Dumézil observed that "the Third Reich could make use of it in its criticism of revenue policies or to justify its dynamic economy."[10]

And yet we should remember that according to Dumézil, the conscious continuity between Germanic traditions and the Third Reich, occasionally emphasized by propaganda, was a superficial, if not actually negligible phenomenon, next to the unconscious, spontaneous, and deep-rooted continuity revealed in the formula of "preestablished congruence between past and present." That such a thesis pleased, with a reservation or two, the reviewer of the *Deutsche Literaturzeitung*, is a fact. But if we should conclude from this that Dumézil's theories only echoed, perhaps with greater subtlety, the arguments of Nazi propaganda, we would be simplifying the issues connected with the problem, including a decisively embarrassing one, the review by Bloch.

I do not have any special information concerning relations between Bloch and Dumézil. One way or another there had to be connections through the school of Durkheim. More specifically, either Antoine Meillet or Marcel Granet, both teachers of Dumézil (despite tensions on a personal level with the former),[11] could have served as intellectual intermediaries to Bloch. From his youth Bloch had been connected with Granet; and he looked to Meillet's works in the field of Indo-European linguistics as indispensable points of reference.[12]

The publication in 1938 in the *Annales* of an essay by Dumézil ('Jeunesse, éternité, aube: Linguistique et mythologies comparées indo-européennes'), strictly speaking outside the vast scope of even this journal, which had not yet added "civilizations" to its subtitle, probably can be explained because it interested Bloch. Moreover, in addition to the comparative approach they shared, there was still another research element in common between them: the serial study of mentalities. A reference to the *Rois thaumaturges* (1924) is obvious. But even in the other splendid book, *Caractères originaux de l'histoire rurale française* (1930), where the intellectual debt to Meillet is continually present, Bloch attempted to explain the contemporary phenomenon of the breakup of landed property by reading agrarian history retrospectively in terms of particular mentalities. He searched for the key to the present not in the recent or relatively recent past – the period of the French Revolution, for example – but in a distant, protohistoric, or even prehistoric past, about which we have only very indirect evidence. Bloch reconstructed ancient forms of landholding through toponyms or such physical data as the existence or absence of enclosures. Only by unrolling the film of history backwards did the last frame, the present, become comprehensible.[13] Bloch was not attempting to reach more or less mythical origins (a fetish which he always opposed right through the posthumous pages of the *Mètier d'historien*).[14] Rather, it was his opinion that in the history of human societies the will for change clashes against deeply rooted physical and, especially, mental inertias.

We can understand how Bloch might have been fascinated by Dumézil's attempt to explain contemporary Germany through a remote Indo-European past. Bloch read *Mythes et dieux des Germains* in the perspective of his own research, and inversely. He singled out the theme of the origins of the Germanic conception of sacral kingship in Dumézil's chapter "Mythes de la souveraineté" – a notion, Bloch observed, based on evidence radically opposed to what was "purest" in Christianity, and destined to prolong its own effects well beyond the Middle Ages ("I have attempted to demonstrate them elsewhere and M. Dumézil, I believe, will not contradict me"). After this reference to the *Rois thaumaturges* – which, after all, Dumézil had cited approvingly – Bloch indirectly alluded to ideas expressed in the just published *Société féodale*: the origins of chivalry from ancient rites of youthful initiation, transformed, however, by a completely different social environment;[15] the emergence in "Romania," following the barbarian invasions, of an apparently buried past, destined to leave a profound mark on medieval civilization. Bloch remarked, and it was no trivial criticism, that many of the characteristics that Dumézil considered specifically Germanic were in reality shared by a number of very different ethnic groups. But this reservation, in his eyes, did not invalidate Dumézil's basic question: what was that attribute which was Germanic first and German later, and how should it be explained? Bloch felt the answer had to be searched for in a profound cultural crisis in a prehistoric age. Bloch maintained that from lack of competence, he could not himself venture to such a distant past; but he had found identical characteristics in the Middle Ages, a period with which he was more familiar. At the end of his review he reformulated the irreducible antithesis between the Germanic conception of sacral kingship and what was "purest" in Christianity by recognizing in the Germanic world the presence of "sentimental, religious, and social tendencies, which were clearly foreign to the universalism of Latin Christendom." If the disconcerting diversity of the Germans presented itself to Bloch in these terms (hardly clear despite appearances) on the eve of war or even after the inception of hostilities, we can understand how Dumézil's book on Germanic myths and gods might offer him an answer.

An answer, yes – but only if one accepted the initial postulate: that of continuity with the Indo-European past. We are dealing, in fact, with a postulate. Dumézil never declared himself on the nature of this continuity in his *Mythes et dieux des Germains*. S. Gutenbrunner's reservations in the *Deutsche Literaturzeitung* can be attributed to the absence of an explicit acknowledgement of race as a unifying element: "The German reader sees the issue differently than Dumézil." From a wholly divergent perspective, such a favorable reviewer as the archaeologist A. Grenier expressed his own uneasiness over the thesis of "a preestablished congruence" between a prehistoric past and the present. He asked himself whether Dumézil had not extracted from the documentation formulae so generic that they could be applied to both Germanic folk as well as Germans, "who, after all, are another people."[16] Bloch, for his part, chose to ignore Dumézil's more radical notions implying a strong and unconscious continuity over time ("preestablished congruence," "social and mystical patterns of whose conformity with the most ancient Germanic structures and mythologies they were not always aware"). Dumézil's emphasis on the "spontaneous movement" of return to Germanic myths occurring in "societies which were the most direct heirs of ancient Germany" revealed a continuity that was more cultural than ethnic.

Each reviewer, in other words, confronted or constructed for himself a different Dumézil. This process has continued until very recent times, often owing to the efforts of readers intent on twisting the same texts, even the same phrases, into new meanings. When Dumézil was inducted into the Académie Française in 1979, Claude Lévi-Strauss delivered the ritual speech of welcome to the new member. On the verge of concluding, he paused over the general, "in many senses prophetic" characteristic of Dumézil's work: that of having faced up to the problem "of the function of ideology in human society, that ideology which we have seen return to the fore, after some centuries dominated by triumphant reason." And here Lévi-Strauss cited from memory that sentence in *Mythes et dieux des Germains* dealing with German masses and their leaders who, without always being aware of it, had "instinctively directed their actions and responses into social and mystical molds inherited from a distant past." Today, Lévi-Strauss continued, "we are witnessing similar phenomena in Iran and in southeast Asia. Impelled by ideologies, people become filled with doubts or are driven to fratricidal strife; sects proliferate and religious controversies are rekindled." On our continent we hear voices that appeal to the "Indo-European soul." But Dumézil's work constitutes precisely the most efficacious antidote against these "illusions." He has shown that Indo-European ideology is only an "empty vessel," or, better yet, a vessel that from time to time, in the course of the centuries or of the millennia, has been filled with a variety of philosophical, political, or social elements.[17]

We have no way of knowing whether, or to what degree, Dumézil recognized himself in Lévi-Strauss's portrait. I am tempted to discern in the page from which I have just quoted an episode in that singular intellectual skirmish which in the last few years joined and, equally often, ceremoniously divided the two scholars.[18] To be sure, the recent endeavor by the *nouvelle droite* to coopt the work of Dumézil, interpreting it (especially the tripartite Indo-European ideology) as an exemplary archetype, has frequently been repudiated in no indefinite terms by Dumézil himself.[19] I have noted, however, in *Mythes et dieux des Germains* the tendency here and there to interpret the data in a normative sense. The expression "empty vessel" used by Lévi-Strauss reflects Dumézil's metaphor of "social and mystical molds," but devalues the continuity of the content, "conformity with the most ancient organizations, the most ancient Germanic mythologies" – a phrase that is, curiously, dropped from the quotation recited by heart cited above. This is a reading of Dumézil's work in a transcendental key, completely different from the archetypal one proposed, for example, by Eliade. Let us leave to students of Dumézil's entire *oeuvre* the task of deciding how reliable these interpretations are (though both are probably misrepresentations). Let us, rather, consider the following question: To what extent does the assumption of an ideological continuity between Indo-European mythology in its Germanic variant and the political, social, and institutional realities of the Third Reich contribute to a better understanding of the latter?

This question is as relevant today as ever. On several occasions in recent years, a historiography oriented only to short-run contemporary political events in a narrow sense has proved woefully inadequate when confronted by the emergence of unforeseen occurrences such as those evoked by Lévi-Strauss (Khomeini's Iran, Pol-Pot's Cambodia). Lévi-Strauss reminds us, once more, that in an age of rampant ideologies, precious assistance in understanding the world can come from historians of religion and of comparative mythology. On this terrain objections on principle lack a raison d'être. Naturally, the construction of long, even extremely lengthy, diachronies does not exclude the utility of synchronic comparisons. To understand the SA, a look at other contemporary paramilitary groups, beginning with the Italian *squadristi*, is inevitable. This does not detract from the fact that even the parallels suggested by Dumézil between the SA and the berserkir in the Icelandic sagas can bring important elements to light.

I could close the discussion which began with *Mythes et dieux des Germains* on this Solomonic and disappointing conclusion. But an explication of such a controversial and elusive text cannot be reduced to a discussion of the reactions it has provoked. Further study is needed to identify Dumézil's sources and how he used them. Judgment on the *opus operatum* obviously cannot exclude consideration of the *modus operandi*. The sample that I have chosen for this analysis is the chapter devoted to the *guerriers-fauves* that I have already rapidly summarized.

The scholarly problem occupying Dumézil had entered a new phase about a decade earlier as the result of an encounter between two previously separate currents of research: the first, on the berserkir; the second, on male societies or associations (*Männerbünde*). Credit for this development, thanks to which the phenomenon of the berserkir could be studied for the first time in a context that provided a key to its interpretation, belonged, as Dumézil observed, to two scholars: Lily Weiser (later Weiser-Aall) and Otto Höfler. The connection between their research is very close (both were students of the Germanist Rudolf Much); but under closer scrutiny, differences are also evident.

In her thoughtful book *Altgermanische Jünglingsweihen und Männerbünde* (1927), Weiser studied "male societies" of a religio-initiatory variety. Typologically they resembled groups already categorized by H. Schurtz in various locations around the world, building in a systematic if somewhat abstract manner on work by Usener.[20] But while Schurtz, from a rigidly evolutionary perspective, had presented these "male groups" as an essential stage on the path towards the formation of society, Weiser's interests differed, at least initially. After reading Theodor Reik on puberty rites among primitive peoples, she identified the "conflict between two generations" behind the initiation ceremonies. Oedipal tensions charge relationships between fathers and sons with ambivalent feelings, a combination of hate and love; the initiation expresses symbolically, through terrifying rituals, the bridling of youthful energies.[21] These ideas, scarcely impaired by a fairly predictable distinction between the interpretations of the Freudian school and the wealth of data which it produced, reveal the probable nonscientific genesis of Weiser's work (shrewdly noted by W. E. Peuckert),[22] namely, the grandiose, composite youth movement through which the cultural gap created between fathers and sons in the early decades of twentieth-century Germany found expression.[23]

Probably this was the origin of Weiser's view of initiation rites as a part of generational conflict. But this idea was allowed to drop, together with the polemical allusion to the importance of female initiation, generally undervalued by scholars.[24] Research took another course, demonstrating the existence of "male societies" in Germanic antiquity through an array of sources that included Tacitus (*Germania*), the Icelandic sagas, the *Historia Danica* by Saxo Grammaticus, and the fables collected by the brothers Grimm. And from the pages of Saxo and the Icelandic sagas, written between the thirteenth and sixteenth centuries, leaped the berserkir, an initiatory group of chosen warriors. In rich and sophisticated analysis, impossible to recapitulate here in detail, Weiser demonstrates that they had been portrayed as human beings, although periodically capable of extraordinary feats when they fell into states of unrestrained fury, and also as mythical beings, able to assume animal appearances (wolves, bears). By comparing them with similar Germanic phenomena, Weiser concluded the enigma could be explained: the berserkir "originally personified the army of the dead" (*Totenheer*), and the authors of the sagas were perfectly aware of the twofold identity.[25] This comparison was based in part on the myths and rites still to be found in Germanic folklore, specifically on "the army of the dead" or "Wild Hunt" (*wilde Jagd*), and in part, following E. Mogk, on beliefs in werewolves.[26] Such elements as ecstasy, the ability to be transformed into animals, and the connection with the army of the dead always led back to that warlike divinity whom the berserkir followed: Odin.

Otto Höfler took these conclusions (later accepted as a whole by Dumézil) as a starting point in his book *Kultische Geheimbünde der Germanen* (1934), the sole volume to appear in a work intended to be joined by two others, which, although partly written, remained unpublished.[27] Its immediate impact internationally was far deeper than Weiser's and touched areas of research ranging from folklore to Iranian studies. In addition to Dumézil and Weiser, other scholars such as Stig Wikander and Karl Meuli responded to the book favorably (though Meuli ended by distancing himself from Höfler).[28] There was also no lack of criticism, some of it harsh, over Höfler's peculiar criteria of interpretation. I noted that Weiser had integrated literary sources (sagas), evidence attesting to the myth of the Wild Hunt, and descriptions of folkloric rituals to argue that the berserkir "originally personified the army of the dead." Höfler went a step further. He interpreted all or virtually all the evidence linked to apparitions of the Wild Hunt as proof of the existence of "male societies" of a religio-initiatory type. In other words, behind the presumed manifestations, there were groups of flesh-and-blood youths who believed that they were personifying the army of the dead. Thanks to Höfler's enormous erudition the amount of evidence collected by Weiser was tremendously expanded, and with disconcerting results. Höfler's explication of the sources in his *Kultische Geheimbünde* in almost every instance presents a challenge to elementary common sense. His method of interpretation, characterized by a sort of ingenuous positivism, was completely paradoxical in a scholar who did not hesitate to rail against positivistic flatness in the name of superior spiritual "realities."[29]

Determining the link between myths and rites has always been a delicate and uncertain process in the work of historians of religion, anthropologists, and folklorists. With nothing less than an interpretative *coup de main*, Höfler obliterated every distinction between myths and rites, explaining documents connected with the former as proof of the existence of the latter. The English Egyptologist Margaret Murray, on the basis of an equally indefensible assumption, though founded on totally different ideological presuppositions, had accepted in part descriptions of the sabbat furnished by accused witches as proof of the existence of a secret cult based on fertility rites. Not surprisingly, Höfler accepted Murray's assumptions in full.[30]

The Witch-Cult in Western Europe (Oxford, 1921), Murray's best-known book, was considered authoritative for decades but is totally discredited today.[31] *Kultische Geheimbünde der Germanen* has experienced a different fate. The existence of secret male societies of a ritual type, accepted by many scholars of Germanic areas, has also been discovered elsewhere, for example in Iran. The objections raised by Höfler's critics have had limited impact, with the exception of F. Ranke's extreme views. According to the latter, all the evidence concerning apparitions of the army of the dead was the fruit of hallucinations pure and simple, and pathological rather than mythico-religious statements.[32] But this rationalistic, reductionist interpretation seems to be as baseless as Höfler's.

I have mentioned that the documentation collected in *Kultische Geheimbünde* was much richer than what had been available to Weiser. Nevertheless, Höfler ignored a number of themes. First, Weiser had compared the ecstasy of Eurasian shamans to the unbridled warlike frenzies (*Raserei*) of the berserkir. Secondly, she had also pointed out the presence of feminine divinities at the head of the Wild Hunt and had investigated the relationship between the Germanic Perchta and the Mediterranean Artemis. It was from the first that Weiser presumably traced her cautiously advanced hypothesis that the mythico-rural complex she was studying actually had pre-Indo-European as well as Indo-European roots; from the second, her allusions connected with fertility themes.[33] Behind the Germanic warrior associations Weiser glimpsed something vaster and more complex which was not exclusively martial nor exclusively Germanic.

Höfler decisively minimized the significance of these possible ramifications. The ecstasy of the Germanic warriors was not an individual phenomenon, but a controlled release of restraints obtained through communion with the dead, "an immense source of social and statal energies." As for female divinities and the connotations that had been attached to fertility, Höfler definitely considered them to be of marginal importance. For him the core of "the ecstatic cult of the Germanic religion of the dead" was the "bond (re-ligio), understood as a sacred duty, with the living dead and their guide."[34] The heroic and martial myth of the Germanic army of the dead was not reducible to "general concepts in the positivistic study of religion, namely, fertility magic and protective magic." Höfler rejected attempts to link Germanic warrior frenzy and shamanistic ecstasy, as well as, in general, the superimposition of "oriental concepts" on Germanic mythology: Wodan=Odin was not a god of licentiousness (*Ausschweifung*), but "the god of the dead, of warriors, of kings and of the state."[35]

The above passages, except for the last two, are from the concluding pages of *Kultische Geheimbünde der Germanen*; the last two appear in a polemical reply to a review by F. von der Leyen. A peculiar accident had befallen Höfler between these two publications: he had discovered, *in extremis*, thanks to a reference by Meuli, the proceedings of a late-seventeenth-century trial against an old Livonian werewolf.[36] We recall that Weiser, pursuing a suggestion by Mogk, had already proposed adding werewolves to the evidence connected with male societies. Now, through this document the voice of a follower of a secret male society had reached Höfler without passing through the filter of literary tradition. The commentary which accompanied the republication of the trial records in an appendix revealed an obvious embarrassment: the stories told by the old werewolf were full of fabulous elements and difficult to accept as literal descriptions of rites; moreover, they were based explicitly on the theme of battles fought periodically against witches and warlocks over the fertility of the harvests; and, finally, the documents actually mentioned the participation in these combats of female werewolves. Höfler attempted to extricate himself by saying that the werewolf was a braggart, and a Balt besides. The Germanic warrior groups, instead, were strictly male and not concerned with questions of fertility – to sum up, they were something totally different.[37]

Clearly, Höfler's interpretative somersaults were required to save the basic framework of his research; its ideological matrix is clear and confirmed by the closing words in his book: "The specific vocation of the Nordic race, its creativity in bringing states into being, found its proper fulfillment in the male societies [*Mannerbünde*], giving them the possibility of flourishing in the richest manner possible. In the fullness of their power they constitute both a productive element and an aggressive force: fighting, educating, and dominating, they entered the history of the world."[38] Such statements certainly did not have an original ring in the Germany of the period. A. Krebs had already written in the journal *Partei und Gesellschaft: Nationalsozialistische Briefe* (1928) that the male *Bund* was the nucleus from which "all states have their origin."[39] Höfler, unlike Weiser, found the inspiration for his research in that current, typified by Krebs and exemplified by the youth movement merging with Nazism. But after having given its stamp to the first phase of Nazism, the *bündisch* current ended up being relegated drastically to the background.[40] This, among other factors, explains the violent attack on Höfler's book published in 1936 in the journal *Rasse*. The author, H. Spehr, judged *Kultische Geheimbünde der Germanen* and M. Ninck's *Wodan und germanischer Schicksalglaube* to be "grave dangers for the contemporary politico-cultural situation." The criticism was not only, nor even primarily, based on scholarly considerations: by modeling the Germanic image on that of the Viking warriors (the berserkir!) who had cut themselves off from their native soil, the two authors had forgotten that "the Germanic man of the pagan period, especially on German soil, was primarily a peasant and a warrior too, of course." He differed greatly from primitive demonic horsemen, from crazed members of secret societies, from ecstatics. The distinctive trait in the soul of the Nordic race and of the original Indo-Germanic religion, Spehr concluded, was moderation, *eusebeia*, combined with *sophrosyne*, not *ekstasis*, the sacred orgy that characterizes the racial soul of Asia Minor.[41] Evidently, in the eyes of the *Rasse* reviewer, the exaltation of the martial ferocity of the Germanic male societies conjured up the memory of the SA, which had been purged in a blood bath two years earlier. Höfler was slightly out of step with the times in regard to that solidly rural image, custodian of traditional virtues, that the Nazi regime wanted to project for itself at that particular moment.

Let us return to *Mythes et dieux des Germains*. Dumézil used Höfler's book in his own work without expressing the slightest critical detachment from it. But Dumézil's juxtaposition of berserkir and the SA was already implicit in *Kultische Geheimbünde der Germanen*, where the berserkir were explained in terms of the SA, and vice versa. It's the case of a vicious circle more than a hermeneutic one.

There remains Bloch's review. Should we interpret it as the fruit of a casual misunderstanding, of a superficial reading? This suggestion, quite improbable in itself, is contradicted by the fact that Bloch was well acquainted with one of the books used by Dumézil, Höfler's *Kultische Geheimbünde der Germanen*. Bloch wrote favorably about it in a 1937 issue of the *Revue historique*: "The erudition is astonishing; the psychological refinement, the sense of life, no less so. Rarely has anyone penetrated further through that substratum of superimposed popular beliefs from which Europe has for so long nourished itself, nor analyzed better, in a mythology considered to be as one, such as that of the ancient Germans, the coexistence of nature deities and warrior gods." Bloch's favorable opinions (all somewhat debatable, except for the tribute to Höfler's erudition) outweighed by far his criticism of the latter's refusal (probably preconceived) to take into account research on the superimposition of Christianity over the ancient myths. Equally downplayed – actually relegated to a footnote – is Bloch's observation apropos the interpretation of a passage in the edict of Rothari condemning disguises contrived "in order to steal" (*latrocinandi animo*). In these travesties Höfler had, as usual, perceived the traces of ancient cults, eliciting this comment from Bloch: "Without being exceedingly prosaic, I believe, one may deplore the scorn in which some mythologists hold the simplest explanations." Curiously, Bloch did not carry this criticism, undermining the very foundations of Höfler's thesis, to its logical conclusion. Stranger still is the fact that he did not make something of the ideological implications so patent in such a book as *Kultische Geheimbünde der Germanen*, especially since he was discussing it in a review dominated by his anxiety, his "anguish," over the nationalistic and racist distortions in German scholarship during these years.[42]

Bloch's intellectual and political biography in the period preceding the war is practically unexplored. Even his correspondence with Lucien Febvre remains unpublished. To discover some of the reasons for Bloch's favorable response to the books by Dumézil and Höfler, we shall have to make an indirect approach.

In 1936 Elie Halévy presented a paper to the Société Française de Philosophie entitled "L'ère des tyrannies," which was later published in the society's *Bulletin*, together with some letters of commentary, one of which was by Marcel Mauss. Mauss fully approved of the links which Halévy had suggested between Bolshevism on one side, and Fascism and Nazism on the other. He noted the importance of Sorel's writings, to which Lenin, Mussolini, and, indirectly, Hitler (through Mussolini) were indebted. The Bolshevik party, he continued, remains a secret society with its own armed body (the KGB), ensconced in the heart of Russia, just as the Fascist and Hitlerian parties, which have neither artillery nor fleet, but possess a police apparatus, inhabit Italy and Germany. And Mauss added: "Here I easily recognize events which often occurred in Greece, and which Aristotle describes well, but which are characteristic of ancient societies in general and, who knows, perhaps of the entire world. I am referring to the 'Society of Men,' with its confraternities that are public and secret at the same time. In this male society it is the young who act." Mauss concluded that this might be a necessary, but sociologically backward, form of activity. It satisfies the craving "for secrecy, for influence, for action, for youth and, often, for tradition.... These are new beginnings, identical sequences."[43]

Neither Dumézil nor, probably, even Bloch could have overlooked this letter, reprinted in 1938 when "L'ère des tyrannies" appeared in book form, immediately after Halévy's death. In *Mythes et dieux des Germains*, which openly acknowledged its dependence on Mauss, the juxtaposition of Nazi paramilitary organizations with ancient "youth societies" was revived and carried further, but in a wholly different spirit. Reading between the lines of Dumézil's detached account, one discerns here and there, as Momigliano clearly perceived (and as I have tried to demonstrate here), a thinly disguised ideological sympathy for Nazi culture.

Mauss's recognition of the archaic components surviving in twentieth-century dictatorships was accompanied by moments of painful self-criticism.[44] A deeper analysis of this subject is obviously needed. It suffices to say at this point that his implicit appeal for an analysis of the contemporary political situation with the tools of anthropology was accepted forthwith. The Collège de Sociologie came into being in Paris in 1937. It was a singular grafting of Maussian themes to an institution that, in addition to its open acknowledgement of such avant-garde movements as Dadaism and Surrealism, proposed to recreate a secret society or a religious order. But we may speak of Dumézilian even more than of Maussian themes. One of the principal moving spirits of the Collège, Roger Caillois (the other was Georges Bataille), enjoyed the closest collaboration and friendship with Dumézil. Several of Caillois's contributions to the activity of the Collége, later collected in the volume *L'homme et le sacré*, third in the series launched by *Mythes et dieux des Germains*,[45] were inspired by Dumézil's research, which at that time was unpublished.

The program of the Collège stressed the contradiction between the progress made by the "sciences de l'homme" in the preceding half century and the delay in analyzing instincts and "myths" in contemporary society: "A significant result of this deficiency is that an entire side of modern collective life, its most serious aspect, its deepest strata, escape understanding." To overcome this, a "sociology of the sacred" was proposed to study "social existence in all its manifestations where the active presence of the Holy is revealed": in particular, power, the sacred, myths.[46] It is easy to identify the principal currents in Dumézil's research in the pre-occupations (or obsessions) that dominated the leaders of the Collège, Bataille and Caillois. To simplify, we might say that for Bataille these were the connection between death (and sexuality) and the sacred; for Caillois, between the sacred and power. In both cases, these themes implied an extremely equivocal attitude towards Fascist and Nazi ideologies. Already, in a letter written in 1934 from Rome to Raymond Queneau, immediately after a visit to an exposition on the Fascist revolution, Bataille had admitted his fascination at the sight of the mortuary symbols, the black pennants, and skulls. He observed that, in spite of everything, there was something serious about all this which should not remain the exclusive domain of Fascist propaganda.[47] In a lecture on power at the Collège on February 19, 1938, Bataille, substituting for an indisposed Caillois, expressed his fascination with Fascist symbolism in his contrast of the fasces portrayed in Italy "on the bellies of locomotives" and the crucifix associated, *à la* Frazer, to a "haunting representation of the king's execution." The lictor's axe, Bataille commented, inasmuch as it is an instrument of capital punishment, "is juxtaposed ostensibly to the image of the slain king."[48] The same climate of morbid, intimately guilty attraction for the mortuary rites of Nazism forms the background for the novel *Le bleu du ciel*, written in 1935, but not published until more than twenty years later.

Caillois's fantasies about an aristocratic community composed of merciless, tyrannical individuals, impatient to confront the rigors of an imminent ice age and the implacable selection accompanying it, had an even more equivocal ring. Its fascistic connotations were promptly noted by critics of the left, both socialist and communist, as well as by such a regular frequenter of the Collège's lectures as Walter Benjamin.[49] But Benjamin's diffidence is significant. The program of the Collège had assembled men who differed broadly among themselves, supporting positions that very quickly revealed themselves incompatible. We find among the organizers both the anti-Semite Pierre Libra, who rapidly disappeared from the scene, and Michel Leiris, who first stood aloof and later communicated to Bataille his firm disagreement, on scholarly grounds, with the general stand of the group. Among the lecturers was Anatole Lewitzky, a Mauss student, who would be shot by the Nazis in 1942 with two colleagues for having established a center of clandestine activity in the Musée de L'Homme. The text of Bataille's lecture "Hitler and the Teutonic Order" (January 24, 1939) has not survived. We can only conjecture about his probable divergence from the lucid reconstruction by Hans Mayer, "The Rites of Political Associations in Romantic Germany" (April 18, 1939), as connected with proto-Nazi and Nazi groups.[50]

Alexandre Kojève, who also lectured at the Collège on "Hegelian ideas," observed ironically that the program of Bataille and Caillois could be compared to a conjurer's attempt to make himself believe in magic through his own tricks.[51] In fact, in the two years of the Collège's activity (November 1937-July 1939), roughly from the eve of the Munich pact to the outbreak of war, novice shamans such as Bataille and rigorous students of shamanism such as Lewitzky, aspiring founders of secret societies such as Caillois and historians of sects such as Mayer, found a common ground for discussion. Looking back, we are struck especially by the ambiguity of the structure and the heterogeneity of the participants. And yet that equivocal project of a "sacred theology" of contemporary reality, rightly criticized by Leiris, attracted at that particular moment even some objective observers little inclined towards mysticizing and aestheticizing muddles.

I have spoken of the extremely close relationship, through Caillois, between Dumézil and the activities of the Collège de Sociologie. There is no evidence that Bloch had any connections with this group. But Lucien Febvre's famous essays "History and Psychology" (1933) and "How to Reconstruct the Emotional Life of a Period: Sensibility and History" (1941), even if written by a man of another generation and of totally different intellectual background, suggest interests not far removed from those of the Collège. Especially in his second essay, under a veil of reticence and ambiguity intended to sidetrack Nazi censorship, Febvre insisted on the political implications of a historical psychology which extends

> to the most ancient as well as the most modern history. To a history of primitive sentiments *in situ*, as well as to that of revived primitive emotions, and our history of continual resurgences and sentimental resurrections. Cult of the blood, of red-hot blood, of that which has the most animal and most primitive about it. Cult of elementary powers.... Resurrection compensating for a species of cult of Mother Earth, on whose bosom it is so sweet at night to stretch one's suffering limbs.... Exaltation of primal sentiments with an abrupt break in orientation and values; exaltation of toughness at the expense of love, of animality at the expense of culture – but animality proved and tested as superior to culture.[52]

Bloch's language is certainly different. But against this background of uncertainty, ambiguity, doubts, and attempts to comprehend that phenomenon Nazism, which seemed to be beyond the grasp of even the most serious historiography, both social and economic as well as political, Bloch's reviews of Höfler's and Dumézil's books seem less surprising.

Various historical as well as theoretical questions requiring further study emerge from that confusing situation which I have attempted to disentangle. The first concerns the impact of Nazism on a number of disciplines, including Indo-European studies. It would be convenient to suppose that propagandistic intrusions and serious research travelled separate roads. But the reality was more complicated, as demonstrated, on the one hand, by the cases of purely physical contact between scholarly contributions and racist trash;[53] and on the other, by the examples (evidently more complex) of such scholars as Höfler who, starting from Nazi or philo-Nazi positions, obtained questionable or unfounded scholarly results, which were not, however, totally lacking in significance. The second question concerns attempts to analyze Nazism as a phenomenon not reducible to its political, economic, and social components. A book such as *Mythes et dieux des Germains* suggests that it is not always easy to distinguish between the two questions.

There is, however, a third question of a more general character. It is both possible and necessary to demarcate scholarly investigation from ideologically motivated theses, and documentary data from their interpretation. The process permits specific research to be used in a different perspective from the one producing it. In some cases, however, this data, even though vitiated by ideological options, was obtained precisely *because* of them. The wheat can be separated from the chaff only through the process of internal criticism. We would be mistaken, for example, if we rejected unilaterally, on ideological grounds, research which explains long continuities in racial (Höfler) or archetypal (Eliade) terms.[54] All the more reason, then, to apply this to the much richer and more original work of Dumézil. And also, work so much more elusive: the unconscious continuity between Germanic myths and aspects of Nazi Germany loomed, in *Mythes et dieux des Germains*, as a phenomenon related neither to race nor to the collective unconscious. In his later writings Dumézil stressed, instead, the conscious continuity of what he ended up calling Indo-European "ideology" of the three functions.[55] Even this tacit self-critical revision of a theoretically crucial point indicates that, after *Mythes et dieux des Germains*, Dumézil had turned a page.

❧ Freud, the Wolf-Man, and the Werewolves

Among the clinical cases studied by Sigmund Freud, the most famous may be the one of the wolf-man. Although written up in 1914, it was not published until the end of the war, in 1918, with the title "From the History of an Infantile Neurosis."[1] The critical point in this work is a dream experienced in early infancy by the patient, a young Russian from an upper-middle-class family who was twenty-seven years old in 1914. Here is his account:

> I dreamt that it was night and that I was lying in my bed. (My bed stood with its foot towards the window; in front of the window there was a row of old walnut trees. I know it was winter when I had the dream, and night time.) Suddenly the window opened of its own accord, and I was terrified to see that some white wolves were sitting on the big walnut tree in front of the window. There were six or seven of them. The wolves were quite white, and looked more like foxes or sheep-dogs, for they had big tails like foxes and they had their ears pricked like dogs when they are attending to something. In great terror, evidently of being eaten up by the wolves, I screamed and woke up. My nurse hurried to my bed, to see what had happened to me. It took quite a long while before I was convinced that it had only been a dream; I had had such a clear and life-like picture of the window opening and the wolves sitting on the tree. At last I grew quieter, felt as though I had escaped from some danger, and went to sleep again.
>
> The only piece of action in the dream was the opening of the window; for the wolves sat quite still and without any movement on the branches of the tree, to the right and left of the trunk, and looked at me. It seemed as though they had riveted their whole attention upon me. – I think this was my first anxiety dream. I was three, four, or at most five years old at the time. From then until my eleventh or twelfth year I was always afraid of seeing something terrible in my dreams.[2]

Through a long and minute analysis Freud discovered, behind this infantile dream reconstructed a posteriori, the elaboration of an experience lived by the patient at an even more precocious age, when he might have been a year and a half old: the primal scene of coitus

146

between his parents. I will return to this point later. First a digression is necessary that will permit us to look at certain elements in the case of the wolf-man from an angle that differs from Freud's.

In a book written several years ago, I studied, on the basis of about fifty inquisitorial trials, a strange sect encountered in the Friuli between the end of the sixteenth and early seventeenth centuries. Its members were men and women who called themselves *benandanti*, well-farers or good-doers. They asserted that they had been born with the caul, and thus were compelled to go forth in spirit four times yearly to fight witches and warlocks for the success of the harvest, or (alternately) participate in processions for the dead. The inquisitors recognized in their accounts a distorted echo of the witches' sabbat: but only after pressure exerted over several decades did they succeed in extorting from the *benandanti* the admission that they were not in fact the adversaries of witches and warlocks, but themselves witches and warlocks.[3]

The beliefs of the *benandanti* – which differed profoundly from the stereotypes of diabolical witchcraft familiar to inquisitors – were not limited to the Friuli. The myth of the procession of the dead is widespread in European folklore, while that of the nocturnal battles over fertility, instead, is much rarer. Originally, I succeeded in uncovering only one parallel connected with fertility rites, in a trial held in Livonia against an old werewolf at the end of the seventeenth century. The man in question, Thiess by name, told the judges that three times yearly he traveled with other werewolves "beyond the sea" to battle witches and warlocks over the fertility of the harvests. The analogy with the *benandanti* is obvious, but difficult to explain. My initial hypothesis, of a substratum of Slavic credences common to the Friuli and Livonia,[4] was confirmed by an essay of R. Jakobson and M. Szeftel which I had missed. This work demonstrates that in Slavic folklore exceptional powers, such as the ability to become a werewolf, were attributed to people born with the caul.[5] The shamanistic characteristics which I had recognized in the *benandanti* now appear to be shared by other figures in European folklore: Slavic and Baltic werewolves, Hungarian *táltos*, Dalmatian *kersniki*, Corsican *mazzeri*, and so forth. All these personages claimed to be able to travel periodically (in spirit or in animal form) to the world of the dead. Their destiny was indicated by special characteristics: having been born with their teeth (*táltos*), with the caul (*benandanti*, *kersniki*, werewolves), or during the twelve days between Christmas and Epiphany (werewolves).[6]

[handwritten margin note: Caul-born on Christmas Day]

Let us return to the wolf-man. We learn from Freud's published account that the patient was a Russian, that he had been born with the caul, that he had been born on Christmas day.[7] There is an obvious cultural homogeneity between these facts and the infantile dream focusing on the appearance of the wolves. A series of casual coincidences is really quite improbable. The intermediary between the sphere of folkloric beliefs connected with werewolves and Freud's future patient, who belonged, as I have said, to an upper-middle-class family, undoubtedly must have been the nurse, the *njanja*, described as a "pious and superstitious" woman.[8] The child was deeply attached to the old nurse (it was she, after all, who comforted him after his anguished dream about the wolves). It was from her that he would have learned what extraordinary (not necessarily negative) powers were conferred by the fact that he had been born with the caul. And it was she who would have told him his first fairy tales, before the English governess read to him Grimm's in a Russian translation. Even the fable of the tailor and the wolves, drawn forth during the patient's analysis, which his grandfather (and, who knows? perhaps his nurse too) had recited, was part of the Russian folklore, and Afanasjev included it in his celebrated collection.[9] But the dream, imbued with fairy-tale echoes of the seven wolves on the tree, also recalls the initiatory dreams with which the vocation of the future benandanti or of the future táltos manifested itself in infancy or adolescence. The Friulian child, for example, who carried around his neck the caul with which he was born and which had been saved by his mother, was visited by an apparition one night many years later: a man who said to him, "You must come with me because you have something of mine."[10] In the case of the táltos, what appeared was an animal, generally a stallion or a bull.[11]

In the wolf-man's nightmare we discern a dream of an initiatory character, induced by the surrounding cultural setting or, more precisely, by a part of it. Subjected to opposing cultural pressures (the nurse, the English governess, his parents and teachers) the wolf-man's fate differed from what it might have been two or three centuries earlier. Instead of turning into a werewolf, he became a neurotic on the brink of psychosis.[12]

It is not so surprising that Freud (who, incidentally, was himself born with the caul) should have allowed these elements to elude him in the end: the patient came from a cultural world too different from his own. When it was a matter of interpreting the dreams of his Viennese patients (or, even better, his own) Freud was in full command of the everyday context, capable of deciphering literary and other allusions, some of a hidden, innermost nature. In the present case, instead, he did not perceive that in a fable in Afanasjev's collection ("The Imbecile Wolf") he would have found the answer to the question about the number of wolves (why six or seven?) asked by his patient.[13] But the failure to make the connection between being born with the caul and wolves (werewolves) had more serious consequences from a hermeneutic point of view. Freud, who years before had written a work on dreams in folklore in association with D.E. Oppenheim,[14] did not recognize the element of folklore present in the wolf-man's dream. Thus, the cultural context behind the dream was ignored: what remained was only the individual experience, reconstructed through the network of associations deduced by the analyst.

One could object that this is not enough to warrant an alternative interpretation to Freud's. The cultural implications that being born with the caul possessed in Slavic folklore integrate, but do not abolish, the psychological implications that this fact had assumed in the patient's psyche. Similarly, they integrate but do not confute Freud's interpretation:

> The world, he said, was hidden from him by a veil; and our psychoanalytic training forbids our assuming that these words can have been without significance or have been chosen at haphazard .... It was not until just before taking leave of the treatment that he remembered having been told that he was born with a caul. He had for that reason always looked on himself as a special child of fortune whom no ill could befall. He did not lose that conviction until he was forced to realize that his gonorrhoeal infection constituted a serious injury to his body. The blow to his narcissism was too much for him and he collapsed. It may be said that in so doing he was repeating a mechanism that he had already brought into play once before. For his wolf phobia had broken out when he found himself faced by the fact that such a thing as castration was possible; and he clearly classed his gonorrhoea as castration.
>
> Thus the caul was the veil which hid him from the world and hid the world from him. The complaint that he made was in reality a fulfilled wish-fantasy that represented the return to the womb; and was, in fact, a wish-fantasy of flight from the world.[15]

Even the general interpretation of the wolf-man's dream as a reelaboration of the primal scene would not appear, at first glance, to have been even slightly impaired by what I have observed thus far.

But what complicates the question is precisely the term "primal scene" (*Urszene*). Although it was used here probably for the first time in a text intended for publication, it had already appeared in a plural form (*Urszenen*) in a letter from Freud to Fliess dated May 2, 1897, and in an accompanying document.[16] The term reemerged with a different meaning, however, after seventeen years. In 1897, in fact, the "primal scenes" referred not to coitus between parents but to acts of seduction perpetrated on children by adults (frequently parents); a decisive aetiological role in the formation of neuroses, especially hysteria, was attributed to these acts. As we know, after having upheld this thesis even publicly in an 1896 lecture, Freud abandoned it suddenly in the summer of the following year, with the beginning of his own autoanalysis. He explained in his famous letter to Fliess of September 21, 1897, that all his certainties had vanished: his patients' accounts about the sexual seductions experienced in infancy now appeared to him to be pure and simple fantasies. From this turning point, coinciding with the identification of the Oedipus complex, psychoanalysis was born.[17] The term *Urszenen* had emerged immediately before this dramatic crisis, almost as if to crown the seduction theory, after a series of reflections had taken an unexpected turn in that same decisive year, 1897. In two agitated letters to Fliess (dated respectively January 17 and 24), Freud revealed that his theories on the origins of hysteria had been discovered and formulated centuries before by judges in witchcraft trials. Besides comparing witches to hysterics (as Charcot and his followers had already done) Freud identified himself implicitly with the judges: "Why are [the witches'] confessions under torture so like the communications made by my patients in psychic treatment?" He concluded: "Now I understand the harsh therapy of the witches' judges."[18] This twofold analogy was based on an infantile trauma which associated judge and defendant (and thus, implicitly, therapist and patient): "Once more, the inquisitors prick with needles to discover the devil's stigmata, and in a similar situation the victims think of the same old cruel story in fictionalized form (helped perhaps by disguises of the seducers). Thus, not only the victims but also the executioners recalled in this their earliest youth."[19]

A few months later, these painful reflections led to "the surprise that in all cases, the father, not excluding my own, had to be accused of being perverse – the realization of the unexpected frequency of hysteria, with precisely the same conditions prevailing in each, whereas surely such widespread perversions against children are not very probable"; the abandonment of the seduction theory followed from this.[20] But in January 1897 Freud was still convinced that witches' confessions could be explained by that theory since they were symbolic expressions of actual infantile sexual trauma, revived in the course of the trial. He had ordered a *Malleus Maleficarum*, and he proposed to study it. He was leaning towards the belief that in perversion there "could be the remnant of a primeval sexual cult, which once was – perhaps still is – a religion in the Semitic East (Moloch, Astarte)."[21] The term *Urszenen*, when referring explicitly to ontogenesis (infantile sexual trauma that set off neuroses), thus had obvious phylogenetic implications for Freud in 1897. That ontogenesis recapitulated phylogenesis was for Freud, then and later, as it was for a large part of European culture at the turn of the century, an indisputable dogma.

Let us return now to the case of the wolf-man. As I have said, the term "primal scene" was introduced here to designate not infantile seduction but coitus between parents. Freud pondered at length the reality of this scene. Had it been an actual experience on the patient's part or a retrospective fantasy? "I acknowledge that this is the most ticklish question in the whole domain of psycho-analysis," Freud wrote in a note, adding, "No doubt has troubled me more; no other uncertainty has been more decisive in holding me back from publishing my conclusions." He had a different opinion in a passage added in 1918 before the work went to press: "The answer to this question is not in reality a matter of very great importance." But there is no need to consult the famous essay "Negation" (not yet written at that date)[22] to state that the question was indeed of great significance for Freud. The sentence immediately following confirms it: "These scenes of observing parental intercourse, of being seduced in childhood, and of being threatened with castration are unquestionably an inherited endowment, a phylogenetic inheritance, but they may just as easily be acquired by personal experience."[23] Freud's outspoken polemic against Jung's hasty phylogenetic explanations (to which I shall return in a moment) thus led the former unexpectedly to rehabilitate the theory of infantile seduction which he had rejected in 1897. A few pages earlier, Freud had actually written about the final stages in the analysis of the wolf-man,

"The old trauma theory which was after all built up upon impressions gained from psycho-analytic practice, had suddenly come to the front once more."[24] This statement flatly contradicted another made in the same year, 1914, in Freud's "On the History of the Psycho-Analytic Movement," where he stated that the theory of seduction constituted "an obstacle ... that was almost fatal for the young science."[25]

Such fluctuations demonstrate the inadequacy, even philologically, of the thesis recently proposed by J. Moussaieff Masson that Freud's rejection of the seduction theory in 1897 was definitive – and had impaired, with serious consequences, the claims of psychoanalysis to reality.[26] However, it is not my intention to discuss here what is unquestionably a decisive chapter in Freud's intellectual biography. I should prefer, rather, to respond to the following question: what is the significance of the reappearance, after an interval of seventeen years, of the term "primal scenes" (*Urszenen*)?

The possibility of an insignificant coincidence can be eliminated straight-off. Granted, in the piece devoted to the wolf-man, *Urszene* has a different meaning than in Freud's letter to Fliess of May 2, 1897; but, as we saw, the reappearance of the term meant a reflowering of the seduction theory within which it had been originally formulated. To this consideration, internal to Freud's writings, another of an external character needs to be added. The *Urszene* of 1897 had emerged, in its phylogenetic implications, after reflection on witches' accounts of the sabbat; the primal scene of 1914, after reflection upon a dream – the wolf-man's – which, as I have stressed, has folkloristic implications associated with beliefs in werewolves. Now, *from a historical point of view*, there is a connection between werewolves and the sabbat which has the benandanti as an intermediate link: both can be considered figures in a vast, half-obliterated stratum of beliefs imbued with shamanistic overtones that under pressure from judges and inquisitors merged with the image of the sabbat.[27] Freud was unaware of this link; even the folkloristic aspects of the wolf-man's dream had escaped him completely. How, then, can one explain the reappearance, at a distance of so many years, of the same key concept, *Urszene*?

In Freudian terms the reply to the question might go like this: the existence of a traumatic sexual nucleus was *perceived clearly* by Freud in 1897 (apropos the witches' confessions), and *discerned dimly* in 1914 (in regard to the dream of the wolf-man). In both cases the original valence suggested by Freud with the prefix *Ur* is ascribable both to the ontogenetic and the phylogenetic spheres. Thus, the folklore beliefs connected with the sabbat and werewolves were thought to preserve the memory, reelaborated, of sexual trauma experienced not just by individuals but by the human race in a remote past. Freud would undoubtedly have subscribed to this interpretation. His disagreement with Jung, brought out into the open in a passage added in 1918 to his study of the wolf-man, did not hinge on whether phylogenetic heredity existed or not, but on the role that the recollection of this heredity should play in the analytical strategy. According to Freud it was permissible to have recourse to phylogenesis for the purpose of explication, but only after having tested all the possibilities for interpretation offered by ontogenesis. The importance Freud attributed to phylogenesis is also testified to by the theory (or anthropological romance) expounded in *Totem and Taboo*, a text which he refers to, significantly, even in the case of the wolf-man.[28]

However, this interpretation, sketched in summary fashion in Freudian terms, is basically unacceptable, for two reasons. First, it rests (just like Jung's theories on the collective unconscious) on an absolutely undemonstrated hypothesis of Lamarckian character: namely, that the psychological and cultural experiences lived by progenitors are part of our cultural baggage. To be sure, Freud, in his piece on the wolf-man, postulates alongside a "phylogenetic experience," inasmuch as it is a repository of specific contents (not too remote from Jungian archetypes), a presumed hereditary disposition of the individual to relive, "in similar situations," events that had occurred in prehistoric periods.[29] But even this disposition still remains an unverifiable conjecture whose potential for explanation does not differ significantly from that *virtus dormitiva* evoked by Molière's physician. The second of the objections is linked to the fact that the identification of a traumatic sexual nucleus in the beliefs connected with the sabbat, with werewolves, and so forth, becomes translated into an arbitrary simplification. When Róheim, for example, reads a sexual initiation into the oneiric initiation of the táltos – shamanistic figures in Hungarian folklore in many respects resembling the benandanti – the discrepancy between the obscure, intricate documentation and the orderliness of the analysis is all too evident.[30] This interpretation, like others, catches a side, but one side only, of a much richer mythical complex.

All this, obviously, leads to Jung. His break with Freud occurred over the question of myth (with personality differences contributing).

Disagreements began to reveal themselves, almost imperceptibly, from the very first letters exchanged by the two in November 1909. On the eighth Jung wrote to Freud, who at the time was reading Herodotus and Creuzer's work on symbolism, commenting that here "rich lodes open up for the phylogenetic basis of the theory of neurosis." Freud replied three days later in an exultant mood: "I was delighted to learn that you are going into mythology .... I hope you will soon come to agree with me that in all likelihood mythology centers on the same nuclear complex as the neuroses."[31] The seeds of irreversible discord were already beginning to take root behind this apparent sharing of interests. We can try to describe it in these terms. For Freud the theory of neurosis includes the myth; for Jung it was just the opposite.

Jung's fuzzy-mindedness and lack of rigor caused the failure of a project that, on this point, was potentially much more fruitful than Freud's. The archetypes identified by Jung were the consequence of a superficial intuition (and superficially ethnocentric); his theory of the collective unconscious aggravated Freud's already unacceptable Lamarckianism. Jung's responses to the problem of myth constitute, in a final analysis, the loss of a wonderful opportunity.

The case of the wolf-man poses forcefully that interweaving of myths and neuroses which so engrossed Freud and Jung, albeit from different points of view. I shall not try to explain the neuroses of the wolf-man by the myth of the werewolves. We cannot ignore, however, that the dream of the wolf-man was impregnated by a much more ancient mythical element, visible also in the dreams (in the ecstasies, in the swoons, in the visions) of the benandanti, the táltos, werewolves, and witches. In obviously different ways, this mythical content impressed itself, through other channels, on Freud, first in 1897 and later, unknown to him, in 1914 – and on this writer. It is not an archetype in a Jungian sense: phylogenetic heredity is not at issue. The go-betweens are historical, identifiable, or plausibly conjecturable: men, women, books, and archival documents that tell of men and women. The mothers of the Friulian benandanti; the wolf-man's nurse; Charcot and his disciples, intent on deciphering the contortions of the hysterics in the Salpêtrière through the descriptions of the possessed (and vice versa); the trial against the benandante drover Menichino da Latisana, discovered by chance in the Archivio di Stato, Venice. We could ask, in a brutal simplification of the problem, are we the ones who think up myths, or is it myths who think us up?

We know that Lévi-Strauss replied to this question by opting for the second alternative, thereby taking a position that unquestionably lends itself to a number of ambiguous, more or less irrational interpretations. In general, it is easy to object that there is a great difference between individual variants of the myth, and especially between the individual contexts within which the myth comes into being and functions. There is an even greater distance between passively living a myth and the attempt to interpret it critically in the broadest and most comprehensive manner possible. But after drawing all these distinctions, we still find ourselves confronting something that our interpretations succeed only in approaching, but not exhausting. Against the hypertrofic (actually solipsistic) image of the interpretative I, today in fashion, the formula "myths think us up" underscores, provocatively, the perpetual inadequacies of our analytical categories.

what you can discover about folk religion/belief by deciphering in the right way the inquisitional records — Ginzburg doing the same as Freud in dream interpretation — whats hidden beneath

✥ The Inquisitor as Anthropologist

The analogy which is the subject of this brief essay struck me for the first time several years ago in Bologna while I was attending a colloquium on oral history. Historians of contemporary European societies and distinguished Africanists and anthropologists such as Jan Vansina and Jack Goody were debating the different ways of dealing with oral evidence. Suddenly it occurred to me that even historians of early modern Europe – a noncontemporary society which has left enormous amounts of written evidence – sometimes use oral sources, or, more precisely, written records of oral speech. For instance, the judicial proceedings of lay and ecclesiastical courts might be comparable to the notebooks of anthropologists, recording fieldwork performed centuries ago.[1] It should be interesting to test this analogy between inquisitors and anthropologists, as well as between defendants and "natives." I intend to discuss some of the implications, primarily from the point of view of a historian who has worked on inquisitorial records, with a particular interest in late medieval and early modern European witchcraft.

The discovery of inquisitorial records as an extremely valuable historical source is a surprisingly late phenomenon. For a long time historians of the Inquisition concentrated on the mechanisms of that peculiar institution, in a rather descriptive (although often polemical) way: the documents themselves remained largely unexploited, even though in some cases they were accessible to scholars. As is widely known, they first began to be used by Protestant historians to show the heroic attitudes of their forefathers in the face of Catholic persecution. A book entitled *I nostri protestanti* (Our Protestants [Venice, 1897]), written at the end of the nineteenth century by the Italian erudite Emilio Comba, can be regarded as a typical example of the continuation on the archival level of a tradition started in the sixteenth century by Crespin's *Histoire des Martyrs*. On the other hand, Catholic historians exhibited a remarkable reluctance to use inquisitorial records in their own research. There was a conscious or unconscious tendency to lessen the impact of the Reformation, as well as a certain uneasiness in dealing with an institution which had become so unpopular – even among Catholics. The historian who kindly introduced me to the ecclesiastical archives in Udine – the learned Catholic priest Pio Paschini, who was Friulian-born – had never thought to exploit inquisitorial trials in his books on heresy and the Counter-Reformation in Friuli.[2] When I was admitted for the first time to the large room which housed in perfect order nearly two thousand inquisitorial trials, I felt the sudden thrill of discovering an unexplored gold mine.

It must be emphasized, however, that in the case of witchcraft, the reluctance to use inquisitorial records has been shared for a long time by confessional (both Catholic and Protestant) and liberal historians alike. The reasons were obvious. Religious, intellectual, or emotional identification was lacking in all cases. The evidence provided in witchcraft trials was usually regarded as a mixture of theological oddities and peasant superstitions. The latter was by definition irrelevant; the former could be better and more easily studied on the basis of printed demonological treatises. For scholars who thought that the only "proper" historical topic was the persecution of witchcraft, and not its target, to dwell on the long and supposedly repetitive confessions of men and women accused of witchcraft would have been a tedious, even useless task.

This sounds like an old story – though the same attitude was still echoed twenty years ago by Hugh Trevor-Roper.[3] In the meantime, however, the situation has changed rather dramatically. Witchcraft has shifted from the periphery to the center of "proper" (not to mention fashionable) historical topics. It is just one symptom of a now well-established historiographical tendency, one immediately perceived by Arnaldo Momigliano several years ago: the study of such sexual or social groups as women or peasants, usually underrepresented in what we may call "official" sources.[4] The "archives of repression" certainly provide us with rich evidence about these people. But the relevance ascribed to witchcraft in this perspective must be connected to a more specific, though related phenomenon, namely the growing influence of anthropology upon history. It is not by chance that the classic book on witchcraft among the Azande, written by Evans-Pritchard over a half century ago, has provided a frame of reference to Alan Macfarlane and Keith Thomas for their works on seventeenth-century witchcraft.[5] The variety of insights provided by Evans-Pritchard is, of course, undeniable – even though the comparison between seventeenth-century English witches or warlocks and their Azande counterparts should be supplemented by a comparison (systematically avoided in the recent literature) with Continental witches persecuted in the same period.

It has been suggested that the peculiar features of English witchcraft trials (particularly the conspicuous lack of confessions related to the witches' sabbat) should be explained also in terms of legal insularity. There is no doubt that Continental trials performed by the Inquisition provide much more rewarding evidence to historians attempting to reconstruct the beliefs about witchcraft held by ordinary people. Here, the analogy between inquisitors and anthropologists (and historians as well) begins to reveal its ambiguous implications. The elusive evidence that inquisitors were trying to elicit from defendants was not so different, after all, from our own objectives: what was different, of course, were their means and ultimate ends. While reading inquisitorial trials, I often felt as if I was looking over the judges' shoulders, dogging their footsteps, hoping (as they presumably did) that the alleged offenders would be talkative about their beliefs – at the offender's own risk, of course. This proximity to the inquisitor somewhat contradicted my emotional identification with the defendant. A different kind of contradiction can be experienced on the intellectual level. The inquisitors' urge for truth (their own truth, of course) has produced for us extremely rich evidence – deeply distorted, however, by the psychological and physical pressures which played such a powerful role in witchcraft trials. Suggestive questioning was especially apparent in inquisitors' interrogations related to the witches' sabbat, the very essence of witchcraft, according to demonologists. When this occurred, defendants echoed, more or less spontaneously, the inquisitorial stereotypes which were diffused throughout Europe by preachers, theologians, and jurists.

The slippery nature of inquisitorial evidence probably explains why so many historians have decided to concentrate on the persecution of witchcraft, analyzing regional patterns, inquisitorial categories, and so on – a more traditional, but obviously safer ground, compared to the attempts to reconstruct witchcraft beliefs. Passing references to Azande witches cannot conceal the obvious fact that very few among the historical studies devoted to European witchcraft in the past twenty years have really been inspired by anthropological research. Some years ago, the debate between Keith Thomas and Hildred Geertz showed that the dialogue between historians and anthropologists is a difficult one.[6] The issue of evidence seems crucial in this context. Historians of past societies cannot produce their sources as anthropologists do. Archival files, seen from this point of view, cannot be a substitute for tape recorders. Do historians have enough evidence to reconstruct witchcraft beliefs in medieval or early modern Europe, to get beyond the judges' stereotypes? Obviously, this is a problem of quality, not of mere quantity. Richard Kieckhefer, in a book somewhat removed from the mainstream of current research, has traced a distinction between learned stereotypes and popular witchcraft, based on a detailed (although still unconvincing) scrutiny of the available evidence. Significantly, he has compared unfavorably the defendants' confessions before the Inquisition both with written complaints made by people who had been previously defamed as witches and with the recorded testimony of witnesses in witchcraft trials.[7] These documents, according to Kieckhefer, give us a more faithful image of popular witchcraft beliefs. Similarly, the comparison between inquisitorial trials and anthropological field notes could have, from the historian's point of view, a negative implication: the presence of those long-ago anthropologists would be so obtrusive as to prevent us from knowing the beliefs and thoughts of the unhappy natives brought before them.

But I don't agree with this pessimistic conclusion, and I would like to reflect further on the analogy. Its bases are textual. In both cases we have texts that are intrinsically *dialogic*. The dialogic structure can be explicit, as in the series of questions and answers that punctuate either an inquisitorial trial or a transcript of the conversations between an anthropologist and his informant. But it can also be implicit, as in ethnographic field notes describing a ritual, a myth, or a tool. The essence of what we call anthropological attitude – that is, the permanent confrontation between different cultures – rests on a dialogic disposition. Its theoretical foundation, on a linguistic (not psychological) level, has been pointed out by Roman Jakobson in a dense passage defining "the two cardinal and complementary traits of verbal behavior": "that inner speech is in its essence a dialogue, and that any reported speech is *appropriated* and remolded by the quoter, whether it is a quotation from an *alter* or from an earlier phase of the *ego* (*said I*)."[8] On a more circumscribed level, another great Russian scholar, Mikhail Bakhtin, has stressed the importance of the dialogic element in his analysis of Dostoyevsky's novels.[9] According to Bakhtin, they exhibit a structure which he calls dialogic or polyphonic: the different characters are seen as conflicting forces;

none of them speaks for the author, from the author's point of view. I am not concerned here with Bakhtin's reflections on the peculiar literary genre which Dostoyevsky's novels occupy. I think, however, that his notion of dialogic texts can shed light on certain features which from time to time come to the surface in inquisitorial witchcraft trials.

Obviously, the conflicting characters who speak in these texts were not on an equal footing. (The same can be said, in a different way, also about anthropologists and their informants.) This inequality in terms of power (real as well as symbolic) explains why the pressure exerted by inquisitors on the defendants in order to elicit the truth they were seeking was usually successful. These trials not only look repetitive but also *monologic* (to use a favorite Bakhtinian word), in the sense that the defendants' answers were quite often just an echo of the inquisitors' questions. But in some exceptional cases we have a real dialogue: we can hear distinct voices, we can detect a clash between different, even conflicting voices. In the Friulian trials that I studied many years ago, the *benandanti* provided long descriptions of the nocturnal battles they fought in spirit against witches for the fertility of the crops. To the inquisitors, all this sounded like a disguised description of the witches' sabbat. Notwithstanding continuous efforts, however, it took half a century to cross over the gap between the inquisitors' expectations and the *benandanti's* spontaneous confessions. Both the gap and the *benandanti's* resistance to inquisitorial pressures indicate that we have here a deep cultural layer which was totally foreign to the inquisitors. The very word benandante was unknown to them: its meaning (was it a synonym of "witch" or, on the contrary, of "counterwitch"?) was, in a sense, the stake in the long struggle which set inquisitors against benandanti in the Friuli between the late sixteenth and mid-seventeenth centuries. In the long run, power settled this semantic dispute (it always does, as readers of *Through the Looking Glass* know). *Benandanti* became witches.[10]

The ethnographic value of these Friulian trials is truly astonishing. Not only words, but gestures, sudden reactions like blushing, even silences, were recorded with punctilious accuracy by the notaries of the Holy Office. To the deeply suspicious inquisitors, every small clue could provide a breakthrough to the truth. It cannot be claimed, of course, either that these documents are neutral or that they convey to us "objective" information. They must be read as the product of a peculiar, utterly unbalanced interrelationship. In order to decipher them, we must learn to catch, behind the smooth surface of the text, a subtle interplay of threats and fears, of attacks and withdrawals. We must learn to disentangle the different threads which form the textual fabric of these dialogues.

In recent years, textual awareness has come to the forefront among anthropologists, in some degree directly inspired by the work of Clifford Geertz.[11] For historians, who usually (though not exclusively) deal with texts, this is not a novelty in itself. But the issue is not so simple. Becoming aware of the textual aspect of ethnographic work ("What does the ethnographer do? – he writes," Clifford Geertz ironically remarked)[12] implies the overcoming of a naive, positivistic epistemology, still shared by too many historians. There are no neutral texts; even a notarial inventory implies a code, which we must decipher. "Any reported speech," as Jakobson said, "is appropriated and remoulded by the quoter." So far, so good. But can this mean, as some historians and anthropologists have recently claimed, or at least implied, that a text is only evidence of itself, of its own order? The refined skepticism which has inspired the rejection of the so-called referential fallacy looks like a dangerous pitfall.[13] Here again, the comparison between inquisitors and anthropologists can be rewarding. As I have shown before, a conflicting cultural reality may leak out even from such heavily controlled texts as inquisitorial trials. The same conclusions can also be extended to ethnographic reports.

An extreme skeptic might object to the term "reality" (or even "cultural reality") as spurious: there are conflicting voices in the same text, not conflicting realities. To reply to such an objection may seem to be a waste of time: after all, the integration of different texts in the writing of history or ethnography rests on their common reference to something which we must call *faute de mieux*, "eternal reality." Still, these skeptical objections, however distorted, point to a real difficulty. Let's take an example.

In 1384 and 1390, two women, Sibillia and Pierina, were tried by the Milanese Inquisition. Their trials are lost; only two detailed sentences (one of them quoting *in extenso* an earlier one) survive. These documents were discovered and analyzed by Ettore Verga in a remarkable essay published at the end of the nineteenth century.[14] They have been subsequently studied on several occasions from different perspectives. Richard Kieckhefer, in his *European Witchcraft Trials*, cited above, interpreted the trials as evidence of a "popular festivity or ritual."[15] This statement seems to be unexpected homage

Murray
thesis

to the notorious "Murray thesis," which implied the physical reality of the witches' sabbat. In fact, the confessions of the two Milanese women are full of details surrounded by a mythical aura. Each Thursday they used to go to a gathering led by a mysterious lady, Madona Horiente. Every kind of animal went there, except the ass and the fox; people who had been beheaded or hanged also attended; dead oxen were brought back to life; and so on. In 1390 one of the women, Sibillia, told the inquisitor Beltramino da Cernusculo that six years earlier she had confessed to his predecessor, Ruggero da Casale, that she used to go "ad ludum Diane *quam appellant* Herodiadem" ("to the games of Diana, whom *they call* Herodiades"), greeting her with the words "Bene stage (stay well) Madona Horiente." This series of names seems puzzling, but the solution is really quite simple. Both Sibillia and Pierina always referred only to Horiente: the latter's identification with Diana and Herodiades had been suggested by the inquisitor Ruggero da Casale. He had obviously been inspired by the famous *Canon episcopi*, a text written at the beginning of the ninth century (or even earlier) in which some superstitious women were labelled as followers of Diana and Herodiades. Needless to say, the same identification was taken for granted by the second inquisitor, Beltramino da Cernuscullo, who tacitly ascribed it to Pierina: she went, the sentence reads, "ad ludum Diane *quam vos appelatis* Herodiadem" ("to the games of Diana *whom you call* Herodiades").[16] We have here, apparently, the customary projection of inquisitorial stereotypes on popular beliefs. But things are actually more complicated than that. These feminine characters of popular religion point to an undeniable underlying unity. Perchta, Holda, dame Abonde, and Madona Horiente are local variants of a single female goddess, profoundly related to the world of the dead. The *interpretatio romana* or *biblica* (Diana or Herodiades) suggested by the inquisitors – was it not an attempt to perceive this underlying unity?

This is not to suggest that comparative mythology originated with inquisitors. What is revealed here is a more embarrassing fact: the existence of a close continuity between our own comparative mythology and the interpretations of inquisitors. They were translating – or, rather, transposing – beliefs fundamentally foreign to them into another, more unambiguous code. What we are doing here is not so different, not only in principle but also in practice, because the evidence available to us is, in the present instance, already contaminated by their interpretation. In a sense, our task is much easier when the inquisitors did not understand – as in the case of the benandanti. When they were more perceptive, the trial lost to some extent its dialogic elements, and we must regard the evidence as less valuable, less pure.

To say "contaminated by their interpretation" is rather unfair toward the inquisitors' anthropological insight: we should add, "but also clarified." Bits and pieces of interpretation suggested by inquisitors, preachers, and canonists provide us with precious elements which fill the gaps in our evidence. Here is another example: Johannes Herolt, a Dominican friar who preached actively in the first part of the fifteenth century, included a long list of names of superstitious people in his collection of sermons. Among them were "those who believe [credunt] that during the night Diana, called in the vernacular *Unholde*, that is *die selige Fraw* [the blessed woman] goes about with her army, traveling great distances [*cum exercitu suo de nocte ambulet per multa spacia*]." This quotation is taken from an edition of Herolt's *Sermones* first printed at Cologne in 1474. Later editions which appeared at Strasbourg in 1478 and 1484 added to Diana's synonyms *Fraw Berthe* and *Fraw Helt* (as a substitute for *Unholde*).[17] Herolt's text obviously carried an echo of the *Canon episcopi*: there are women who "*credunt* se et profitentur *nocturnis horis cum Diana* paganorum dea et innumera multitudine mulierum equitare super quasdam bestias, et *multa* terrarum *spatia intempestae noctis* silentio *pertransire*" ("believe and profess themselves, in the hours of night, to ride upon certain beasts with Diana, the goddess of the pagans, and an innumerable multitude of women, and in the silence of the dead of night traverse great distances of the earth").[18] But Herolt did not quote the *Canon* literally; he used it as a frame of reference, either suppressing or adding details on the basis of his personal experience – his fieldwork, we could say. The allusion to riding animals disappeared; synonyms for Diana, taken from local German lore, were included not only by the author but by his editors as well; Diana herself was provided with an army (*cum exercitu suo*). The last detail is the most intriguing. I can find no parallel to it either in classical or medieval texts. It can be easily explained, however, in the context of European folklore related to the Wild Host or the Wild Hunt beliefs.[19] In Herolt's text Diana is represented as leader of the army of dead souls. This comparatively early evidence seems to support the hypothesis I have proposed elsewhere about the connection between this layer of presabbatical beliefs, already recorded by the *Canon episcopi*, and the world of the dead.[20] One could protest that my interpretation coincides, to some extent, with that of the inquisitors or of preachers such as Johannes Herolt. They were not impartial scholars: they were trying, often successfully, to make people believe what they thought was the truth. Does this continuity between evidence and early interpretations imply that we are inevitably caught up in the web of categories used by those remote anthropologists – preachers and inquisitors?

The question reflects, on a more restricted level, the extreme skeptical objection I recalled before, the criticism of "referential fallacy." Such criticism would, however, lose its universal epistemological implications, because some features of the evidence being dealt with are specific to the individual case. But even this moderate skepticism doesn't seem justified. We can test our interpretation in a comparative context which is much broader than the one available to inquisitors. We can take advantage, moreover, of those invaluable cases in which the lack of communication on a cultural level between judges and defendants permitted, rather paradoxically, the emergence of a real dialogue – in the Bakhtinian sense of an unresolved clash of conflicting voices. Earlier, I mentioned the case of the benandanti, calling it "exceptional." It is not unique, however: the splendid evidence on Sicilian *donne di fuori* ("women from outside") which Gustav Henningsen, the Danish folklorist, discovered some years ago in Spanish archives, demonstrates that in sixteenth-century Europe there were other recorded examples of beliefs still untainted by inquisitorial stereotypes.[21] In any case, the occurrence of a phenomenon cannot be taken as an index of its historical relevance. A close reading of a relatively small number of texts, related to a possibly circumscribed belief, can be more rewarding than the massive accumulation of repetitive evidence. For better or worse, historians of past societies cannot produce tangible evidence, as anthropologists do, and as inquisitors did. But for the interpretation of this evidence they have something to learn from both.

central argument – importance of his Method

- Possible to get at what the accused actually believed
- Want to get at what the common people thought not the learned
- What common person said was misinterpreted by the learned

 Notes

Witchcraft and Popular Piety: Notes on a Modenese Trial of 1519

1. The collection of inquisitorial trials now preserved in the Archivio di Stato, Modena, under the heading "Inquisizione di Modena e Reggio: Processi," was placed in the Archivio Segreto Estense at the time of the suppression of the Inquisition. See F. Valenti, Introduction to *Archivio Segreto Estense, sezione "Casa e Stato": Inventario*, Ministero dell'Interno, Pubblicazioni degli Archivi di Stato, 13 (Rome, 1953), p. xxxix. This archive contains 117 *buste*, or bundles, numbered from 2 to 118, arranged in chronological order (from 1489 to 1784, according to the archival description; but among the documents one encounters the copy of a trial held in Bologna in 1458). Although this material is largely unpublished, it has been discussed on a number of occasions, especially in regard to the question of witchcraft. The first to mention it was a student of local history, who published a few of the more colorful trial passages. See T[ommaso] S[andonnini], "Streghe e Superstizioni," *Il Panaro* (Gazzetta di Modena) 26, no. 111 (April 24, 1887). In his monograph *Pregiudizi e superstizioni del popolo modenese* (Modena, 1890), P. Riccardi dealt with the materials used by Sandonnini in a chapter entitled "Superstizioni e stregonerie in Modena nei secoli xvi e xv." (Actually the trials preserved in the Modena State Archives do not antedate the end of the fifteenth century, as I have noted.) Brief passages from a few trials have been published by N. Corradini, "I processi delle streghe a Modena nella prima metà del sec. xvi," in *Folklore Modenese: Atti e Memorie del I Congresso del Folklore Modenese ...* (Modena, 1959), pp. 44 ff. Delio Cantimori emphasized the importance of this archival collection in his review of L. Febvre, *Au coeur religieux du XVIe siècle*, in *Annales: E.S.C.*, 15 (1960): 567.

   The document which is the object of my attention here is in Busta 2, which contains the oldest series of trials (from 1458 to 1549). They are arranged according to the original order in "libri" (from "liber tertius" on: the first two are lost). The trials of the friar Bernardino da Castel Martino and of Chiara Signorini are preserved in the "liber quartus." The numbering of the leaves is modern.

2. It is impossible to compare the rhythm of activity of the Modenese Inquisition in other periods because there is a break in the trials between 1499 and 1517 (with a single exception in 1503) and between 1520 and 1530 (with two exceptions). Just the same, it is worth noting that in the years 1495-99 and 1530-39 almost all the trials concern cases of witchcraft, magic, and the like. In this regard a comparison with data from the triennium 1518-20 is possible.

3. I have been unable thus far to identify the two individuals positively. I have not come across any Modenese document which refers to the vicar of the Inquisition in these years as "Bartholomeus de Spina." According to the custom of the times he is everywhere referred to by his place of origin, that is, "Bartholomeus de Pisis." On the other hand, Spina's biographies pass over the period extending from his precocious entry into the Order (1494) to his appointment as professor of theology in Bologna (1530). See J. Quétif & J. Echard, *Scriptores Ordinis Praedicatorum* (Lutetiae Parisiorum [i.e., Paris], 1721), 2:126 ff.; and *Memorie Istoriche di più Uomini Illustri Pisani* (Pisa, 1790-92), 3:269-87. The eulogy of Spina is by S. Canovai. Nevertheless, from the introductory "Ad lectorem" in the *Quaestio de strigibus* (Rome, 1576), it emerges that during the years in which the treatise was being written, Spina was in fact serving as a vicar of the Inquisition ("duplici et utraque gravissima lectura, tam inquam naturalis, quam sacrae Theologiae, simul ac Inquisitionis vice alterius onere praegravatus"). Now, the *Quaestio de strigibus* informs us that it was "edita anno Domini 1523." But from an allusion at the beginning of the *Tractatus de Praeeminentia sacrae Theologiae super alias omnes scientias, et praecipue humanarum legum* (included in the 1576 edition of the *Quaestio*), it seems that it was written a few years earlier ("Perfecto de strigibus opere, cum eius impressio per plures annos praeter spem petentium sit dilata," *Quaestio de strigibus*, p. 91). Thus the *Quaestio* came into being precisely during the years in which our not better-identified Fra Bartolomeo "de Pisis" was vicar of the Inquisition in Modena (as was Spina). In addition, even if the *Quaestio* lacks specific references to Modena, it does mention frequently trials held in nearby places, such as Mirandola and Ferrara.

For information on Spina's later career, see A. Walz, O.P., "Die Dominikaner und Trient," in G. Schreiber, *Das Weltkonzil von Trient* (Freiburg im Breisgau, 1951), 2:489 ff. (now in a revised version in Walz's *I Domenicani al Concilio di Trento* [Rome, 1961], pp. 92 ff.). For a list of his writings, see Quétif and Echard, *Scriptores Ordinis Praedicatorum* and the *Memorie Istoriche*. (These two works incorrectly also attribute a manuscript "Cronica Pisana" to Spina; the false attribution, due to R. Roncioni, *Delle istorie pisane libri XVI* [Florence, 1844], 1:549 and n. 4, was passed on to Moreni's *Bibliografia storico-ragionata della Toscana*. Actually, the writing in question is a chronicle very doubtfully ascribed by Muratori to the Dominican theologian Bartolomeo "de Sancto Concordio," also a Pisan, and thus the confusion between the two. See L. A. Muratori, *Scriptores Rerum Italicarum* [Milan, 1725], 6:98.)

4. Archivio di Stato, Modena (henceforth abbreviated ASM), Inquisizione di Modena e Reggio, Busta 2, Liber Quartus. The trial against Fra Bernardino occupies fols. 97*r*-111*v*.

5. Ibid., fols. 98*r-v*.

6. Ibid., fol. 99*r*.

7. Ibid.

8. Ibid., fol. 99*v*.

9. Ibid., fol. 100*v*.

10. ASM, Inquisizione, Busta 2, Liber Quartus. The trial of Chiara Signorini occupies fols. 221*r*-260*r*. The sequence of folios does not reflect the chronological order of the trial sessions.

11. "Spiritus ex ore Gotolle [one of the possessed] dixit quod ipsa testis [Margherita] fuerit malliata a quadam muliere que vocatur Clara uxor Bartholomei Signorini, et quod ad hoc malleffitium faciendum ipsa Clara fecerat quandam imaginem ceream, quam absconderat ipsa Clara extra domum suam ruri sitam" (fol. 108*v*).

12. For information on Forni, see the bibliography cited by A. Mercati, *Il sommario del processo di Giordano Bruno, con appendice di documenti sull'eresia e l'inquisizione a Modena nel secolo XVI*, Studi e Testi, 101 (Vatican City, 1942), p. 129, n. 5.

13. ASM, Inquisizione, Busta 2, Liber Quartus, fol. 230*r*.

14. Ibid., fol. 99*r*.

15. Ibid., fols. 228*r-v*.

16. Ibid., fol. 228*v*.

17. Ibid., fols. 228*v*-229*r*.

18. Ibid., fols. 229*v*-230*r*.

19. Ibid., fol. 225*v* (testimony of Margherita Pazzani, February 1, 1519).

20. Ibid., fol. 256*r*.

21. Ibid., fol. 237*v*.

22. "[Chiara] maledixit ipsi domine Margarite et omnibus qui eam expulerunt de possessione, dicens hec verba vel similia: 'Maledicta sia madonna Margarita Pazzana et quanti n'é de soi che m'anno cacciata fuor de questa possessione, et non possi mai haver né ben né riposo, né lei né suoi figlioli,' …quando maledicebat predicto modo … tenebat in manu candelam quandam, orantibus simul genibus flexis marito eius et filiis, et dicebat hec vel similia: 'Così si possi consummar la vita di madonna Margarita come si consumma questa candela'; et post hec prohiciebat quandam herbam mori silvestri super ignem, maledicens ut supra." Deposition of Paolo Magnano, [February] (document has January), fol. 225*r*. The day is not indicated.

23. ASM, Inquisizione, Busta 2, Liber Quartus, fol. 224*r* (deposition of Ludovico Dienna, February 6, 1519).

24. Ibid., fol. 258*r*.

25. In a deposition of February 18, 1519, Stella Canova accused Chiara of casting a spell on her child: "Postquam ingresa fuerat dicta testis cum viro suo in domo ipsius domine Gentilis, conducta posesione sua quam prius Clara et vir eius colebant" (fol. 254*r*).

26. The question of magic powers was not of interest in that context and was not even raised. For a stimulating discussion of the issue, see E. De Martino, *Il mondo magico* (Turin, 1948).

27. J. Michelet, *La sorcière* (Paris, 1862), had already discerned the character of disguised social rebellion underlying witchcraft in many cases. This suggestion has been revived recently in a small popular volume: J. Palou, *La sorcellerie*, "Que-sais-je?" no. 756 (Paris, 1957). However, it is presented as an original finding ("Ici nous voulons soutenir par de multiples exemples, une thèse qui, à notre connaissance, n'a jamais été encore soutenue. La sorcellerie est fille de la misère. Elle est l'espoir des révoltés." P. 5), although at p. 18 the author acknowledges his debt to Michelet. Some of the texts Palou uses are of special significance, especially a passage from the French version of the *Sermo* (or *Tractatus*) *de secta Vaudensium*, written by Jehan Taincture (Johann

Tinctoris) on the occasion of the *Vauderie* at Arras (1459-61), where it is stated that the triumph of the *Vauderie* (i.e., of witchcraft) would provoke a general uprising in society. The same text had already been cited by J. Hansen in a slightly different and more reliable reading: "Lors guerres, murtres, debas, redicions forsenneront es royaumes, es citez et es champs, les gens sentre-tueront et cherront mors lun sur lautre. Amis et prochains se feront mal, les enfans se esleveront contre les anciens et sages gens et les villains entrepren-deront sur les nobles." J. Hansen, *Quellen und Untersuchungen zur Geschichte des Hexenwahns und der Hexenverfolgung im Mittelalter* (Bonn, 1901), p. 187. But certainly, even more noteworthy are the statements expressing the social aggression in witches' confessions themselves. There is a fine example of this among the documents published by A. Panizza, "I processi contro le streghe nel Trentino," *Archivio Trentino* 8 (1889): 227: in a trial held in 1505, a witch tells how, walking through a field with two companions, "videntes ibique pulcra blada super campaneis et annona prosperare, et quod ipse tres erant pauperes, et non habebant sic talia blada et possessiones, et propter invidiam deliber-averunt ipso die facere tempestatem. Et cusì la dicta Ursula andé quel dii dominico con le altre doe soe diabolice sotie, et quando venivano in la Vall, appresso la Ru, videlicet rivus, ...appresso quella Ru, aut rivulo, taiglaveno de le rame de le arbore de le aunari (ontani) et battevano in l'aqua, et chiamavano el diabolo dicendo: 'Vien, vien, diabolo del inferno, et dane la tempesta.' Et cusì appare, che de fatto veniva una si fatta tempesta." As early as 1444 Felix Haemmerlin, in his *De Nobilitate et Rusticitate Dialogus* (Strasbourg? 1490?), had the nobleman polemically attribute all the blame for witchcraft to the peasants: see chapter 32, "De Rusticorum presentium enormitatibus."

28. ASM, Inquisizione, Busta 2, Liber Quartus, fol. 221r (testimony of Giovan Gerolamo Pazzani, February 6, 1519).

29. Ibid., fol. 260r (testimony of Caterina Bongandi, February 12, 1519). The belief that witches before dying had to leave to some one their own places in the sect, bequeathing to them at the same time a patrimony of magical formulae, sortileges, and so forth was extremely widespread. A curious case was reported by a witch of Colle Vecchio (Perugia) who was tried in mid-seventeenth century: a witch, old and sick and alone in the world, before dying has her hen brought to her to make the hen heir of the "arte della strearia," and she spits on its beak saying, "Va che tu sei mia herede e cusì te concedo tucte mie ordini e rascione della strearia, e vattene via sta per me!" A. Bertolotti, "Streghe, sortiere, e maliardi nel secolo xvi in Roma," *Rivista Europea-Rivista Interna-zionale*, n.s., 14 (1883): 606.

To the vicar who asked Caterina Bongandi "si ipsa Clara esset reputata fatua," she answered, "Quod non, sed erat astutissima femina, et sagacissima, etiam super conditionem suam" (fol. 260r).

30. ASM, Inquisizione, Busta 2, Liber Quartus, fol. 231r.

31. Ibid., fols. 231v-232r.

32. Ibid., fol. 232r.

33. Ibid., fol. 232v.

34. Ibid., fols. 232v-233r. Bartolomeo Spina (about whom see above at note 3) stated that witches "faciunt homagium diabolo de anima et corpore suo, et quandoque filiorum suorum." *Quaestio de strigibus*, p. 19.

35. ASM, Inquisizione, Busta 2, Liber Quartus, fol. 233*r*.
36. Ibid., fol. 233*v*.
37. Ibid., fols. 234*v*-235*r*. The passage reads: "Respondit ... ipsa Clara usa est hoc malleficio verborum et gestorum, videlicet ponendo quinque digitos in muro et dicendo ista verba: cinque dite ficho in muro, cinque diavoli chiamo et sconzuro, nove gozze de sangue ge tochane, sei men daghani et tre sin tegnani per la sua faticha; et lei, intelligendo de domina Margarita Pazana, ut ipsa Clara dixit, non posia mai havere ben né requie, né dormire, né ben havere, né iacere, né potere andare, né per campo stare, finché a mi non vegnite a parlare."
38. Ibid., fol. 235*r*.
39. Ibid., fols. 235*r-v*.
40. Ibid., fol. 236*r*.
41. Ibid., fols. 236*r-v*.
42. In the existing documentation there are some notable examples of such layers of interpretation. In the *inquisitio* drawn up in the course of a trial against a Modenese witch in 1519, after a list of a series of admissions she had made regarding love potions, poisons, and charms, the document also states: "Quum tot et tantas superstitiones fecerit in nomine diaboli ... et actus illos idolatrie egerit, magna suspitio est quod alia pacta expressa habuerit cum diabolo cum expressa apostasia a fide catholica et assumptione ipsius in dominum suum, maxime quum omnes alie persone professores talis secte sic comuniter faciant. Item quod crucem concalcaverit et alia nephanda fecerit que facere consueverunt huiusmodi criminose persone." The process is clear: the superstitious rites performed with such interjections as "in nomine diaboli" or "in nomine magni diaboli" are defined as "actus idolatrie," which in turn lead one to suppose ("magna suspitio est") that the defendant has sullied herself with the worst crimes associated with witchcraft proper, as described in the demonological treatises. ASM, Inquisizione, Busta 2, Liber Quartus, fol. 212*v*; the same pattern is repeated in a 1523 trial. That this kind of distortion was not an isolated procedure in witchcraft cases emerges clearly from a passage in the widely circulated *Sacro Arsenale* by Fra Eliseo Masini. After exhorting inquisitors to moderation and caution in dealing with cases of this type (in line with instructions issued by the Holy Office in 1613), the manual cautions: "Di più avvertano i giudici, che quantunque alcuna donna resti convinta, ò confessa d'haver fatti incanti, e sortilegii *ad amorem*, ò vero, *ad sananda maleficia*, ò à qual si voglia altro effetto, non segue però necessariamente, ch'ella sia strega formale, potendo il sortilegio farsi senza formale apostasia al Demonio, tutto che si renda di ciò sospetta, ò leggiermente, ò vehementemente. E strega formale dee reputarsi, ed è colei, ch'havrà fatto patto col Demonio, et apostatando dalla fede, co' suoi maleficii, ò sortilegii danneggiato una, ò piu persone in guisa, che ne sia loro seguita per cotali maleficii, ò sortilegii la morte, ò se non la morte, almeno infermità, divortii, impotenza al generare, ò detrimento notabile à gl'animali, biade, ò altri frutti della terra." F. Eliseo Masini da Bologna Inquisitore, *Sacro Arsenale, overo Prattica dell'Officio della S. Inquisitione ampliata* (Rome, 1639), p. 178. Only if the intricate complex of beliefs and practices that went under the name of "witchcraft" (comprising simple superstitions as well as the sabbat

and adoration of the Devil) are subjected to systematic analysis will it be possible to distinguish on a case-by-case basis the forced interpretations of inquisitors from genuine popular beliefs.

43. ASM, Inquisizione, Busta 2, Liber Quartus, fol. 238*r.*
44. Ibid., fols. 231*v*-232r.
45. Ibid., fol. 236*v.*
46. Ibid., fol. 232*v.*
47. Ibid., fols. 239*r-v.*
48. Ibid., fol. 232*r.*
49. Ibid., fol. 239*r.*
50. Ibid., fol. 239*v.*
51. One thinks in particular of the popular cult of Diana, so intimately connected to witchcraft. On this question, which should be studied in depth, see, for now, E. Verga, "Intorno a due inediti documenti di stregheria milanese del secolo XIV," *Rendiconti del R. Istituto Lombardo di Scienze e Lettere,* 2nd ser., 32 (1899): 165 ff., and the recent volume by G. Bonomo, *Caccia alle streghe* (Palermo, 1959), esp. chs. 3, 4, and 6. The attempt to interpret the name "Diana" as a corruption of "daemonum meridianum" seems untenable, if only because it does not succeed in explaining adequately the extraordinary diffusion of the popular cult of the goddess, still flourishing well into the sixteenth century. See R. L. Wagner, *"Sorcier" et "Magicien"* (Paris, 1939), p. 40, n. 3, with bibliography.
52. ASM, Inquisizione, Busta 2, Liber Quartus, fols. 240*v*-241*v.*
53. Ibid., fol. 240*r.*
54. Ibid., fol. 241*v.*
55. Ibid., fol. 242*v.*
56. Ibid., fol. 243*r.* (In inquisitorial law a sentence to a "carcere perpetuo," or life imprisonment, customarily meant a term of three years' incarceration. – *Trans.*)
57. Ibid., fol. 247*r.*

[The identification of Fra Bartolomeo da Pisa with Bartolomeo Spina, which I here proposed tentatively, was demonstrated subsequently by A. Rotondò in *Rivista storica italiana* 74 (1962): 841. On Spina's activity as inquisitor in Modena, see now M. Bertolotti, "Le ossa e la pelle dei buoi: Un mito popolare tra agiografia e stregoneria," *Quaderni storici,* no. 41 (1979): 470-99.]

From Aby Warburg to E. H. Gombrich: A Problem of Method

1. A. Warburg, *La rinascita del paganesimo antico* (Florence, 1966), with a preface by G. Bing, trans. E. Cantimori; F. Saxl, *La storia delle immagini,* Introduction by E. Garin, trans. G. Veneziani (Bari, 1965), with 247 illustrations; and E. H. Gombrich, *Arte e illusione: Studio sulla psicologia della rappresentazione pittorica,* trans. R. Federici (Turin, 1965).

   Bing's introduction to the Italian edition of Warburg's writings had appeared in the *Journal of the Warburg and Courtauld Institutes* (henceforth *JWCI*) 28 (1965): 299-313, as a greatly revised version of a lecture given at the

Courtauld Institute in 1962. Unlike the German text edited by Bing – *Die Erneuerung der heidnischen Antike: Kulturwissenschaftliche Beiträge zur Geschichte der europäischen Renaissance*, 2 vols. (Leipzig and Berlin, 1932) – the essays in the Italian text are arranged in chronological order. The Italian text drops a few minor writings and the appendices. The latter included additions and supplements inserted by the editors, as well as corrections, some quite significant, from Warburg's own pen; and this material too was omitted in the Italian translation. (See, for example, Bing's preface to the German edition, p. xvi.) On Warburg, see the bibliography cited by Bing in the preface to *La rinascita*, p. 1n., to which should be added the privately printed pamphlet *Aby M. Warburg zum Gedächtnis: Worte zur Beisetzung von Professor Dr. Aby M. Warburg* (Darmstadt, n.d. [but 1929]), speeches and recollections by E. Warburg, E. Cassirer, G. Pauli, W. Solmitz and C. G. Heise. The appendix in this pamphlet contains previously published obituaries by E. Panofsky and F. Saxl.

The foreword of the Italian edition of Saxl's lectures indicates its differences from the English edition (*Lectures*, 2 vols. [London, 1957]), as well as the criteria for the selection. The disorder of the plates in the essays "L'appartamento Borgia" and "La villa Farnesina" is regrettable.

Arte e illusione has a new preface by Gombrich, but, inexplicably, lacks his preface to the second English edition (*Art and Illusion: A Study in the Psychology of Pictorial Representation* [London, 1960; 3rd ed. London, 1968]).

2. E. Panofsky, *La prospettiva come forma simbolica e altri scritti*, ed. G. D. Neri, with a Note by M. Dalai (Milan, 1961): these essays, plus others, accompanied by an up-to-date bibliography of Panofsky's writings, have been reprinted in their original language, with the title *Aufsätze zu Grundfragen der Kunstwissenschaft* [Berlin, 1964]); idem, *Il significato nelle arti visive* (Turin, 1962), in English as *Meaning in the Visual Arts: Papers in and on Art History* (Garden City, 1955).

3. See Bing, preface to Warburg, *La rinascita*, pp. 3, 6, and also her "Ricordo di Fritz Saxl (1890-1948)," published in the appendix to Saxl, *La storia delle immagini*, p. 187: "Saxl always considered the library as the most complete expression of Warburg's ideas, and preoccupied himself to maintain its arrangement unchanged as much as possible." On Bing, see *Gertrud Bing, 1892-1964* (London, 1965), with writings and recollections by E. H. Gombrich, D. Cantimori, D. J. Gordon, O. Klemperer, A. Momigliano, and E. Purdie. The pieces by Cantimori and Momigliano had already appeared, respectively, in *Itinerari* 11 (1964): 89-92, and *Rivista storica italiana* 76 (1964): 856-58.

4. See, in addition, the presentation by J. S. Trapp, "The Warburg Institute," *Studi medievali*, 3rd ser., 2 (1961): 745-50.

5. Bing, appendix to Saxl, *La storia delle immagini*, p. 182.

6. Bing, preface to Warburg, *La rinascita*, pp. 7-8, uses the term *deviazione*.

7. Ibid., F. Saxl, "*Die Bibliothek Warburg und ihr Ziel*," in *Bibliothek Warburg: Vorträge, 1921-1922* (Leipzig and Berlin, 1923), p. 2; idem., "Warburg's Visit to New Mexico," in *Lectures*, 1:325-30. A. Momigliano, "Gertrud Bing (1892-1964)," *Rivista storica italiana* 76 (1964): 857, observes that Saxl and Bing "had a much less 'primitive' notion of paganism than Warburg, and quickly gave a prominent place to Platonic studies in the research program of the Institute."

8. See C. G. Heise, *Persönliche Erinnerungen an Aby Warburg* (Hamburg, 1959), p. 54, and G. Pasquali, "Aby Warburg," in *Vecchie e nuove pagine stravaganti di un filologo* (Turin, 1952), pp. 66-67.

9. On all this see especially Cassirer's contribution in *Aby M. Warburg zum Gedächtnis*.

10. See Heise, *Persönliche Errinerungen*, pp. 37-40.

11. See G. Bing, "Aby M. Warburg," *Rivista storica italiana* 72 (1960): 105, and Bing's preface to *La rinascita*, p. 14.

12. On the theme of Fortune, see especially A. Doren, "Fortuna im Mittelalter und in der Renaissance," *Bibliothek Warburg: Vorträge, 1922-1923* (Leipzig and Berlin, 1924), pp. 71-144. Evidence that contemporaries were aware of the complexity and imperviousness of this representation of Fortune can be found in a drawing prepared for the costumes of the *Masquerade of the Pagan Gods* (*Mascherata degli Dei gentili*), performed in Florence in 1565, an event dealt with by Warburg. It represents Fortune clutching a puffed-out sail in its hand, and a caption that reads: "This is Fortune; the arm that holds the veil is false and will appear real; it will be a beautiful mask and will have great meaning." Biblioteca Nazionale, Florence, MS. Palatino CB 53.3, II, fol. 54.

13. Bing, "Aby Warburg," p. 109.

14. See E. Wind, "Warburgs Begriff der Kulturwissenschaft und seine Bedeutung für die Aesthetik," *Zeitschrift für Aesthetik und Allgemeine Kunstwissenschaft* 25 (1931): appendix (containing the proceedings of the Fourth Congress of Aesthetics and Art Theory, held at Hamburg, October 7-9, 1930, on the theme "Gestaltung von Raum und Zeit in der Kunst," 175; Bing, preface to *La rinascita*, p. 18.

15. E. R. Curtius, *Europäische Literatur und lateinisches Mittelalter* (Bern, 1948) (and index); idem, "Antike Pathosformeln in der Literatur des Mittelalters," in *Estudios dedicados a Menéndez Pidal* (Madrid, 1950), 1:257-63, where the explicit reference to Warburg (not limited to the title) seems especially significant.

16. Bing, "Aby M. Warburg," p. 107.

17. There is a characteristic example apropos Florentine *cassoni* painters: "Now, what confers to that art of furnishings a continuing strong attraction, is not … its artistic value per se, nor the 'romantic' theme, but rather the energetically effulgent delight in existence joyfully alive and resplendent, which, impatiently, awaits ancient battles and poetic triumphs as a cue for its own entrance on stage." Warburg, *La rinascita*, pp. 151-52. And see also the quotation that follows immediately in Warburg's text.

18. The importance of this passage had already been noted by Wind, "Warburgs Begriff," p. 167.

19. This expression was taken over almost verbatim by Saxl to define the scope of Warburg's research, in "Three 'Florentines': Herbert Horne, A. Warburg, Jacques Mesnil," in *Lectures*, 1:341.

20. On iconology, see G. J. Hoogewerff, "L'iconologie et son importance pour l'étude systematique de l'art chrétien," *Rivista di Archeologia Cristiana* 8 (1931): 60-61. This essay, because of the clear distinction it draws between "iconography" and "iconology," constitutes an important antecedent, especially from the point of view of terminology, to Panofsky's "Iconography

and Iconology: An Introduction to the Study of Renaissance Art," in *Meaning in the Visual Arts*, pp. 26-54, originally published as the Introduction to *Studies in Iconology* (New York, 1939). See, for example, the juxtaposition established between "ethnography" and "ethnology" (Hoogewerff, p. 58; Panofsky, *Meaning in the Visual Arts*, p. 32). At any rate the juxtaposition is a mere point of departure, introduced by Panofsky into a different and larger context (see below) which develops ideas formulated in a 1932 lecture now contained in his *Aufsätze zu Grundfragen der Kunstwissenschaft*, pp. 85-97. For the significance of Hoogewerff's essay in Panofsky's formulations, see the important article by J. Bialostocki, "Iconografia e iconologia," in *Enciclopedia universale dell'arte*, vol. 7, cols. 163-77.

21. See Bing, preface to *La rinascita*, pp. 5-6; see also pp. 20-21, for the transmission of astrological images. See also her note apropos Hoogewerff's article cited above, in *Kulturwissenschaftliche Bibliographie zum Nachleben der Antike*, vol. 1, 1931, under the auspices of the Bibliothek Warburg (Leipzig and Berlin, 1934), p. 77.

22. The two volumes of *Die Erneuerung der heidnischen Antike* were supposed to have been followed by others containing notes, letters, and fragments from the atlas of symbols diffused in the Mediterranean world that would have been entitled *Mnemosyne*.

23. F. Saxl, "Ernst Cassirer," in *The Philosophy of Ernst Cassirer*, ed. P. A. Schilpp (New York, 1958), p. 49.

24. Both cited above, notes 14 and 21. To Wind's introduction in the first volume of the *Bibliographie*, R. Oertel replied with a polemical review appearing in *Kritische Berichte zur Kunstgeschichtlichen Literatur* 5 (1932-33): 33-40, which proposed, probably under the influence of H. Sedlmayr (cited on p. 40 of the article), a "structuralist" and "autonomous" interpretation of artistic phenomena.

25. Wind, "Warburgs Begriff," p. 170.

26. Wind, Introduction to the *Bibliographie*, p. vii. Wind also revives Warburg's critical attitude towards disciplinary boundaries, but Warburg's word, *Grenzwächtertum*, was stronger and more sarcastic. Wind also inveighs against Wölfflin and his attempt to found a *Kunstgeschichte ohne Namen* and against Windelband for his notion of a *Problemgeschichte* reflecting the historical context in which philosophical ideas are generated.

27. See the entire section, "Das Symbol als Gegenstand kulturwissenschaftlicher Forschung," pp. viii-xi of the Introduction cited above. Oertel (p. 39 of the review cited in n. 24, above) alluded to Wind's unclear relation with the thought of Cassirer.

28. See Warburg, *La rinascita*, p. 3; Saxl, "Ernst Cassirer," pp. 47-51. Cassirer too, at one point, explicitly cites Vischer, but only to accentuate more emphatically his own concept of "symbol," which he places at the center not only of art, but of cultural life as a whole: "Das Symbol-Problem und seine Stellung im System der Philosophie," *Zeitschrift für Aesthetik und Allgemeine Kunstwissenschaft* 21 (1927): 295, 321-22.

29. F. Saxl, "Rinascimento dell'antichità: Studien zu den Arbeiten A. Warburg's," *Repertorium für Kunstwissenschaft* 43 (1922): 220-72.

30. Saxl, "Die Bibliothek Warburg und ihr Ziel." In this writing, as in the

preceding, Saxl always speaks in the past tense of Warburg, who was hospitalized.

31. E. Panofsky and F. Saxl, "Classical Mythology in Mediaeval Art," *Metropolitan Museum Studies* 4 (1932-33): 228-80. For the contrast between the two scholars proposed by Garin, see note 41, below.

32. Panofsky, *Meaning in the Visual Arts*, p. 330. The allusion to research on the Hercules transformation obviously refers to Panofsky's own book, *Hercules am Scheidewege und andere Antike Bildstoffe in der neueren Kunst*, Studien der Bibliothek Warburg 18 (Leipzig and Berlin, 1930).

33. See E. Panofsky, *Renaissance and Renascences in Western Art* (Stockholm, 1965). For Burckhardt, see *Weltgeschichtliche Betrachtungen: Über geschichtliches Studium* (Munich, 1978), pp. 90-91. Panofsky and Saxl go on to develop, among other things, certain of Gentile's observations on anti-ascetic motifs found in the works of Giannozzo Manetti.

34. Panofsky and Saxl, "Classical Mythology," pp. 270-74, esp. p. 274. Panofsky formulated this comparison, which was so important to him, on several occasions: for example, *Idea: A Concept in Art Theory* (Columbia, S. C., 1968), p. 51; *Meaning in the Visual Arts*, pp. 51 and passim; "Renaissance and Renascences," p. 108. See the text at note 109, below, for Gombrich's critique on this subject.

35. This passage is followed by a mention of the transformation, occurring towards the end of the Renaissance, of this awareness of the distance from antiquity, into a nostalgic and melancholy worship – a sentiment which Panofsky studied for its historical implications a few years later in his great work, "*Et in Arcadia Ego*: Poussin and the Elegiac Tradition," now in *Meaning in the Visual Arts*, pp. 295-320; some of its statements have been challenged recently by F. Della Corte, "Et in Arcadia ego," *Maia*, n.s., 16 (1964): 350-52.

36. See, for example, Garin's *Italian Humanism: Philosophy and Civic Life in the Renaissance* (New York, 1965), and *Medioevo e Rinascimento: Studi e ricerche* (Bari, 1954), pp. 105-7.

37. Garin, Introduction to Saxl, *La storia delle immagini*. Apart from the most recent arbitrary attempts to claim a connection with the Warburg Institute in a context of mediocre and superficial irrationalism (cf. E. Battisti, *L'antirinascimento* [Milan, 1952]), which Garin does not discuss, the introduction pays insufficient attention to the ties and relationships which linked individual Italian scholars and the Warburg group in the years between the two wars, in contrast to the prevailing attitude of indifference or superiority displayed by the dominant idealist culture. Evidence of a certain interest, even if inspired by Crocean orthodoxy, are the notes on Saxl and Panofsky sketched by Leone Ginzburg at an uncertain date, but definitely after 1933, and left in their unfinished form: see *Scritti* (Turin, 1964), pp. 478-79. Apart from the fine essay by Pasquali, cited by Garin (Introduction, pp. x, xii, xviii), it is significant that the first volume of the *Journal of the Warburg and Courtauld Institutes* should contain a substantial study by D. Cantimori, "Rhetoric and Politics in Italian Humanism," *JWCI* 1 (1937-38): 83-102. Cantimori also participated actively in the compilation of volume 2 of *A Bibliography of the Survival of the Classics ... 1932-33*, edited by the Warburg Institute (London, 1938); and, at

war's end, an entire volume of the *Journal*, the ninth, contained exclusively contributions by Italians, a gesture of friendship towards our country, but also testimony of ties with scholars that the war had not succeeded in breaking – ties that were old in some cases and even went back to Aby Warburg himself, as in the case of Augusto Campana (see the latter's "Vicende e problemi degli studi malatestiani," *Studi Romagnoli* 2 [1951]: 15). The ninth volume of the *Journal* contained writings by R. Bianchi Bandinelli, F. Ghisalberti, A. Campana, A. Perosa, G. C. Argan, N. Orsini, R. Pettazzoni, and A. Momigliano. These are details and nuances, but not on that account isolated instances.

38. In this period, says Garin, "not a few conceptual instruments developed by nineteenth-century philosophy had revealed their deficiencies, while an image of man and his history had been deteriorating. The most valid hypotheses and the most important ideas, in fact, emerged precisely from specific research, rather than from general theorizing. Working on the frontiers, almost contemporaneously, historians and students of the 'human sciences,' on the periphery and outside the schema of the prevailing culture, not only corrode those schema, but consume those categories that underlie and justify them. They cause the outlines of new concepts to emerge, revealing unforeseen dimensions of human activity, venturing into unexplored areas, and thereby laying the foundations for a profound restructuring of the concept of man, of his work, of his meaning. The examples are too numerous and too striking to reiterate them here. It is enough to think of certain analyses of depth psychology, or of the renewed research on primitive mentalities." Introduction to Saxl, *La storia delle immagini*, pp. xvii–xviii. It is not quite clear, however, what Garin means by that "image of man and his history" that "had been deteriorating"; what were those "most valid hypotheses" and "most important ideas" that had "emerged"; who were those "historians and students of the 'human sciences' " who not only "corrode those schema" (which?), but actually "consume" the not well defined "categories that underlie them"; etc. Nor does Garin's peremptory conclusion help us very much to understand all this. Once again the reader is forced into guessing. What can be meant by that curious expression "certain analyses of depth psychology"? This is not an allusion to Jung because note 14 on page xviii appears to exclude such an allusion (see, instead, for a rather surprising positive evaluation of Jung's work, Garin's *Medioevo e Rinascimento*, p. 188). Is the allusion to Freud or to one of his followers? Why not come straight out and say it then? Similarly, what is that "renewed research on primitive mentalities"? Can it be Tylor's *Primitive Culture*, which made such an impression on the young Huizinga (see W. Kaegi, *Historische Meditationen*, 2 vols. [Zurich, 1946], 2:250), or the work of Frazer, or of Morgan, or, say, even of Bachofen? With such vagueness any hypothesis becomes legitimate. And, here too, why merely suggest instead of coming to the point?

39. Garin, Introduction to Saxl, *La storia delle immagini*, p. xvii.

40. See Bing, preface to Warburg, *La rinascita*, p. 3. Garin writes, here too without specifying: "Without doubt, not everything in this research and in these assumptions was of equal value; without doubt, much that had been operative in the past has broken down, at least in part, or has been surpassed by new positions and formulations." Introduction, p. xi.

41. "Reading Panofsky one thinks increasingly of 'philosophical' doctrines that matured in nineteenth-century Germany and blossomed between the two wars, not all valid and fruitful; in reading Saxl's works one always thinks less about this; in fact they inspire a spontaneous comparison with the best research of the most progressive historians laboring in the various areas of human culture. Thus we get the impression of a particular durability in his work, which is never without ideas, but where the 'ideas,' instead of being superimposed over 'things,' mix with them, so that questions and answers are related .... When Saxl pursues the representations of astral divinities from the East to the West, he does not allow himself to be seduced by the hypotheses of depth psychology." Introduction, p. xxiv. The reader who might have been confused running up against "certain analyses of depth psychology" (cited in note 38) is quickly reassured: those analyses, those hypotheses, are "seductions" against which the historian must scrupulously guard. And indeed, to take an example, Panofsky's openly acknowledged debt to Cassirer (should we assume that for Garin, Cassirer too was a "philosopher" in quotes?) in Panofsky's essay "La prospettiva come 'forma simbolica' " ("Die Perspektive als 'symbolische Form,' " in *Aufsätze zu Grundfragen*) is enormous, and even more obvious today, now that the cultural climate has changed. But would that work (over which Garin does not pause) have been written without Cassirer's theoretical stimuli? It is also important to note that G. Hauck's observations on perspective in the field of optics remained a dead letter for several decades, before they were revived by Panofsky. Simply to belabor the "philosophizing" and "theorizing" which underlie Panofsky's piece, without recognizing its brilliant results – still obvious today when renowned scholars are posing the problem of perspective from a totally different point of view – would be petty and unenlightened. (See the survey by R. Klein, "Etudes sur la perspective à la Renaissance, 1956-1966," *Bibliothèque d'Humanisme et Renaissance* 25 [1963]: 577-87.) Moreover, the image of Panofsky as "theorizer" is valid for only a few of his works from the German period.

42. Note that, after recalling the names of Burckhardt, Nietzsche, and Usener – who had been mentioned by Saxl in connection with Warburg – Garin states that for Saxl too, "it would be easy to talk about relationships and affinities"; but, out of the usual allusiveness, or reticence, Garin does not communicate these to the reader.

43. F. Saxl, "Veritas filia Temporis," in *Philosophy and History: Essays Presented to Ernst Cassirer*, ed. Raymond Klibansky and H. J. Paton (Oxford, 1936), pp. 197-222; G. Gentile, "Veritas filia Temporis: Postilla bruniana," in *Giordano Bruno e il pensiero del Rinascimento* (Florence, 1920), pp. 89-110. On Gentile's essay, see the just observations by Garin, *Medioevo e Rinascimento*, pp. 195-97, and G. Aquilecchia's Introduction to Bruno's *La cena de le Ceneri* (Turin, 1955), which, among other things, corrects (p. 58, n. 4) a factual error by Gentile.

44. Garin, Introduction to Saxl, *La storia delle immagini*, p. xxix.

45. Saxl, "Veritas filia Temporis," p. 201, notes the connection between Marcolino's device (already mentioned by Gentile in his *Giordano Bruno*, p. 97, n. 1) and Lucian's description of Calumny, and he stresses that Aretino, a friend of Marcolino and the probable inspiration for the printer of Forlì, used

the Lucian text not as an erudite allegory, but as a living and present reality. Cf. Saxl, *Lectures*, 1:167.

46. Saxl,"Veritas filia Temporis," p. 202.

47. Saxl, "Die Bibliothek Warburg," pp. 7-8. See also note 7 above for Momigliano's observation about Warburg's and Saxl's differing attitudes toward classical antiquity.

48. Saxl and Panofsky revive the Warburgian concept of pathos formulae and use it with significantly different meanings. Saxl understands it in a "realistic" sense and does not pursue the question much further, while Panofsky takes it in an "idealistic" sense (with a reference to Goethe's use of the term). See Saxl's essay "Continuity and Variation in the Meaning of Images": there, he says of the representation of Hercules battling with the bull, "The moment this image was invented it became classic; it became classic, however, in the Olympian, not the Delphic, shape; because it was evidently at Olympia that the interplay of forces *found its most logical expression.*" And later, still on the same theme, he says, "A new formula was found, *more realistic and more logical* than the one which the Eastern civilizations had created," and refers to "a new and – in a realistic sense – a more logical form." *Lectures*, 1:5, 6, 11; my italics. For his part, Panofsky writes in "Albrecht Dürer and Classical Antiquity": "[In classical art] not only the structure and movement of the human body, but also the active and passive emotions of the human soul were sublimated, in accordance with the precepts of 'symmetry' and 'harmony,' into noble poise and furious battle, sweetly sad parting and abandoned dance, Olympian calm and heroic action, grief and joy, fear and ecstasy, love and hate. All these emotional states were reduced, to use a favorite expression of Aby Warburg, to 'pathos formulae' which were to retain their validity for many centuries *and appear 'natural' to us precisely because they are 'idealized' as compared to reality – because a wealth of particular observations had been condensed and sublimated into one universal experience.*" *Meaning in the Visual Arts*, p. 268; my italics.

49. Cited by Gentile, *Giordano Bruno*, p. 97, n. 1.

50. Ibid., pp. 102-3.

51. Saxl, "Veritas filia Temporis," pp. 218-19. To avoid ambiguity, note that not even in this documentation does the motto suggest an indefinite opening or progress towards truth. The juxtaposition of the ancient philosopher and Descartes (or Newton) is certainly very significant: but the fact remains that truth reveals itself *entirely* at one precise point in human history. Here historicism has no place.

52. Bing, "Aby Warburg," p. 109.

53. Saxl, "Veritas filia Temporis," pp. 220-21.

54. Saxl's relations with Warburg were not happy after the latter regained his health: see Bing, "Ricordo di Fritz Saxl," in Saxl, *La storia delle immagini*, p. 191.

55. Heise, *Persönliche Errinerungen*, p. 23.

56. Ibid., p. 57: "Qualität im rein ästhetischen Sinne was für ihn nicht die oberste Wertkategorie." Similarly, Saxl remarks (*Lectures*, 1:343) that Warburg lacked "aesthetic refinement" (the comparison is with Jacques Mesnil). This does not contradict the fact that Warburg was becoming increasingly more aware that his studies also had bearing on the aesthetic appreciation of art:

significantly, the sentence which concludes his essay on Francesco Sassetti's testament – "to correct historically a consideration that is unilaterally aesthetic" – he later amended to read "a consideration that is unilaterally hedonistic"; see *Die Erneuerung*, p.xvi.

57. B. Croce, "Gli dei antichi nella tradizione mitologica del Medio Evo e del Rinascimento," *La Parola del Passato* 1 (1946): 273-85, esp. p. 277 (apropos J. Seznec, *La survivance des dieux antiques* [London, 1940]). Gombrich comments on Croce's views in "Icones Symbolicae: The Visual Image in Neoplatonic Thought," *JWCI* 11 (1948): 163, n. 2.

58. In certain cases, as Warburg noted, the slight or non-existent aesthetic value of a work in fact facilitates the reconstruction of the iconographic "program" underlying it. See *Die Erneuerung*, 2:464: "And finally I shall choose the representation of the month of July, because in it a less emphatic artistic personality allows its erudite program to transpire in the most tangible way." Also see ibid., 2:472. I should be careful to note that this is an isolated observation. Warburg is certainly not trying to maintain that loyalty to an iconographic program always hinders the achievement of artistic value (with such a stance we would be relapsing in a sense into Croce's position cited above).

59. Bing, "Aby Warburg," p. 110. The implications of a "history of culture" conceived in terms analogous to Burckhardt's, assuming, in other words, that art is the element that characterizes and unifies a historical period, have been examined by F. Gilbert, "Cultural History and Its Problems," in *Onzième Congrès International des Sciences Historiques: Rapports* (Uppsala, 1960), 1:40-58. For an extreme approach in this sense, see C. J. Friedrich, "Style as the Principle of Historical Appreciation," *Journal of Aesthetics and Art Criticism* 14 (1955): 143-51, and D. Cantimori's rightly severe criticism, "L'età barocca," in *Manierismo, Barocco, Rococò: Concetti e termini: Convegno internazionale – Roma, 21-24 aprile 1960* (Rome, 1962), pp. 395-417. But these discussions are rather remote from the problems raised by Warburg and his followers.

60. See Momigliano, "Gertrud Bing," p. 857. See also the statements by Saxl in "Verzeichnis astrologischer und mythologischer illustrierter Handschriften des lateinischen Mittelalters in römischen Bibliotheken," in *Sitzungsberichte der Heidelberger Akademie der Wissenschaften*, Phil.-hist. Kl., 1915, 6-7 Abh., pp. v-vi.

61. F. Saxl, "The Villa Farnesina," and "The Appartamento Borgia," now in *Lectures*, 1:189-99 and 174-88. The subject of the first paper had earlier appeared in book form: *La fede astrologica di Agostino Chigi: Interpretazione dei dipinti di Baldassarre Peruzzi nella sala di Galatea della Farnesina* (Rome, 1934). The conclusion of "The Appartamento Borgia" is typically Warburgian: "In the process which we call the Renaissance such primeval symbols laden with emotion are re-awakened, re-born to a new life. The bull is one of them, the raving Maenad and the slain Orpheus are others" (p. 188). As we know, the Maenad and Orpheus had been identified as pathos formulae by Warburg himself: see *Die Erneuerung*, 2:445 ff.

62. See Bing, preface to Warburg, *La rinascita*, pp. 10-11.

63. F. Saxl, "Holbein and the Reformation," in *Lectures*, 1:227-85. The fact that this paper and the following ones are simply lectures (but at what a level!) is

irrelevant for my discussion, which is not based on the originality (often very much in evidence) of the findings, but rather on the approach and method of argumentation.

64. Saxl, "Holbein," p. 277. Here we have an echo of Cassirer's thoughts on the "absence of semantics" in figurative art – considerations that Ragghianti strangely deems "a subjugation of human visibility to verbality or even worse to its disintegration into the latter" (preface to K. Fiedler, *L'attività artistica* [Venice, 1963], p. 36). If anything, Cassirer is expressing the exact opposite – namely, a vindication of the specificity of artistic language against any sort of abstract rationalizations. C. Brandi refers to the "polysemy" of the image in another sense and in a different context in *Le due vie* (Bari, 1966), pp. 63-64 and passim. See also note 142 below.

65. Published by E. His, "Holbein's Verhältnis zur Basler Reformation," *Repertorium für Kunstwissenschaft* 2 (1879): 156-59.

66. Saxl, "Holbein," p. 279.

67. Ibid., pp. 281-82.

68. See, specifically for Holbein, the characteristic publishing history of the *Danse Macabre* in Lyons, admirably reconstructed by N. Z. Davis, "Holbein's *Pictures of Death* and the Reformation at Lyons," *Studies in the Renaissance* 3 (1956): 97-130. The printers who issued the work inserted it into a more or less orthodox context, depending on the case, varying the captions but always leaving the images unchanged.

69. For this entire question, see H. Grisar, S. J., and F. Heege, S.J., *Der Bilderkampf in den Schriften von 1523 bis 1545*, Luthers Kampfbilder, fasc. 3 (Freiburg im Breisgau, 1923), pp. 1-23.

70. Ibid., p. 14, and M. Gravier, *Luther et l'opinion publique* (Paris, 1942), p. 293.

71. See Gravier, *Luther*, pp. 294-95. Grisar and Heege, *Der Bilderkampf*, pp. 20-21, state that "without doubt" the two figures of the donkey-pope and the calf-monk were engraved by the author of the *Passional*, namely Cranach. Other scholars attribute them to Cranach's shop.

72. See Saxl, "Holbein's Illustrations to the 'Praise of Folly' by Erasmus," *Burlington Magazine* 83 (1943): 275-79.

73. Saxl, "Holbein," pp. 282-83. For the attribution of the *Hercules Germanicus* to Holbein, for its interpretation, and for the reference to Hugwald's letter, see D. Burckhardt-Werthemann, "Drei wiedergefundene Werke aus Holbeins früherer Baslerzeit," *Basler Zeitschrift für Geschichte und Altertumskunde* 4 (1905): 33-37, and esp. P. Burckhardt-Biedermann, "Ueber Zeit und Anlass des Flugblattes: Luther als Hercules Germanicus," ibid., pp. 38-44. The print (initially attributed to H. Baldung Grien) was erroneously conceived as philo-Lutheran by F. Baumgarten, "Hans Baldungs Stellung zur Reformation," *Zeitschrift für die Geschichte des Oberrheins*, n.s. 19 (1904): 249-55. E. Wind, " 'Hercules' and 'Orpheus': Two Mock-Heroic Designs by Dürer," *JWCI* 2 (1938-39): 217-18, not too convincingly interpreted the *Hercules* as a satirical response to a drawing by Dürer of the *Hercules Gallicus*. But Wind's arguments aside (on which see E. Panofsky, *The Life and Art of Albrecht Dürer* [Princeton, 1948], 1:73-76, 2:26, and R. E. Hallowell, "Ronsard and the Gallic Hercules Myth," *Studies in the Renaissance* 9 [1962]: 249, n. 28), the print cannot be called "satirical." It should be noted first of all that the epithet

"Hercules Germanicus" was used at the beginning of the sixteenth century for Emperor Maximilian I, sometimes represented in the guise of Hercules: see P. Du Colombier, "Les triomphes en images de l'empereur Maximilien Ier," in *Les fêtes de la Renaissance*, II: *Fêtes et cérémonies au temps de Charles Quint* (Paris, 1960), p. 112, n. 33. Moreover, the figure of the Luther-Hercules appears grandly terrible, not grotesque or a caricature. To grasp its significance we should probably look at a group of Erasmian passages which have not been accorded the consideration they deserve. The analogy between Erasmus's own literary burdens and the labors of Hercules, enounced in the proverb "Herculei labores" (see *Adagiorum chiliades quatuor cum sesquicenturia* ... [Geneva, 1558], cols. 615-23), recurs frequently in the letters of Erasmus and is imitated by his correspondents. He alludes to himself as a Hercules whose labors are represented by struggles against friars and scholastics, or by the attempts to expurgate a text which time had covered with accretions and corrupted. See Erasmus, *Opus Epistolarum*, ed. P. S. Allen, 2:86, 406, 539-40; 4:77, 266; 8:71, 117; 9:117, 125; and also *Briefwechsel des Beatus Rhenanus*, ed. A. Horowitz and K. Hartfelder (Leipzig, 1886), p. 393. All this, it seems to me, further clarifies the significance of the *Hercules Germanicus*. It is a subtle and politically very astute attempt (note that the year is 1522, a moment in which Erasmus, though pressed from all sides, has not yet taken an open position regarding Luther) to present Luther in Erasmian vestment, intent on combatting Aristotle, Saint Thomas, Ockham, Duns Scotus, etc., for the purification of theology and letters. Cf. Burckhardt-Biedermann, "Ueber Zeit und Anlass," p. 42. Curiously, the ambiguous epithet "The German Hercules" was adopted by R. H. Bainton, despite its philo-Erasmian implications, as a chapter title in his classic *Here I Stand: A Life of Martin Luther* (Nashville, 1950).

74. Saxl, "Dürer and the Reformation," in *Lectures*, 1:267.
75. Ibid., p. 270.
76. A not too convincing attempt to cast doubt on Dürer's full adherence to the Lutheran reformation has been made by H. Lutz, "Albrecht Dürer und die Reformation: Offene Frage," in *Miscellanea Bibliothecae Hertzianae ...*, Römische Forschungen der Bibliotheca Hertziana, 16 (Munich, 1961), pp. 175-83.
77. Saxl, "Dürer," pp. 271, 273.
78. Note that Panofsky, in his *Life and Art of Albrecht Dürer*, a book that Saxl certainly had in mind when he wrote these pages, was much more cautious in examining the transformations in Dürer's style during the years of the religious crisis. First, he places greater emphasis (p. 199) on the fact that the repercussions were not stylistic alone, but also iconographic (with few exceptions Dürer abandoned nonreligious themes during this period). Second, even when Saxl follows Panofsky's analyses more closely (Saxl, *Lectures*, 1:271, 2: plates 190*a* and *b*; Panofsky, *Life and Art of Albrecht Dürer*, 1:199-200), he tends to accentuate psychological comparisons. Panofsky, all things considered, limits himself to writing that the emphasis in Dürer's art at this time passed "from linear values and dynamic movement to schematized volume" (p. 200). Even more telling is the different interpretation of the "Christ on the Mount of Olives" (1521) furnished by the two scholars. For

Saxl, as we have seen, the gesture of Christ who falls to the ground with his arms outstretched was meant to express "Dürer's mood: salvation lies in complete submission to faith." For Panofsky (*The Life and Art of Albrecht Dürer*, p. 220), it is the echo of an archaic iconography founded on an "unusually literal" interpretation of the apposite passages of the Gospels of Matthew and Mark: Matt. 26: 39: "And going a little farther he fell on his face and prayed"; Mark 14:35: "And going a little farther, he fell on the ground and prayed." It seems obvious to me that Panofsky's interpretation is far more solidly grounded and convincing.

79. For this term, used here in the sense proposed by E. H. Gombrich, see the text at note 124 and note 125.

80. This is valid even for a lecture on Velásquez given by Saxl in 1942 (not one of his better ones, to be frank), a lecture that can be situated midway between the stylistic deductions of the essays on Holbein and Dürer and a utilization of the work of art as "Photoersatz der Vergangenheit." (For this expression see G. Bandmann, "Das Kunstwerk als Gegenstand der Universalgeschichte," *Jahrbuch für Aesthetik und Allgemeine Kunstwissenschaft* 7 [1962]: 146-66, which on the whole offers a lot less than what the title promises.) In his essay Saxl establishes an actually quite mechanical parallelism between political events in Spain and the portraits of Philip IV executed by Velásquez. With this approach, Saxl is able to discern in the first portrait an elegantly dressed youth "whose main interests at that period were horses and love, and whom Olivares had to make attend to his royal business by threats" ("Velasquez and Philip IV," in *Lectures*, 1:313); in another, a certain *joie de vivre* joined to a quiet dignity (p. 314); in a still later portrait, a monumental physiognomy, full of self-assurance, no longer fearful of reproaches on the part of Olivares (pp. 314-15); in yet another, the countenance of a king "who is bent on recovering what Olivares had lost during the preceding ten years" (p. 319). The positivistic assumption that to know Philip IV in the various periods of his life, it sufficed to study the portraits of Velásquez, is not weakened by Saxl's insistence on the progressive stylistic maturity of the painter. Note that H. I. Marrou, *De la connaissance historique* (Paris, 1962), pp. 231-32, 295-96, twice refers to the example of portraits, Cleopatra's and Louis XIV's, to demonstrate, against positivistic concepts, "the inextricable confusion of subject and object" that characterizes historical knowledge.

81. Examples are unnecessary. One need merely recall the use that has always and increasingly been made of figurative evidence by historians of antiquity.

82. See, for instance, the passage in A. Grenier dealing with the statue of Augustus discovered at Prima Porta and the comment by R. Marichal in *L'histoire et ses méthodes*, ed. C. Samaran, Encyclopédie de la Pléiade, 11 (Paris, 1961), p. 1352 (the reference to Bloch is on the previous page). Note that Bloch's own views on the subject were quite different: see the passage cited P. Francastel in "Art et histoire: Dimension et mesure des civilisations," *Annales: E.S.C.* 16 (1961): 297.

83. See E. Wind, "Some Points of Contact between History and Natural Science," in *Philosophy and History*, pp. 255-64 (quotation on p. 257); Panofsky, *Meaning in the Visual Arts*, pp. 9-10.

84. See below, note 99.

85. See Panofsky, *Meaning in the Visual Arts*, pp. 8-10.
86. The full implications of Panofsky's theoretical essays from his German period elude, in large part, someone like myself who does not have even remotely adequate knowledge of the discussions taking place in Germany on these themes between the two world wars. Similarly, it is difficult for me to comprehend to what degree there was continuity between the Panofsky of the German and American periods. (He emigrated to the United States in 1933.) At any rate, however precociously and closely he was bound to the Warburg group, Panofsky had a distinctive background and education which he never completely rejected. Symptomatic of this, just to give an example, is the fact that Wind and Saxl disagreed with Wölfflin and Riegl, but especially the former, in the name of an ever closer relationship between the history of art and other historical disciplines. Panofsky, on the other hand, in his early essays, criticized the psychological and physiological implications of Riegl's and Wölfflin's theories for the sake of a transcendental philosophy of art which bore a decisively Kantian stamp.
87. See Bialostocki, "Iconografia e iconologia," col. 168. Panofsky's essay "Zum Problem der Beschreibung und Inhaltsdeutung von Werken der bildenden Kunst" is now published in *Aufsätze zu Grundfragen*, pp. 85-97.
88. Panofsky: "A description that was indeed *purely formal* could not even use such expressions as 'stone,' 'man,' or 'rocks'; it should limit itself, rather, on principle, to connecting colors that are distinguished from each other through various shadings and that at the very most can be related with formal complexes that are almost ornamental and almost tectonic; it should limit itself to describing them as composite elements totally devoid of meaning and ambiguous even from a partial point of view .... It is not always possible 'to recognize' what the painting represents. We all know what a mandrill is; but 'to recognize' it in this painting [by Franz Marc at the *Kunsthalle* in Hamburg] we must be 'attuned,' as it is customary to say, in accordance with the principles of expressionist representation that here dominate the work of art." "Zum Problem der Beschreibung," pp. 86 ff.
89. See above, note 20.
90. "Zum Problem der Beschreibung," pp. 93-94.
91. Panofsky, "Das Problem des Stils in der bildenden Kunst," in *Aufsätze zu Grundfragen*, p. 25.
92. Panofsky, "The Concept of Artistic Volition," trans. Kenneth J. Northcott and Joel Snyder, *Critical Inquiry* 8 (1981-82): 26. The complicating element introduced by Panofsky in this essay is the following. He rejects the interpretation of artistic volition (*Kunstwollen*) not only in reference to the artist's psychology but also in regard to "the psychology of a period." And he does this for two reasons. Either "it is a question of intentions and evaluations which have become conscious as they find their formulation in the contemporary theory of art or in contemporary art criticism" (p. 23), and thus they need to be considered "phenomena parallel to the artistic products of the epoch" and need to be interpreted by the same measure as the latter. Or – and here the discussion grows in interest – "we experience trends or volitions which can only be explained by precisely those artistic creations which in their own turn demand an explanation on the basis of these trends and volitions.

Thus 'Gothic' man or the 'primitive' from whose alleged existence we wish to explain a particular artistic product is in truth the hypostatized impression which has been culled from the works of art themselves" (p. 23). Here, there is perceptive recognition of the danger of falling into a vicious circle which is implicit in an "explanation" of artistic phenomena that uses historico-cultural categories drawn from an often very superficial consideration of the artistic phenomena themselves. Nevertheless, the reader who bears in mind Panofsky's successive formulations regarding the iconological method might be led to believe that this "circle" could easily be broken if, as Panofsky himself will propose later, artistic phenomena, instead of being considered (as here) in a sort of artificial isolation, were inserted in a comprehensive review of the cultural products of a determinate society. But it is not by chance that Panofsky pauses before the prospect of the introduction of artistic phenomena in a more general historical context. In this essay there is a distinct antithesis between the "history of meaning immanent" in artistic phenomena, and art history (see below, note 94).

93. Panofsky, *Meaning in the Visual Arts*, pp. 39-40 and, in contrast, *Aufsätze zu Grundfragen*, p. 95. See also Garin, Introduction to Saxl, *La storia delle immagini*, p. xxi. On the preface to *Studies in Iconology*, see the just observations of R. Klein, "Considérations sur les fondements de l'iconographie," *Archivio di Filosofia* (1963), 419-36.

94. See Panofsky, "The Concept of Artistic Volition," p. 26: The history of meaning "is not to be confused with the deceptive generic explanation which the psychologistic view of artistic volition presented to us." And see also pp. 30-31: "And if in this case such a transcendental aesthetic mode of looking at things is being advocated, this is not done in any sense to supplant previous historically oriented writing of art history but merely to secure for this mode a right to stand side by side with it. Far from displacing purely historical work, the method which adopts the history of meaning (*sinngeschichtlich*) is the only one competent to complement it." A few pages earlier Panofsky had stated that the assignment of this "history of immanent meaning" is the deduction of a real and actual table of transcendental categories, valid a priori: "It is certainly the task of aesthetics – going beyond historical understanding, formal analysis, and explanation of content – to embrace the artistic volition which is realized in artistic phenomena and is the basis of all their stylistic qualities. Just as certainly as we ascertained that artistic volition can of necessity only signify a work of art's immanent meaning, so it is equally certain that the task of aesthetics is to create categories which are valid a priori, which, like causality, can be applied to linguistically formulated judgments as a standard for determining their nature as part of epistemology, and which can be applied, to some extent, to the work of art being studied as a standard by which its immanent meaning can be determined. These categories, however, would designate not the form taken by the thought which creates experience but rather the form of the artistic intuition." Ibid., p. 28. A product of this stage in the thought of Panofsky is the essay "Über das Verhältnis der Kunstgeschichte zur Kunsttheorie: Ein Beitrag zu der Erörterung über die Möglichkeit 'kunstwissenschaftlicher Grundbegriffe'," *Zeitschrift für Aesthetik und Allgemeine Kunstwissenschaft* 18 (1925): 129 ff.

184 / *Notes to Pages 39–40*

95. See the synoptic table in *Meaning in the Visual Arts*, p. 41: The "corrective principle of (iconological) interpretation" is furnished by the "history of *cultural symptoms* or '*symbols*' in general (insight into the manner in which, under varying historical conditions, *essential tendencies of the human mind* were expressed by specific *themes* and *concepts*)." The italics are Panofsky's.

96. See C. Gilbert, "On Subject and Not-Subject in Italian Renaissance Pictures," *Art Bulletin* 34 (1952): 202-16. The examples selected by Gilbert (who informs us, among other things, that in reactionary American circles "iconologist" had become an ambivalent term, almost an insult, virtually the same as "intellectual") are not always convincing. He concludes (p. 216) with an expression of hope for an "iconology of richer scope" which might also include the interpretation of "non-subject pictures." Panofsky replied briefly to Gilbert in the new preface to the second edition (1962) of *Studies in Iconology*, pp. v-vi. For a problem touched on by Gilbert, see also E. H. Gombrich, "Renaissance Artistic Theory and the Development of Landscape Painting," *Gazette des Beaux Arts*, 6th ser. 42 (1953): 335-60, esp. p. 360 (for an opinion on Gilbert's essay which agrees with what has been said above).

97. Panofsky, "The Neoplatonic Movement and Michelangelo," in *Studies in Iconology*, p. 178, n. 18.

98. Ibid., p. 229.

99. Panofsky, "Introductory," in *Studies in Iconology*, pp. 14-15. At this juncture a comparison between Panofsky's iconological method and the stylistic criticism of L. Spitzer might be in order. The point of departure is the clear analogy between the "methodical circle" that Panofsky borrows from E. Wind, and the "philological circle," or the proceeding "from periphery to center," described by Spitzer. Both ideas come from Dilthey (even though Wind does not quote him), who, in turn, went back to Schleiermacher's hermeneutics. (For Spitzer, see *Critica stilistica e semantica storica* [Bari, 1966], pp. 94, 273-77; and the splendid essay by C. Cases, "Leo Spitzer e la critica stilistica," now in *Saggi e note di letteratura tedesca*, [Turin, 1963], pp. 267-314.) This analogy could be probed further, bearing in mind the obvious differences in personality, background, and interests of these two great scholars, since there are difficulties common to both methods. Panofsky, like Spitzer, though perhaps more cautiously, postulates a method of interpretation – the iconological – that is based on an irrational intuition. Both, on the other hand, invoke the objective control of texts and of documentary materials when confronted by distortions and obviously irrational arbitrariness (the case of Heidegger for Panofsky; the school of Stefan George for Spitzer). Moreover, Spitzer, after having indicated in 1930 his objective of "making evident the unconscious formal will (*Formwillen*) of an art work," retreated (1948) to the analysis of only the known significance, explicitly cautioning against "the investigation of the poet's unconscious intentions" (see Cases, "Leo Spitzer," pp. 270-71). Panofsky has moved along an almost identical course: the very expression "unconscious formal will" recalls his words cited earlier. Even the impossibility of attaining a judgment of aesthetic value, the risks of bias in the iconological approach, the accompanying danger of ending up in a final analysis with judgments or historiographical categories that had not been

adequately discussed, find a certain echo in Spitzer's stylistic critique (where, however, the arbitrary quality is no doubt more pronounced). (See *Cases*, pp. 294 ff., 280-81). Obviously, these observations are simply intended to point, not to reciprocal influences, but to a cultural context common to both scholars which has influenced to some extent their methodology.

100. Panofsky, *Studies in Iconology*, p. 16.

101. This has been noted by E. Garin, Introduction to Saxl, *La storia delle immagini*, p. xxi, who comments that "it is worthwhile underscoring the disappearance," but does not specify in what sense. Of Panofsky's more recent iconographic research, see especially *The Iconography of Correggio's "Camera di San Paolo"* (London, 1961). Panofsky's *Tomb Sculpture: Four Lectures on Its Changing Aspects from Ancient Egypt to Bernini*, ed. H. W. Janson (London, 1964), in contrast, is rich in iconological analysis, strictly understood.

102. See O. Pächt, "Panofsky's Early Netherlandish Painting, II," *Burlington Magazine* 98 (1956): 276. I should like to acknowledge that in this section I have found Bialostocki, "Iconografia e iconologia," most useful. One should also read by this author, *Teoria i twórczość: O tradycji i inwencji w teorii sztuki i ikonografii* (Poznan, 1961) (with English summary, pp. 210-13).

103. E. H. Gombrich, "Botticelli's Mythologies: A Study in the Neoplatonic Symbolism of His Circle," *JWCI* 8 (1945): 13.

104. For Saxl, see Bing, in the appendix to *Storia delle immagini*, p. 179; Saxl also contributed to the *Festschrift für Julius Schlosser* (1927) with an essay entitled "Aller Tugenden und Laster Abbildung." For Schlosser's collaboration with the *Vorträge*, see his article "Von modernen Denkmalkultus," in *Bibliothek Warburg: Vorträge, 1926-1927*, (Leipzig and Berlin, 1930), pp. 1-21.

105. See O. Kurz, Introduction to J. von Schlosser, *L'arte del Medioevo* (Turin, 1961), p. xxviii.

106. The ironic thrust is typical: see Gombrich, *Art and Illusion*, p. 218 (cf. *Arte e illusione*, p. 311). Only rarely does impatience in pursuing a close theoretical argument cause Gombrich not to pay due attention to the requirements of philological research. This is, let me underline, a rare tendency to oversimplify (not to be confused with the theoretical "extremism" mentioned by R. Arnheim) for which Gombrich has been chided by the anonymous reviewer of *Art and Illusion* in the *Times Literary Supplement*, April 8, 1960, pp. 217-18. For another, related example, see Gombrich, "Light, Form and Texture in Fifteenth-Century Painting," *Journal of the Royal Society of Arts* 112 (1963-64): 844, apropos Alberti's acquaintance with Flemish painting.

107. E. H. Gombrich, "Botticelli's Mythologies," *JWCI* 8 (1945): 7-60; idem., "Icones Symbolicae," ibid., 11 (1948): 163-92. Note that the image of History taken from C. Giarda, *Icones Symbolicae*, reproduced by Gombrich as plate 32c in his "Icones Symbolicae" (and see also p. 192) is derived, as the three-headed figure and the caption indicate, from the iconographic type studied by Panofsky in his essay "Titian's 'Allegory of Prudence': A Postscript," in *Meaning in the Visual Arts*, pp. 146-68. Another very obvious example of Gombrich's prevailing theoretical interests is his study "Raphael's *Madonna della Sedia*" (London, 1956), now in *Norm and Form* (London, 1966).

108. E. H. Gombrich, *A Bibliography of the Survival*, pp. 3-5.

109. Ibid., pp. 100-101. A partial echo of this criticism, although without any

mention of Panofsky, is in G. Tonelli, "E. H. Gombrich e l'estetica delle arti figurative," *Filosofia* 13 (1962): 62-64.

110. See the extremely just general observations made in this regard by E. Garin in his review of A. Chastel, *Marsile Ficin et l'art* (Geneva, 1954), in *Bibliothèque d'Humanisme et Renaissance* 17 (1955): 455. D. Cantimori, "Il problema rinascimentale di Armando Sapori," now in *Studi di storia* (Turin, 1959), p. 377, remarks that "if we understand mechanically and statically the relationship of economic-social, political, 'cultural' life as a relationship of *coincidence*, we embark on a direction that ... precludes any real historical comprehension," and concludes, "It seems to me that the preoccupation with coincidence ends up in a blind alley, as Antal's failure demonstrates, since everything cannot be reduced to the relationship patron-artist." The problem discussed here is different, but the observation is pertinent. Antal, as we know, referred back to studies by Warburg and his followers, but took them in a general, sociological vein (see, for example, "Remarks on the Method of Art History: I," *Burlington Magazine* 91 [1949]: 50).

111. E. H. Gombrich, "Wertprobleme und mittelalterliche Kunst," *Kritische Berichte zur Kunstgeschichtlichen Literatur* 6 (1937): 109-16; now in English in E. H. Gombrich, *Meditations on a Hobby Horse and Other Essays on the Theory of Art* (London, 1963), pp. 70-77.

112. Gombrich, "Wertprobleme," p. 114 (*Meditations*, p. 75). The rejection of the analogy between linear perspective and historical consciousness was formulated in virtually identical terms: see Gombrich, *A Bibliography*, p. 100. I am translating *physiognomisch* as "physiognomic," and not as "expressive," to preserve the implicit allusion to Lavater. (See also the brilliant essay by Gombrich, "On Physiognomic Perception" [1960], now in *Meditations*, pp. 45-55, esp. pp. 45, 48, 49.) This theme of "physiognomic fallacy" is continually repeated in his writings (see also below). It has been given precise formulation by M. Shapiro, in "Style," *Anthropology Today: Selections*, ed. S. Tax (1953; Chicago, 1962), esp. pp. 296-300, in terms very similar to Gombrich's, who is not cited, however. (Gombrich refers to Shapiro's article in *Meditations*, p. 168, and *Art and Illusion*, pp. 16, 18.) The reference to Gombrich's elaboration of this term is explicit, instead, in L. D. Ettlinger, *Art History Today: An Inaugural Lecture Delivered at University College, London, 9 March 1961* (London, 1961).

113. Gombrich, "Wertprobleme," pp. 114-15 (*Meditations*, p. 76), also adopted closely and developed further by Shapiro, "Style," p. 299: "A common tendency in the physiognomic approach to group style has been to interpret all the elements of representation as expressions, etc."

114. With particular emphasis in Gombrich's preface to *Art and Illusion*, p. ix. Gombrich declares that he had come into contact with Popper before Hitler's troops entered Vienna. On the other hand, in the essay being examined here, written in 1935, only a short time before the author emigrated to London (*Meditations*, p.xi), one discerns a likely clue to Popper's influence in the polemical reference, "There is no 'historicism of world literature' which is comparable to the historicism of expressionist art history" ("Wertprobleme," p. 115*n*; *Meditations*, p. 76*n*). Popper's criticism of historicism is well known: and in the preface to the English edition of *The Poverty of Historicism* (London,

1960), the author recalls that a first draft of the book, written in 1935, was already circulating at the beginning of 1936 with the same title that obviously alludes to Marx and before him to Proudhon (*Poverty*, p. vii). On Popper's peculiar use of the term "historicism" see the critical observations by E. H. Carr, *What Is History?* (New York, 1963), pp. 119*n*, 140-41*n*.

115. See *Art and Illusion*, pp. 16-17, and the extremely harsh review of the volume by a group of Sedlmayr's students in the *Art Bulletin* 46 (1964): 418-20. I have not seen Gombrich's chapter "Kunstwissenschaft" in *Das Atlantisbuch der Kunst*, ed. M. Hürlimann (Zurich, 1952). Sedlmayr's introduction to Riegl's essays has been reprinted in *Kunst und Wahrheit: Zur Theorie und Methode der Kunstgeschichte*, Rowohlts deutsche Enzyklopädie, 71 (Hamburg, 1958), pp. 14-34, with the title "Kunstgeschichte als Stilgeschichte: Die Quintessenz der Lehren Riegls." The Gombrich of *Art and Illusion* has been juxtaposed to Sedlmayr and his "structural analysis" by W. Hofmann, in response to a recent survey "Strutturalismo e critica" (*Casa editrice Il Saggiatore: Catalogo generale, 1958-1965* [Milan, 1965], pp. xxxv-xxxix).

116. For the anti-Hegelian polemic, based explicitly on assumptions taken from Popper, see in particular Gombrich's "Social History of Art," now in *Meditations*, esp. pp. 88-89, a review of A. Hauser's book by the same title. These are not Gombrich's best pages.

117. Gombrich, "Wertprobleme," p. 115 (*Meditations*, p. 76).

118. Gombrich has been greatly influenced by Freud and by psychoanalysis (see the text below at note 164 for his collaboration with E. Kris) but never in a servile way. Cf. his "Psycho-Analysis and the History of Art" (1953), in *Meditations*, pp. 30-44, and "Freud e l'arte," *Tempo Presente* 11 (February 1966): 22-40. Gombrich has always expressed himself critically about Jung, and rightly so: see, e.g., *Meditations*, p. 13, and *Art and Illusion*, p. 87; and in connection with his debate against critical impressionism, his review of K. Clark, "Piero della Francesca," *Burlington Magazine* 94 (1952): 178. Justifiable observations, but coming from different concerns, are in Brandi, *Le due vie*, pp. 174-79. Gombrich forcefully states: "The artist's private feelings at the moment of production clearly do not enter here, and as to his personality – we have long learned to see the immense complexity that shields behind this simple word" (*Meditations*, p. 26). Here too it seems clear that, contrary to what generally takes place, the influence of psychoanalysis does not lead Gombrich to hurried simplifications and explanations – quite the contrary. But the rejection of superficial connections between the artist's "personality" and the work of art, as suggested even by such a scholar as Saxl in regard to Dürer, cannot lead us willy-nilly to deny the existence of the problem. But in his actual analysis Gombrich attenuates the rigidity of this, as well as of other, theoretical statements: see, for example, his "Psycho-Analysis and the History of Art," apropos Picasso.

119. See Gombrich, "Visual Metaphors of Value in Art," in *Meditations*, esp. pp. 25-27 (but the essay is outstanding and should be read in its entirety).

120. See Gombrich, "Expression and Communication," in *Meditations*, pp. 56-59. We find a less extreme position in *Art and Illusion*, p. 18: "If we really want to treat styles as symptomatic of something else (which may, on occasion, be very interesting), we cannot do without some theory of alternatives." But see also

Gombrich's critique of Croce's aesthetics in his essay "Tradition and Expression in Western Still Life" (1961), in *Meditations*, pp. 95-105.

121. It would be useless here to provide bibliographical citations on Gombrich's attempts to apply information theory or semiotics to aesthetics. For an outline of his cautious position (he states, among other things, that "the use I propose to make of the analysis of communication ... is not to explain art, but to criticize certain assumptions about art," *Meditations*, p. 60), see his critical review of C. Morris, "Signs, Language, and Behaviour," *Art Bulletin* 31 (1949): 68-73.

122. Gombrich employs such terms indifferently, and occasionally in a metaphorical sense (see, e.g., *Meditations*, p. 56). Cf., however, ibid., pp. 25-27.

123. Panofsky, "The Neoplatonic Movement," p. 178.

124. Panofsky's own *Gothic Architecture and Scholasticism* (Latrobe, 1951) cannot totally avoid the criticism of "physiognomic" connections. To be sure, the author, after suggesting that the relationship between Scholastic philosophy and Gothic architecture is a question of influences by diffusion, and thus not an individual matter, discards every purely analogical connection, hinging his argument on an intermediate term, "mental habit," introduced by Scholasticism (pp. 20-21). Nevertheless, the reader cannot avoid the impression that, despite the customary richness and sophistication in Panofsky's argumentation, this intermediate term is somewhat elusive and that the author frequently skips over it completely to fall back on "immediate," "physiognomic" analogies. To take an example: at page 43 Panofsky asserts that pre-Scholasticism had erected a barrier similar to a Romanesque edifice between faith and reason (and here refers us to an illustration showing the abbey of Maria Laach, 1093-1156). Isn't this a tacit assumption that style is an integrally "expressive" whole? And yet we cannot disagree with M. Shapiro (who revives Gombrich's "anti-physiognomic" criticisms) when he writes, alluding to but not citing, this work of Panofsky's: "The common element in these two contemporary creations [Gothic architecture and Scholastic philosophy] has been found in their rationalism and in their irrationality, their idealism and their naturalism, their encyclopedic completeness and their striving for infinity, and recently in their dialectical method. Yet one hesitates to reject such analogies in principle, since the cathedral belongs to the same religious sphere as does contemporary theology." Shapiro, "Style," p. 297. This implicit difference between Panofsky and Gombrich has not been noted, to the best of my knowledge. P. O. Kristeller, for example, totally misreads the latter's position in his review of A. Chastel, "Marsile Ficin et l'art," *Art Bulletin* 40 (1958): 78, where he writes that Panofsky, Saxl, Wind, Gombrich, and Tolnay attempted in their work to grasp "*the stylistic analogies* between the different expressions of the same period and the other signs that may indicate that certain works of art and of thought originated in a common intellectual climate or were conceived as a response to common problems or situations" (my italics).

125. Gombrich, "The Social History of Art" (1953), in *Meditations*, p. 91. For an observation resembling Panofsky's, see above, note 92. Cf. also Gombrich's extremely efficacious views in "Botticelli's Mythologies," pp. 10-13, and in his *Meditations*, p. 51.

126. Gombrich, "André Malraux and the Crisis of Expressionism," in *Meditations*, p. 79. See in this connection the passage by S. K. Langer (a Cassirer student),

introduced, significantly, into a debate with the intention of considering art under the profile of communication: "The concept of art as a sort of *communication* has its dangers because, through the analogy of language, we naturally expect to have *communication* between the artist and his public, something that I consider an aberrant notion. But there is something that can, without risk of being taken too literally, be called *communication through art*, particularly the information that the arts can offer for one epoch and people to persons of another epoch. Not even a thousand pages of history can illustrate Egyptian mentality better than a visit to a museum or exhibition of Egyptian art." Cited by Brandi, *Le due vie*, pp. 43-44. It follows, obviously, that Gombrich considers Langer's position to be based on an "expressionist assumption" (*Meditations*, p. 57).

127. Gombrich, "Art and Scholarship," in *Meditations*, pp. 106-19.

128. J. Huizinga, *The Waning of the Middle Ages* (London, 1924), p. v. A reference to this question by C. L. Ragghianti in his preface to K. Fiedler, *L'attività artistica*, p. 31, misses the point.

129. Saxl, "Why Art History?" in *Lectures*, 1:353.

130. Gombrich, "The Social History of Art," p. 91.

131. A. Momigliano, "Problemi di metodo nella interpretazione dei simboli Giudeo-Ellenistici," *Athenaeum*, n.s., 34 (1956): esp. 239-41. The materials on symbolism collected by the Warburg Institute are discussed at p. 243*n*.

132. Gombrich, "Art and Scholarship," p. 116. On the same page Gombrich expresses his skepticism over Warburg's explanations on individual mentality.

133. See, for example, Gombrich's *Meditations*, p. 10; *Art and Illusion*, p. 7; and especially a passage from his review, cited earlier, of C. Morris, "Signs, Language, and Behaviour," p. 72.

134. Gombrich, "Art and Scholarship," p. 117.

135. Edgar Wind, *Pagan Mysteries in the Renaissance* (1958), 2nd ed. (London, 1960), p. 7. It is typical of Wind, in a sense, that after having insisted on the close formal resemblance between Michelangelo's lost *Leda* and the *Night* of the Medici Chapels, and after having stated that "aesthetically the two works are separate, and it is a form of antiquarian curiosity to look at them together" (p. 138), he should pursue precisely that association Leda-Leto-Night, alluded to in passing by Plutarch, which is definitely irrelevant for the comprehension of Michelangelo's two works, as Wind himself recognizes. (This point has been criticized also by R. Klein in his careful review published in *Zeitschrift für Kunstgeschichte* 23 [1960]: 285.) It seems that in this book (whose themes and structure in general seem heavily inspired by Panofsky's *Studies in Iconology*), Wind has chosen precisely the role of the antiquarian for himself: a Renaissance antiquarian, thoroughly imbued with Neoplatonism and the philosophy of Pico.

136. Wind, *Pagan Mysteries*, p. 22.

137. Ibid., p. 144. The italics are mine.

138. Ibid.

139. And again, at p. 155, in the flayed Saint Bartholomew of Michelangelo's *Judgment*, who holds in his hand his own skin with the artist's self-portrait, Wind sees a parallel with the Neoplatonic Marsyas which he had discerned in the first canto of the *Paradiso*: "As in Dante, of whom Michelangelo was

known to be a profound expounder, the Marsyas-like portrait is a prayer for redemption, that through the agony of death the ugliness of the outward man might be thrown off and the inward man resurrected pure, having shed the *morta spoglia.*" It is clear that here Wind is content with even thinner evidence: first, he had seen testimony in his favor in the presence of Dante in the *Parnaso* and in the *Disputa*; now it actually suffices for him that Michelangelo was "a profound expounder" of Dante to establish the connection between Dante's Marsyas, interpreted as we have seen, and the Saint Bartholomew of the *Judgment*. Moreover, the reference to Dante is not only contradictory, but also useless: it would have sufficed to recall Michelangelo's Neoplatonism and the interpretation of the myth of Marsyas circulating in Neoplatonic circles. But on this basis the connection between Marsyas and Saint Bartholomew really seems ill-founded.

140. Venice, Pietro Quarengi, October 11, 1497, fol. ccxxiii *r*: "Entra nel pecto, ne la mente et spira in me tal canto quale usasti quando vincesti Marsia, etc." ("Enter my breast, my mind and breathe into me that song which you used when you conquered Marsyas, etc.") And see also Vellutello's commentary (Venice, 1564), p. 283.

141. A. Chastel, *Art et Humanisme à Florence au temps de Laurent le Magnifique* (Paris, 1959), p. 8, n. 2, rightly criticizes Wind's book and his methodology. Curiously, however, he then proceeds to provide an interpretation of Dante's verses that closely resembles Wind's own and that is based on an identical misunderstanding (see Chastel, pp. 51-52 and n. 109). At p. 52, n. 2, Chastel rejects P. Renucci's useful suggestion to interpret Dante's Marsyas as an example of foolish pride, evoked to suggest the poet's intention to submit "to the celestial intelligence that will deign to inspire him." He does so for the singular reason that "the so obvious interest of the poet in the 'mysteries of the pagan religion' ... invites one to accept 'the mystic sense' under 'the moral sense.' " (And see also in this connection Y. Batard, *Dante, Minerve, et Apollon: Les images de la Divine Comédie* [Paris, 1952], p. 27.)

142. Ettlinger (*Art History Today*, p. 16) observes that for some scholars iconology (here synonymous with "iconography") "becomes simply a meaningless display of free associations." The consciousness of this risk to which iconographic interpretation is exposed should not lead us to accept C. Brandi's conclusions (*Le due vie*, pp. 179-87), who, anyway, considers these investigations wholly superfluous to the aesthetic fruition of the work of art: "In the exegesis of the cultural and semantic background of an image, which, as we have said and repeated, is polysemantic by nature, we can never be certain to have touched bottom and to have exhausted all the possibilities" (p. 185). But here the many meanings of this image are not a factor. Brandi himself observes (p. 180) that "the search for these messages, whether innate or collateral in a work, naturally experiences all the uncertainty and possible upheavals familiar to historical and philological research; the discovery of a new source or historical fact frequently suffices to subvert the previous interpretation." But this also applies to a poem, in which it is often far from easy to identify "the cultural and semantic background." Furthermore, even "polysemy" is not an exclusive characteristic of the image. "More than of 'polysemy,' " Brandi writes, "one should speak of *availability*, of the inertia of

the image from the semiotic point of view. We can make an image say whatever is desired, even with a work of art. Look at the example of the *Mona Lisa* used in an advertisement for a laxative" (p. 63). Even a verse from the *Divine Comedy* was used as a publicity slogan for a similar product.

143. See the *Art Bulletin* 44 (1962): 75-79 (the reference to the term *illusion* is at p. 76). The observations found here concerning Arnheim's review (see the text below at note 156) are also present in what G. Previtali wrote in *Paragone* 13 (September 1962): 74-79. See also Previtali's review of *Art and Illusion*, ibid. 12 (September 1961): 44-48, which I found too dismissive. Objections to the use of the term *illusion* are advanced also by J. Beloff, "Some Comments on the Gombrich Problem," *British Journal of Aesthetics* 1 (1960): 62-70, and R. Wollheim, "Art and Illusion," ibid., 3 (1963): 15-37, esp. pp. 26 ff. Wollheim brings great perception and methodological refinement to his examination of Gombrich's book and raises technical objections that only indirectly touch upon the problems discussed here. (For a useful survey of the reviews of *Art and Illusion*, see Tonelli, "Gombrich e l'estetica," p. 54, n. 5.)

144. Gombrich, *Art and Illusion*, pp. 330 ff.

145. See the article "The Vogue of Abstract Art" (1956), now in *Meditations*, pp. 143-50; frankly, this is the least convincing of the essays collected in this volume. Similar doubts have been raised by J. Stolnitz in his review in the *British Journal of Aesthetics* 4 (1964): 271-74.

146. Gombrich, *Art and Illusion*, p.78.

147. Ibid., p. 30.

148. Similar objections (but excessively formalistic ones in my view) have been advanced on this issue by Wollheim, "Art and Illusion," p. 33, and by Arnheim, in the *Art Bulletin* (1962), p. 77. I have not seen Wollheim's *On Drawing an Object* (London, 1965), reviewed by H. Osborne in the *British Journal of Aesthetics* 6 (1966): 70-74. On the possible "fortuitousness" of the schema, see H. W. Janson, "The 'Image Made by Chance' in Renaissance Thought," in *De artibus opuscula xl: Essays in Honor of Erwin Panofsky* (1960), ed. M. Meiss, 2 vols. (New York, 1961), 1:254-66, which appeared contemporaneously with the book by Gombrich and is based on very similar documentation.

149. See the review of *Art and Illusion* in the *Times Literary Supplement*, April 8, 1960, p. 218. Above all, it is not clear if the *schema* should be understood in a transcendental sense (see the Kantian inscription to the chapter) or as a historically determined condition.

150. Gombrich, *Art and Illusion*, p. 198.

151. Ibid., p. 265.

152. Ibid., p. 266.

153. E. H. Gombrich, *The Story of Art* (1950), rev. ed. (London, 1966).

154. See Gombrich's essays "Expression and Communication" and "Tradition and Expression in Western Still Life," in *Meditations*, pp. 56-59 and 95-105.

155. Arnheim, *Art Bulletin* (1962), p. 79.

156. See, for Arnheim's objection concerning the "first image," Gombrich, *Art and Illusion*, pp. 90 ff. and 265-66, and especially the hypothesis in the essay "Meditations on a Hobby Horse" (1951), which Arnheim does not seem to have seen, now reprinted in the collection of that title, pp. 1-11. Other

objections are raised by Arnheim, who, as we know, is a devoted follower of Gestalt psychology, concerning Gombrich's eclectic use of theories of the psychology of perception (but see *Art and Illusion*, p. ix). Actually Gombrich makes generous use of the results of the Gestalt school: the very insistence on the need to consider stylistic data in their own context rather than atomistically is probably also due to the psychology of form (however, see "Raphael's *Madonna*," p. 15). In any case Arnheim does not reply to certain rather serious objections advanced by Gombrich on the question of the minimizing of learning through experience by the Gestalt school (see *Art and Illusion*, pp. 221-23). Moreover, Arnheim considers irrelevant Gombrich's use of the example of superficial details to emphasize the active intervention of the spectator in the deciphering of the image, inasmuch as one is dealing with a "marginal" experience (*Art Bulletin*, 74-79, 77). This is a futile observation, since this is hardly the first time that seemingly secondary data helped to raise a particular scholarly point of view (and, moreover, haven't Gestalt psychologists themselves used optical illusions for this purpose?).

157. Gombrich, *Art and Illusion*, p. 77.
158. Arnheim, in *Art Bulletin* (1962), p. 79.
159. Gombrich, *Art and Illusion*, p. 268.
160. Ibid., p. 3.
161. Ibid., pp. 19-20. In regard to Warburg's successors, Gombrich, in the notes, cites principally works by Saxl and Panofsky.
162. *Gertrud Bing, 1892-1964*, p. 3.
163. These conclusions differ substantially from those of L. D. Ettlinger (*Art History Today*), who in rightly underlining the tremendous importance of Gombrich's work, sees (too simplistically in my opinion) a sort of uninterrupted evolution, without lapses and dissent, from Warburg to Panofsky and Gombrich himself.
164. Ernst Kris and E. H. Gombrich, "Principles of Caricature," reprinted in E. Kris, *Psychoanalytic Explorations in Art* (London, 1953), pp. 189-203. Some of the essays in this collection are indeed notable: see, for example, the employment of works of art in psychological diagnosis in F. X. Messerschmidt, "A Psychotic Sculptor of the Eighteenth Century," ibid., pp. 128-50.
165. Kris and Gombrich, "Principles of Caricature," p. 195 (here followed almost to the letter).
166. The authors recognize, however, that the formation of this atemporal psychological mechanism within the confines of the figurative arts was made possible by the presence of specific historical conditions – the Neoplatonic conception of the artist as creator and a stylistic development which permitted such a calculated regression as caricature. Ibid., pp. 197-98.
167. Gombrich, "Raphael's *Madonna*," p. 23 and "Freud e l'arte."
168. Gombrich, "Art and Scholarship," in *Meditations*, p. 118.
169. Gombrich, *Art and Illusion*, p. 101.
170. Ibid., pp. 103-7.
171. Ibid., pp. 107-13.
172. Ibid., p. 78.
173. Ibid., pp. 123-25.

174. Ibid., p. 53.
175. Gombrich, "Expression and Communication," in *Meditations*, pp. 58, 60.
176. Gombrich, *Art and Illusion*, p. 157.
177. See the text above at note 159. Cf. the review of *Art and Illusion* by G. Boas in the *Journal of Aesthetics and Art Criticism* 19 (1960): 229.
178. Gombrich, *Art and Illusion*, p. 196.
179. Gombrich, *Arte e illusione*, p. xxxiv. A little earlier, in controversy with Arnheim, Gombrich stated: "However difficult it may be to realize this intention, I insist again that we would do better, and for a long time to come, to keep the study of images and the study of visual beauty separate" (p. xxxiii). And see also the allusion to the "borders of aesthetics, that promised land which [the reader] will only glimpse from afar." *Art and Illusion*, p. 25.
180. For "The Early Medici," see *Italian Renaissance Studies: A Tribute to the Late Cecilia M. Ady*, ed. E. F. Jacob (London, 1960), pp. 279-311. Cf. Gombrich's "Light, Form, Texture," and "Moment and Movement in Art," *JWCI* 27 (1964): 293-306, which carry on brilliantly themes mentioned in passing in *Art and Illusion*, pp. 279-82. In addition to his well-known polemic against Hegel and his successors, and against the "physiognomic" interpretation of works of art, Gombrich significantly advances the need for closer ties between artistic phenomena and other aspects of history at the conclusion of a lecture entitled "Hegel and His Followers" given at the Courtauld Institute in 1963. Thanks to the great courtesy of the author, to whom I express my heartfelt thanks, I have been able to see the unpublished manuscript of this talk, as well as of the other commemorative address which he gave at Hamburg and, in a slightly revised version, in London on the centenary of Warburg's birth. To this day the latter remains the richest and most penetrating interpretation of Warburg. Unfortunately, since I saw it only after this piece had been written, I have not been able to refer to it specifically. I should also like to thank Robert Klein, who read my own essay in proofs, for his valuable suggestions.

[Author's addendum: A great deal has been written in recent years about the scholars whose work is discussed in the preceding pages. I shall limit myself to a few references. On Warburg, the bibliography in the appendix to *Ausgewählte Schriften und Würdigungen*, ed. D. Wuttke (Baden-Baden, 1979), is indispensable. See also E. H. Gombrich, *Aby Warburg: An Intellectual Biography, with a Memoir on the History of the Library by Fritz Saxl*, 2nd ed. with a new preface and additional bibliography (Chicago, 1986); W. Hofmann, G. Syamken, and M. Warnke, *Die Menschenrechte des Auges: Ueber Aby Warburg* (Frankfort a.M., 1980); S. Settis, "Warburg continuatus," *Quaderni storici*, n.s., no. 58 (April 1985), pp. 5-38. On Saxl, see the introduction by S. Settis to the Italian translation of his astrological writings, *La fede negli astri: Dall'antichità al Rinascimento* (Turin, 1985); in addition, a selection from the *Lectures (La storia delle immagini)* has been published with an introduction by E. Garin (Bari, 1982). For a bibliography of Panofsky's writings, see *Aufsätze zu Grundfragen der Kunstwissenschaft*, ed. H. Oberer and E. Verheyen, 2nd expanded and corrected edition (Berlin, 1974). See also M. A. Holly, *Panofsky and the Foundations of Art History* (Ithaca, 1984). There is a bibliography of Gombrich, which will need to be updated, in *Kunst und Fortschritt: Wirkung und Wandlung einer Idee* (Cologne, 1978). A challenging answer to one of the crucial questions asked in this essay – can we analyze pictorial style as an indicator of broad historical phenomena? – has been given by M. Baxandall in his *Painting and Experience in Fifteenth-Century Italy* (Oxford, 1972)].

The High and the Low: The Theme of Forbidden Knowledge

1. This is the text of the passage: "Quod si aliqui ex ramis fracti sunt, tu autem, cum oleaster esses, insertus es in illis et socius radicis et pinguedinis olivae factus es: noli gloriari adversus ramos. Quod si gloriaris, non tu radicem portas, sed radix te. Dices ergo: Fracti sunt rami ut ego inserar. Bene, propter incredulitatem fracti sunt; tu autem fide stas: noli altum sapere, sed time. Si enim Deus naturalibus ramis non pepercit, ne forte nec tibi parcat." *Bibliorum sacrorum nova editio*, ed. L. Gramatica (Rome, 1951), p. 1066.

2. See W. E. Plater and H. J. Whyte, *A Grammar of the Vulgate* (Oxford, 1926), p. 29, and F. Blass and A. Debrunner, *A Greek Grammar of the New Testament and Other Early Christian Literature*, trans. and ed. R. W. Funk (Chicago, 1961), p. 65. The religious and moral significance of φρονειν is underlined by W. Jaeger, *The Theology of the Early Greek Philosophers* (1947; Oxford [photographic reprint], 1967), pp. 113-14.

3. Ambrosius, *De fide* 5:17.209 (*Sancti Ambrosii Opera*, vol.8, ed. O. Faller, *Corpus scriptorum ecclesiasticorum Latinorum* [henceforth *CSEL*] [Vienna, 1866-], 78: 295); see also ibid., p. 300.

4. Pelagius, *Expositiones tredecim epistolarum Pauli*, in *Epistolam ad Romanos* (*Patrologiae cursus completus: Series Latina* [henceforth *PL*], ed. J.-P. Migne, 221 vols. and *Supplementum* [Paris, 1844-64, 1958-74], *Supplementum*, vol.1, ed. A. Hamman, col. 1161).

5. See L. Valla, *In Novum Testamentum annotationes … cum Erasmi Praefatione* (Basel, 1541), pp. 141*v*, 142*r-v*. Cf. Valla's *De libero arbitrio*, ed. M. Anfossi (Florence, 1934), pp. 50-52, in which the Pauline passage is cited in a cognitive context – an attack against the presumptuous speculations of theologians over the *libero arbitrio* and predestination.

6. See Desiderius Erasmus Roterodamus, *Opera omnia*, 10 vols. (Leiden, 1703-6), 10.1726; 6.625.

7. See *Novum Testamentum Graece et Latine*, ed. A. Merk, 5th ed. (Rome, 1944).

8. Lactantius, *Divinae Institutiones* 2.7 (ed. S. Brandt and G. Laubmann, *CSEL*, 19:125): "Sapere id est veritatem quaerere."

9. G. Luck, "Zur Geschichte des Begriffs 'sapientia,'" *Archiv für Begriffsgeschichte* 9 (1964): 203-15. See also E. F. Rice, *The Renaissance Idea of Wisdom* (Cambridge, Mass., 1958).

10. Smaragdus, *Collectiones epistolarum et evangeliorum de tempore et de sanctis*, Dominica prima post Theophania (*PL*, 102.76-77); *Rabanus Maurus, Enarrationum in epistolas beati Pauli libri triginta* 6.11; 7.12 (*PL*, 111. 1532, 1544-46). See also Primasius, *Commentaria in epistolas S. Pauli, Epistola ad Romanos*, 11 and 12 (*PL*, 68.491, 494); Luculentius, *In aliquot novi Testamenti partes commentarii*, 3 (*PL*, 72.813-14); Alulfus, *De expositione novi Testamenti*, 6.29 (*PL*, 79.1304); Sedulius Scotus, *Collectanea in omnes B. Pauli epistolas*,

1.11, 12 (*PL*, 103.105, 111); Bruno Carthusianus, *Expositio in epistolas Pauli, Epistola ad Romanos* 11-12 (*PL*, 153.96, 102); Hugo de Sancto Victore, *Quaestiones et decisiones in espistolas D. Pauli, In Epistolam ad Romanos*, q. 288 (*PL*, 175.502-3); Guillermus abbas Sancti Theoderici prope Remos, *Expositio in epistolam ad Romanos* 6.11; 7.12 (*PL*, 180.662, 672); Herveus Burgidolensis, *Commentaria in epistolas divi Pauli, Expositio in epistolam ad Romanos*, 11-12 (*PL*, 181.754, 765-66). All these commentators interpret Rom. 12:3 in a context of knowing (illicit curiosity, etc.). Some (Luculentius, William of St. Theodoric, Herveus Burgidolensis) explicitly cite Rom. 11:20.

11. *Biblia vulgare historiata …*, trans. Niccolò Malermi (Venice, 1507), fol. CLXX v.

12. See S. Timpanaro, *The Freudian Slip: Psychoanalysis and Textual Criticism* (London, 1976; rpt. Shocken Books, 1985).

13. In studying a lapsus of this kind I had as a model E. Panofsky, "*Et in Arcadia ego*: Poussin and the Elegiac Tradition," in *Meaning in the Visual Arts* (Garden City, N.J., 1955), pp. 295-320.

14. See, in general, G.E.R. Lloyd, *Polarity and Analogy: Two Types of Argumentation in Early Greek Thought* (Cambridge, 1966).

15. See L. von Bertalanffy, "An Essay on Relativity of Categories," *Philosophy of Science* 22 (1955): 243-63. For a recent discussion of the problem, see H. Gipper, *Gibt es ein sprachliches Relativitätsprinzip? Untersuchungen zur Sapir-Whorf Hypothese* (Frankfort a.M., 1972), with bibliography.

16. R. Needham, ed., *Right and Left* (Chicago, 1973).

17. See G. Róheim, "Primitive High Gods," in *The Panic of Gods and Other Essays* (New York, 1972), pp. 52-53 and passim (not convincing, but highly stimulating). Some psychological implications of the archetype of "verticality" are emphasized by J. Laponce, "Hirschman's Voice and Exit Model as a Spatial Archetype," *Social Science Information* 13, no. 3 (1974): 67-81.

18. R. Pettazzoni, *The All-Knowing God: Research into Early Religion and Culture* (London, 1956).

19. "Noli ergo extolli de ulla arte vel scientia: sed potius time de data tibi notitia.… Noli altum sapere (Rom. 11:20): sed ignorantiam tuam magis fatere." Thomas à Kempis, *De imitatione Christi libri quattuor, editio ad codicem autographum exacta* (Rome, 1925), p. 6.

20. See Desiderius Erasmus Roterodamus, *Opus epistolarum*, ed. P. S. and H. M. Allen, 12 vols. (Oxford, 1906-58), 5: 176-77 (to John Carondelet). Cf. ibid., pp. 338-39, and *Opera Omnia*, 2.250. On the motto, "Quae supra nos, ea nihil ad nos," see A. Otto, *Die Sprichwörter und sprichwörterlichen Redensarten der Römer* (Leipzig, 1890), p. 335. I intend to study the use of this slogan by sixteenth- and seventeenth-century skeptics in a broader context.

21. See M. Praz, *Studies in Seventeenth-Century Imagery* (Rome, 1964); and see also the review by W. S. Heckscher and C. F. Bunker of *Emblemata: Handbuch zur Sinnbildkunst des XVI und XVII Jahrhunderts*, ed. A. Henkel and A. Schöne, in *Renaissance Quarterly* 23 (1970): 59-80.

22. Icarus and Prometheus can both be found in Andrea Alciati's *Emblematum liber* (Augsburg, 1531), probably the oldest and undoubtedly the most influential of the emblem book collections. Note, however, that in the first edition the poem entitled "In astrologos" was accompanied by an illustration

of an astrologer ready to stumble as he gazes at the stars (see figure 3). In subsequent editions the figure (Thales, according to an ancient tradition) was replaced by Icarus. Here is the text of the poem: "Icare per superos qui raptus et aëra, donec / In mare praecipitem cera liquata daret. / Nunc te cera eadem fervensque resuscitat ignis, / Exemplo ut doceas dogmata certa tuo. / Astrologus caveat quicquam praedicere, praeceps / Nam cadet impostor dum super astra vehit." And here is a virtually literal translation: "Icarus, you who were snatched through the upper air, until the molten wax sent you headlong to the sea, now the same wax and burning fire are reviving you, so that you might teach us sure lessons by your example. Let the astrologer be wary of predicting anything; for the impostor will fall headlong, while he is flying beyond the stars." (The English version is taken from *Andreas Alciatus, 1: The Latin Emblems: Indexes and Lists*, ed. Peter M. Daly with Virginia W. Callahan, assisted by Simon Cuttler [Toronto, 1985], emblem 104. – *Trans.*)

23. See Alciati, *Emblematum liber*, pp. 55-56; P. Pomponazzi, *Libri quinque de fato, de libero arbitrio et de praedestinatione*, ed. R. Lemay (Lugano, 1957), p. 262. In general, see O. Raggio, "The Myth of Prometheus: Its Survival and Metamorphoses up to the Eighteenth Century," *Journal of the Warburg and Courtauld Institutes* 21 (1958): 44-62; R. Trousson, *Le thème de Prométhée dans la littérature européenne*, 2 vols. (Geneva, 1964) (superficial).

24. John Donne, *Ignatius His Conclave: An Edition of the Latin and English Texts with Introduction and Commentary*, ed. T. S. Healy, S.J. (Oxford, 1969), p. 17.

25. Previous versions of this article incorrectly give the date as 1619. – *Trans.*

26. Archivio di Stato, Venice, Sant' Uffizio, b. 72 ("Costantino Saccardino"). The "dovecote" here metaphorically signifies the less privileged classes in society. On this episode, for the moment, see C. Ginzburg, "The Dovecote Has Opened Its Eyes," in *The Inquisition in Early Modern Europe: Studies on Sources and Methods*, ed. G. Henningsen and J. Tedeschi in association with Charles Amiel (De Kalb, 1986), pp. 190-98.

27. See R. Pintard, *Le libertinage érudit dans la première moitié du XVIIe siècle*, 2 vols. (Paris, 1943).

28. G. Galilei, *Dialogue Concerning the Two Chief World Systems – Ptolemaic and Copernican*, trans. Stillman Drake, 2nd ed. (Berkeley and Los Angeles, 1967), p. 37.

29. R. Descartes, *Discourse on Method ...*, trans. E. S. Haldane and G.R.T. Ross (Chicago, 1952), p. 45.

30. Some reactions to the idea of the plurality of worlds, as an extension of the Copernican cosmology, are analyzed by P. Rossi, "Nobility of Man and Plurality of Worlds," in *Science, Medicine, and Society in the Renaissance: Essays to Honor Walter Pagel*, ed. A. G. Debus, 2 vols. (London, 1972), 2:131-62.

31. S. Pallavicino, *Del bene* (Rome, 1644), pp. 346-47.

32. V. Malvezzi, *Davide perseguitato* (Bologna, 1634), p. 9.

33. Pallavicino, *Del bene*, pp. 248, 168.

34. On curiosity, see the important study by H. Blumenberg, *Der Prozess der theoretischen Neugierde* (Frankfort a.M., 1973).

35. M. Marciano, *Pompe funebri dell' universo nella morte di Filippo Quarto il Grande re delle Spagne* (Naples, 1666), p. 101 and the table facing p. 102; the emblem

was dedicated to Emperor Matthias. The slogan is from Horace (*Carmina* 1.3.37).

36. See A. de Boodt, *Symbola varia diversorum Principum, Archiducum, Ducum, Comitum & Marchionum totius Italiae, cum facili isagoge* (Amsterdam, 1686), pp. 292-94. The Latin saying "Nil linquere inausum" is from Vergil (*Aeneid* 7.308).

37. D. Bartoli, *Dell'huomo di lettere difeso et emendato* (Venice, 1689), pp. 115 ff.

38. See F. Schoonhovius, *Emblemata … partim moralia partim etiam civilia* (Gouda, 1618; other eds., 1626; Amsterdam, 1635, 1648).

39. See D. Nobbs, *Theocracy and Toleration: A Study of the Disputes in Dutch Calvinism from 1600 to 1650* (Cambridge, 1938).

40. *Praestantium ac eruditorum virorum Epistolae ecclesiasticae ac theologicae*, ed. C. Hartsoecker and P. à Limborch, 2nd ed. (Amsterdam, 1684), pp. 492, 378.

41. Horace, *Epistolae*, 1.2.40 ("ad Lollium").

42. All this confirms L. Firpo's brilliant hypothesis in "Ancora a proposito di 'Sapere aude!' " *Rivista Storica Italiana* 72 (1960): 114-17.

43. See C. Vivanti, *Lotta politica e pace religiosa in Francia fra Cinque e Seicento* (Turin, 1963), pp. 325-62.

44. *Praestantium ac eruditorum virorum Epistolae*, p. 288.

45. See Firpo, "Ancora a proposito," pp. 116-17.

46. A van Leeuwenhoek, *Epistolae ad Societatem Regiam Anglicam et alios illustres viros* (Leiden, 1719).

47. See F. Venturi, "Was ist Aufklaerung? Sapere aude!" *Rivista Storica Italiana* 71 (1959): 119-28; idem, *Utopia e Riforma nell'Illuminismo* (Turin, 1970), pp. 14-18.

[For a recent contribution to one of the themes discussed above, see E. Peters, "*Libertas inquirendi* and the *vitium curiositatis* in Medieval Thought," in *La notion de liberté au Moyen Age: Islam, Byzance, Occident*, ed. G. Makdisi (Paris, 1985) (with bibliography).]

Titian, Ovid, and Sixteenth-Century Codes for Erotic Illustration

1. Terence, *The Eunuch*, in *Terence with an English Translation by John Sargeaunt*, Loeb Classical Library (Cambridge, Mass., and London, 1929), 1:293, 295.

2. See D. Freedberg, "Johannes Molanus on Provocative Paintings: *De historia sanctarum imaginum et picturarum*, Book II, Chapter 42," *Journal of the Warburg and Courtauld Institutes* 34 (1971): 242, n. 24. F. Orlando alludes to the passage in Saint Augustine, but in a different context: "Su teoria della letteratura e divisione del lavoro intellettuale," *Strumenti Critici*, no. 29 (February 1976), p. 115.

3. See J. L. Connolly, Jr., in *Woman as Sex Object: Studies in Erotic Art, 1730-1970*, ed. T. B. Hess and L. Nochlin (New York, 1972), p. 1, and the piece by Nochlin, ibid. pp. 9 ff. I will discuss the problem of images that are explicitly homosexual, or intended for a homosexual public, on another occasion.

4. See I. Calvino, "Considerazioni sul sesso e sul riso," *Il Caffè* 17, no. 2 (1970): 3-5. The classical and medieval distinction between various stylistic levels is accepted here in E. Auerbach's sense (*Mimesis: The Representation of Reality in Western Literature* [Princeton, 1953]).

5. See the Pompeian fresco reproduced by W. S. Heckscher, "Recorded from Dark Recollection," in *De artibus opuscula XL: Essays in Honor of Erwin Panofsky*, ed. M. Meiss (New York, 1961), fig. 5.

6. In contrast, I would define as pornographic those illustrations which are intended exclusively to arouse the spectator sexually.

7. See Freedberg, "Johannes Molanus," p. 233.

8. This distinction is based principally on P. Burke, *Culture and Society in Renaissance Italy, 1420-1540* (London, 1972), pp. 144, 158, passim.

9. See Freedberg, "Johannes Molanus," p. 241, n. 15.

10. See G. Vasari, *Le vite*, ed. G. Milanesi (Florence, 1879), 4:188.

11. P. Barocchi, "Un 'Discorso' sopra l'onestà delle immagini di Rinaldo Corso," in *Scritti ... in onore di Mario Salmi* (Rome, 1963), 3:173-91.

12. See J. S. Held, "Flora, Goddess and Courtesan," in *De artibus opuscula XL*, pp. 201-18.

13. A. Catarino Politi, *Disputatio ... de cultu et adoratione imaginum* (Rome, 1552), pp. 142-43.

14. H. Tietze, "An Early Version of Titian's Danae: An Analysis of Titian Replicas," *Arte Veneta* 8 (1954): 199-208.

15. E. Panofsky, *Problems in Titian, Mostly Iconographic* (London, 1969).

16. *Raccolta di lettere sulla pittura, scultura ed architettura* (Rome, 1757), 2:22.

17. *Raccolta* (Rome, 1759), 3:259-60.

18. The truncated passage is in R. Pallucchini, *Tiziano* (Florence, 1969), 1:140-41.

19. M. L. Shapiro, "Titian's 'Rape of Europa,' " *Gazette des Beaux Arts* 77, no. 1225 (1971): 109-16. The previously formulated hypothesis of a derivation from "such more recondite authors as Moschus" is rejected by Panofsky (*Problems in Titian*, p. 165) in favor of the traditional Ovidian theory, on which more below.

20. D. Stone, Jr., "The Source of Titian's *Rape of Europa*," *Art Bulletin* 54 (1972): 47-49. (And see now, following a similar line of interpretation, but with the addition of new elements, P. F. Watson, "Titian's 'Rape of Europa': A Bride Stripped Bare," in *Storia dell'Arte*, no. 28 [1976], pp. 249-58.)

21. Shapiro, "Titian's 'Rape,' " p. 114. Note that Stone does not exclude (with excessive prudence in my opinion) the Stoic implications proposed by Shapiro.

22. Panofsky, *Problems in Titian*, pp. 140-41.

23. It does not seem to me that all the implications of the relationship between Titian and Aretino have been exhausted. On the significance of the latter's literary success, see the perceptive comments by C. Dionisotti, *Geografia e storia della letteratura italiana* (Turin, 1967), pp. 193-94. On the sixteenth-century *poligrafi*, see the useful work by P. F. Grendler, *Critics of the Italian World (1530-1560): Anton Francesco Doni, Nicolò Franco, and Ortensio Lando* (Madison, 1969).

24. G. Campori, "Tiziano e gli Estensi," *Nuova Antologia* 27 (1874): 587.

25. In Vinegia, per Curtio Navo e fratelli, 1538.
26. E. Panofsky, "Der gefesselte Eros (Zur Genealogie von Rembrandts *Danae*)," *Oud Holland* 50 (1933): 203 ff.
27. Ovid, *Le Methamorphosi cioè transmutationi tradotte dal latino diligentemente in volgar verso ... per Nicolò di Agustini* (Venice: Bernardino de' Bindoni, 1538), fol. 42r.
28. Panofsky, *Problems in Titian*, pp. 157, 159. The second citation alludes to Diana and Actaeon as well as to Diana and Callistus.
29. Ibid., p.157.
30. *Delle metamorfosi d'Ovidio libri III ... Di Giovanni Andrea dell'Anguillara* (In Vinegia, nella bottega d'Erasmo, appresso Vincenzo Valgrisi, 1555), fols. 36r-v.
31. See V. Golzio, *Raffaello nei documenti, nelle testimonianze dei contemporanei, e nella letteratura del suo secolo* (Vatican City, 1936), p. 86. The passage is recalled in connection with the *Actaeon* also by Panofsky, *Problems in Titian*, p. 158, n. 47, and by Vasari, *Le vite*, 1:138. According to Wethey (*The Paintings of Titian*, vol. 3, *The Mythological and Historical Paintings* [London, 1975], p. 73, the Gothic aspect of the grotto is due to a mistaken interpretation by Panofsky; nevertheless, he too remarks that in Ovid's text there is no trace of that "architectural design" introduced by Titian (on the basis of Anguillara's translation, in my opinion).
32. G. B. Cavalcaselle and J. A. Crowe, *Tiziano, la sua vita e i suoi tempi* (Florence, 1878), 2:250-51.
33. See Panofsky, *Problems in Titian*, pp. 167-68.
34. *Le Methamorphosi*, fols. 43v-44v.
35. See C. Gould, "The *Perseus and Andromeda* and Titian's *Poesie*," *Burlington Magazine* 105 (1963): 112-17.
36. According to Panofsky (*Problems in Titian*, p. 167) this last solution was suggested by Bernard Salomon's Ovidian illustration (Lyons, 1557). But Charles Hope informs me that *Perseus and Andromeda* could already be found in Spain from the preceding year. I also owe to Hope the reference to a passage in Achille Tazio which describes a painting representing Perseus and Andromeda (*Dell'amore di Leucippe e Clitophonte* [Venice, 1551], fols. 35v-37r), which is quite different from Titian's.
37. For all this see F. Zambrini, *Le opere volgari a stampa dei secoli XIII e XIV* (Bologna, 1884), pp. 730-31; P. Tommasini-Mattiucci, "Fatti e figure di storia letteraria di Città di Castello," *Bollettino della Regia Deputazione di Storia Patria per l'Umbria* 7 (1901): 24-33; C. Marchesi, "Le allegorie ovidiane di Giovanni del Virgilio," *Studi Romanzi* 6 (1909): 119-27, 135-45; and the entry for "Bonsignori, Giovanni," in the *Dizionario Biografico degli Italiani*.
38. See F. Ghisalberti, *Giovanni del Virgilio espositore delle "Metamorfosi"* (Florence, 1933) (reprinted from the *Giornale Dantesco*), who publishes excerpts from the paraphrases and, in an appendix, the entire text of the allegories.
39. See Biblioteca Casanatense, MS. 1369, fol. 29v (which contains the notes for the Ovidian paraphrase dictated by Giovanni del Virgilio in the *Studio* at Bologna); Ovid, *Metamorphoseos vulgare* (Venice per Christofolo de Pensa ad in stantia del nobile homo miser Lucantonio Zonta fiorentino, 1501), fol. XXXXIIIIr (this is the second printing of Bonsignori's vernacular version,

identical, according to Zambrini, to the first, which appeared in Venice in 1497); *Le Methamorphosi*, fol. 41*r*.

40. For one attempt, see my *Cheese and the Worms: The Cosmos of a Sixteenth-Century Miller* (Baltimore, 1980).
41. See E. W. Monter, "La sodomie à l'époque moderne en suisse romande," *Annales: E.S.C.* 29 (1974): 1023-33, esp. p. 1030.
42. D. Herlihy offered some interesting observations on the subject at the Venetian roundtable in September 1976.
43. B. Caimi, *Interrogatorium sive confessionale* (n.p., 1474), unpaginated.
44. See the stimulating remarks by L. Febvre, *Le problème de l'incroyance au XVI siècle: La religion de Rabelais* (1942; Paris, 1968). The subject of a "history of the senses" was proposed by Marx in a famous page of the Parisian *Manuscripts*.

[The present article was reprinted (without the illustrative material, owing to editorial oversight) in the proceedings of the conference, *Tiziano e Venezia* (Venice, 1980). In that volume see the contributions by C. Hope and H. Zerner, who discuss themes treated here. On vernacular versions of Ovid I should have cited B. Guthmüller, "Die literarische Uebersetzung im Bezugsfeld Original-Leser am Beispiel Italienischer Uebersetzungen der Metamorphosen Ovids im 16. Jahrhundert," *Bibliothèque d'Humanisme et Renaissance* 36 (1974): 233-51. See also, by the same author, "Ovidübersetzungen und mythologische Malerei: Bemerkungen zur *Sala dei Giganti* Giulio Romanos," *Mitteilungen des Kunsthistorischen Instituts in Florenz* 21 (1977): 35-68 (brought to my attention by Carlo Dionisotti). On Dolce's dedication to Titian, discussed above, see the clarifications by Dionisotti, "Tiziano e la letteratura," in *Tiziano e il manierismo europeo*, ed. R. Pallucchini (Florence, 1978) (but his entire essay is important). In the same volume see also the contribution by M. Gregori, "Tiziano e Aretino." A. Chastel, following Dionisotti, has insisted on the significance for Titian of vernacular versions of Ovid: "Titien et les humanistes," in *Tiziano Vecellio*, Atti dei convegni dei Lincei, 29 (Rome, 1977), pp. 31-48. A. Gentili takes a different position (*Da Tiziano a Tiziano* [Rome, 1980], pp. 173 ff.) and argues against my interpretation. I have corrected an error in the name of Achille Tazio's translator, and specified that the reference to Titian's *Danae* applied to both versions. For the rest, however, it does not seem to me that Gentili grasped the sense of my argument, which intended to deny not Titian's capacity for invention (imagine!), but simply his direct dependence on Ovid's text, assumed by Panofsky. The attempts to devaluate the importance of the quite clear passage in Dolce's dedication are doomed to fail.]

Clues: Roots of an Evidential Paradigm

1. I use the term in the sense proposed by T. S. Kuhn, *The Structure of Scientific Revolutions* (Chicago, 1962), disregarding the clarifications and distinctions introduced later by the author (see "Postscript–1969") in the second, revised edition of his work (Chicago, 1974), pp. 174 ff.
2. On Morelli, see especially E. Wind, *Art and Anarchy*, 3rd ed. (Evanston, 1985), pp. 32 ff., 117 ff., and the bibliography cited there. For his biography,

see also M. Ginoulhiac, "Giovanni Morelli, la vita," *Bergomum* 34, no. 2 (1940): 51-74. Attention has recently been paid to Morelli's method by R. Wollheim, "Giovanni Morelli and the Origins of Scientific Connoisseurship," in *On Art and the Mind: Essays and Lectures* (London, 1973), pp. 177-201; H. Zerner, "Giovanni Morelli et la science de l'art," *Revue de l'art*, 1978, nos. 40-41: 209-15; and G. Previtali, "A propos de Morelli," ibid., no. 42: 27-31. Other contributions are cited in note 12, below. Unfortunately, we still lack a comprehensive study on Morelli which considers – in addition to his works on art history – his education, his relations with German circles, his friendship with De Sanctis, and his involvement in political life. In regard to De Sanctis, see the letter in which Morelli proposed him as instructor in Italian literature at the Zurich Polytechnic Institute (F. De Sanctis, *Lettere dall' esilio, 1853-1860*, ed. B. Croce [Bari, 1938], pp. 34-38), as well as the indices of De Sanctis's *Epistolario*, 4 vols. (Turin, 1956-69). On Morelli's political commitment, see for now the brief remarks in G. Spini, *Risorgimento e Protestanti* (Naples, 1956), pp. 114, 261, 335. For the European impact of Morelli's works, see what he wrote to Marco Minghetti from Basel on June 22, 1882: "Old Jakob Burckhardt, whom I went to visit last night, gave me the warmest welcome, and insisted on spending the entire evening with me. He is an extremely original man both in thought and action, and you would like him too, but he would especially please our Donna Laura. He spoke to me of Lermolieff's book as if he had consigned it to memory, and he used it to ask me a thousand questions – a thing which certainly tickled my vanity. I am to meet with him again this morning." Bologna, Biblioteca Comunale dell' Archiginnasio, Carte Minghetti, XXIII, 54.

3. Next to the "great" Cavalcaselle, Longhi judged Morelli "less great, but notable just the same"; he spoke immediately after, however, of "suggestions of ... materialism" which rendered Morelli's "method presumptuous and esthetically unserviceable." R. Longhi, "Cartella tizianesca," in *Saggi e ricerche, 1925-1928* (Florence, 1967), p. 234. On the implications of this and other similar opinions of Longhi's, see G. Contini, "Longhi prosatore," in *Altri esercizi (1942-1971)* (Turin, 1972), p. 117. This damaging comparison with Cavalcaselle is revived, for example, by M. Fagiolo in G. C. Argan and M. Fagiolo, *Guida alla storia dell'arte* (Florence, 1974), pp. 97, 101.

4. See Wind, *Art and Anarchy*, pp. 40 ff. Croce, instead, spoke of "the sensuality of details, immediate and out of context." B. Croce, *La critica e la storia delle arti figurative: Questioni di metodo* (Bari, 1946), p. 15.

5. Longhi, *Saggi*, p. 321, speaks of "the sense of quality ... in Morelli" being "so little developed or frequently corrupted by the arrogance of the simple acts of the connoisseur"; immediately after, he actually calls Morelli "the sad and mediocre critic from Gorlaw" (the Russian disguise for Gorle, a place near Bergamo where Morelli-Lermolieff resided).

6. Wind, *Art and Anarchy*, p.38.

7. E. Castelnuovo, "Attribution," in *Encyclopaedia universalis*, 2 (1968): 782. More generally, A. Hauser (*The Philosophy of Art History* [New York, 1959], pp. 109-10) compares Freud's detective technique to Morelli's (cf. note 12, below).

8. A. Conan Doyle, "The Cardboard Box," in *The Complete Sherlock Holmes*

Short Stories (London, 1976), p. 932.

9. Ibid., pp. 937-38. "The Cardboard Box" appeared for the first time in the *Strand Magazine* 5 (1893): 61-73. W. S. Baring-Gould, editor of *The Annotated Sherlock Holmes* (London, 1968) 2:208, noted that a few months later the same journal published an anonymous article on the different shapes of the human ear ("Ears: A Chapter On," *Strand Magazine* 6 [1893]: 388-91, 525-27). According to Gould, the author of the article could have been Conan Doyle himself, who might have ended up writing Holmes's contribution to the *Anthropological Journal* (for *Journal of Anthropology*). But this is just a gratuitous assumption: the article on ears had been preceded in the *Strand Magazine* 5 (1893): 119-23, 295-301, by an article entitled "Hands" signed "Beckles Willson." At any rate the page of ear illustrations from the *Strand* reminds us of those accompanying Morelli's writings – confirmation that themes of this sort were popular at the time.

10. It cannot be excluded, however, that this is more than a parallelism. One of Conan Doyle's uncles, Henry Doyle, painter and art critic, became the director of the National Art Gallery in Dublin in 1869 (see P. Nordon, *Sir Arthur Conan Doyle: L'homme et l'oeuvre* [Paris, 1964], p. 9). Morelli met Henry Doyle in 1887 and wrote about it in French to his friend Sir Henry Layard: "What you tell me about the Dublin gallery interested me very much, especially because I had the opportunity in London to meet that excellent Mr. Doyle personally, who made the best of impressions on me … alas, instead of a Doyle just think who one ordinarily finds directing our European museums?!" British Library, Add. MS. 38965, Layard Papers, vol. 35, fol. 120v. The fact that Henry Doyle knew the Morellian method (obvious to an art historian of the day) is proved by the *Catalogue of the Works of Art in the National Gallery of Ireland* (Dublin, 1890), which Doyle compiled and which uses (see p. 87, for example) Kugler's manual, thoroughly revised by Layard in 1887 under Morelli's guidance. The first English translation of Morelli's writings appeared in 1883 (see the bibliography in *Italienische Malerei der Renaissance im Briefwechsel von Giovanni Morelli und Jean Paul Richter, 1876-1891*, ed., J. and G. Richter [Baden-Baden, 1960]). The first Holmes story, "A Study in Scarlet," was published in 1887. The possibility emerges from all this that Conan Doyle had direct knowledge of Morelli's method through his uncle. But this supposition is not essential, since Morelli's writings were not the only vehicle for the ideas I have been attempting to study here.

11. Wind, *Art and Anarchy*, p. 38.

12. In addition to a precise reference in Hauser (*The Philosophy of Art History*, pp. 109-10), see also J. J. Spector, "The method of Morelli and Its Relation to Freudian Psychoanalysis," *Diogenes*, 1969, no. 66: 63-83; H. Damisch, "La partie et le tout," *Revue d'esthétique* 2 (1970): 168-88; idem, "Le gardien de l'interprétation," *Tel Quel*, 1971, no. 44: 70–96; R. Wollheim, "Freud and the Understanding of Art," in *On Art and the Mind*, pp. 209-10.

13. See S. Freud, "The Moses of Michelangelo," in Freud's *Collected Papers* (New York, 1959), 4:270-71. R. Bremer, "Freud and Michelangelo's Moses," *American Imago* 33 (1976): 60-75, discusses Freud's interpretation of the *Moses* without mention of Morelli. I have not been able to see K. Victorius,

"Der 'Moses des Michelangelo' von Sigmund Freud," in *Entfaltung der Pyschoanalyse*, ed. A. Mitscherlich (Stuttgart, 1956), pp. 1-10.

14. See S. Kofman, *L'enfance de l'art: Une interprétation de l'esthétique freudienne* (Paris, 1975), pp. 19, 27; Damisch, "Le gardien," pp. 70 ff.; Wollheim, "Freud and the Understanding of Art," p. 210.

15. Spector's excellent essay is an exception; however, it too denies the existence of a real relationship between the methods of Freud and Morelli ("The Method of Morelli," pp. 68-69).

16. S. Freud, "The Interpretation of Dreams," in *The Basic Writings of Sigmund Freud*, trans. and ed. with an Introduction by A. A. Brill (New York, 1938), p. 339n.

17. See M. Robert, *The Psychoanalytic Revolution: Sigmund Freud's Life and Achievement* (New York, 1966), p. 84.

18. See E. H. Gombrich, "Freud's Aesthetics," *Encounter* 26, no. 1 (1966): 30. Curiously, in this essay Gombrich does not mention Freud's reference to Morelli.

19. I. Lermolieff, *Die Werke italienischer Meister in den Galerien von München, Dresden, und Berlin: Ein kritischer Versuch*, aus dem Russischen übersetzt von Dr. Johannes Schwarze (Leipzig, 1880).

20. G. Morelli (I. Lermolieff), *Italian Masters in German Galleries: A Critical Essay on the Italian Pictures in the Galleries of Munich, Dresden, and Berlin*, translated from the German by L. M. Richter (London, 1883).

21. H. Trosman and R. D. Simmons, "The Freud Library," *Journal of the American Psychoanalytic Association* 21 (1973): 672. I am grateful to Pier Cesare Bori for this reference.

22. See E. Jones, *The Life and Work of Sigmund Freud*, 3 vols. (New York, 1962), 1:335.

23. See Robert, *The Psychoanalytic Revolution*, p. 180; Morelli (I. Lermolieff), *Della pittura italiana*, pp. 88-89 (on Signorelli) and 159 (on Boltraffio).

24. Morelli (Lermolieff), *Della pittura italiana*, p. 4.

25. Vergil, *Aeneid* 7.312 (Loeb Classical Library). Freud's choice of the Vergilian passage has been interpreted in various ways: see W. Schoenau, *Sigmund Freuds Prosa: Literarische Elemente seines Stil* (Stuttgart, 1968), pp. 61-73. The most convincing view, in my opinion, is E. Simon's (ibid., p. 72); he suggests that the epigraph signifies that the hidden, invisible part of reality is not less important than the visible. On the possible political implications of the epigraph, already used by Lassalle, see the excellent essay by C. E. Schorske, "Politique et parricide dans 'L'interprètation des rêves' de Freud," *Annales: E.S.C.* 28 (1973): 309-28, esp. 325 ff.

26. Morelli (Lermolieff), *Della pittura italiana*, p. 71.

27. See Morelli's epitaph written by Richter (ibid., p. xviii): "Those particular clues [discovered by Morelli] ... which such a master is wont to advance out of habit and almost unconsciously."

28. Steven Marcus, Introduction to A. Conan Doyle, *The Adventures of Sherlock Holmes: A Facsimile of the Stories as They Were First Published in the "Strand Magazine"* (New York, 1976), pp. x-xi. See also the bibliography in the appendix to *The Seven Percent Solution; Being a Reprint from the Reminiscences of John H. Watson, M.D., as Edited by Nicholas Meyer* (New York, 1974), a novel

based on Holmes and Freud which enjoyed an undeserved success.

29. See *The Wolf-Man by the Wolf-Man*, ed. M. Gardiner (New York, 1971), p. 146; T. Reik, *Ritual: Psycho-Analytic Studies* (London, 1931). For the distinction between symptoms and clues, see C. Segre, "La gerarchia dei segni," in *Pscicanalisi e semiotica*, ed. A. Verdiglione (Milan, 1975), p. 33, and T. A. Sebeok, *Contributions to the Doctrine of Signs* (Bloomington, 1976).

30. See W. S. Baring-Gould, "Two Doctors and a Detective: Sir Arthur Conan Doyle, John A. Watson, M.D., and Mr. Sherlock Holmes of Baker Street," *Introduction to the Annotated Sherlock Holmes*, 1:7 ff., regarding John Bell, the physician who was the inspiration for the creation of Sherlock Holmes. See also A. Conan Doyle, *Memories and Adventures* (London, 1924), pp. 25-26, 74-75.

31. See A. Wesselofsky, "Eine Märchengruppe," *Archiv für slavische Philologie* 9 (1886): 308-9, with bibliography. For the later success of this fable, see notes 89 and 90, below, and accompanying text.

32. See A. Seppilli, *Poesia e magia* (Turin, 1962).

33. See the famous essay by R. Jakobson, "Two Aspects of Language and Two Types of Aphasic Disturbances," in *Fundamentals of Language,* by Roman Jakobson and Morris Halle (The Hague and Paris, 1971), pp. 67-96.

34. See E. Cazade and C. Thomas, "Alfabeto," in *Enciclopedia Einaudi* (Turin, 1977), 1:289. Cf. Etiemble, *The Orion Book of the Written Word* (New York, 1961), pp. 23-24. See in general, Walter Benjamin, "Über das mimetische Vermögen," in *Angelus Novus: Ausgewählte Schriften 2* (Frankfort a.M., 1966), pp. 96-99.

35. I am using the excellent essay by J. Bottéro, "Symptômes, signes, écritures," in *Divination et rationalité* (Paris, 1974), pp. 70-197.

36. Ibid., pp. 154 ff.

37. Ibid., p. 157. For the connection between writing and divination in China, see J. Gernet, "La Chine: Aspects et fonctions psychologiques de l'écriture," in *L'écriture et la psychologie des peuples* (Paris, 1963), esp. pp. 33-38.

38. This is the inference which Peirce called "presumptive" or "abductive," distinguishing it from simple induction: see C. S. Peirce, "Deduction, Induction, and Hypothesis," in *Chance, Love, and Logic* (New York, 1956), pp. 131-53, and "Abduction and Deduction," in *Philosophical Writings of Peirce*, ed. J. Buchler (New York, 1955), pp. 150-56. In his own essay, Bottéro constantly emphasizes, instead, the "deductive" characteristics (as he calls them, "for lack of something better") of Mesopotamian divination ("Symptômes," p. 89). This is a definition which unduly simplifies, to the point of distorting it, the complicated trajectory which had been so well reconstructed by Bottéro himself (ibid., pp. 168 ff.). This oversimplification seems to be dictated by a narrow and one-sided definition of "science" (p. 190), disavowed in fact by the significant analogy proposed at one point between divination and such a loosely deductive discipline as medicine (p. 132). The parallelism proposed above between the two tendencies of Mesopotamian civilization and the mixed character of cuneiform writing develops some of Bottéro's observations (pp. 154-57).

39. Ibid., pp. 191-92.

40. Ibid., pp. 89 ff.

41. Ibid., p. 172.

42. Ibid., p. 192.
43. See the essay by H. Diller, "Οψισ Αδηλων Τα Φαιηομενα," in *Hermes* 67 (1932): 14-42, esp. 20 ff. The juxtaposition proposed there between analogical and semiotic methods will have to be corrected, interpreting the latter as the "empirical use" of analogy: see E. Melandri, *La linea e il circolo: Studio logico-filosofico sull'analogia* (Bologna, 1968), pp. 25 ff. J.-P. Vernant's statement ("Parole et signes muets," in *Divination et rationalité*, p. 19) according to which "political, historical, medical, philosophic and scientific progress consecrates the break with divinatory mentality," seems to identify the latter exclusively with inspired divination (but see what Vernant himself states at p. 11 in regard to the unresolved problem constituted by the coexistence, even in Greece, of the two forms of divination, inspired and analytical). An implicit devaluation of Hippocratic symptomatology is evident on p. 24; cf., instead, Melandri, *La linea*, p. 251, and especially the book by Détienne and Vernant cited at note 45, below.
44. See the introduction by M. Vegetti to Hippocrates, *Opere* (Turin, 1965), pp. 22-23. For Alcmeon's fragment, see *Pitagorici: Testimonianze e frammenti*, ed. M.Timpanaro Cardini (Florence, 1958), 1:146 ff.
45. On all this see the rich study by M. Détienne and J.-P. Vernant, *Cunning Intelligence in Greek Culture and Society*, trans. Janet Lloyd (New York, 1978). The divinatory attributes of Metis are alluded to at pp. 104 ff.: but see also pp. 145-49 for the connection between the types of knowledge listed and divination (apropos sailors) and pp. 270 ff. On medicine, see pp. 297 ff.; on the relationship between disciples of Hippocrates and Thucydides, see Vegetti's introduction to Hippocrates, *Opere*, p. 59 (but also Diller, *Hermes* 67:22-23). The ties between medicine and historiography should also be investigated from the reverse perspective: see the studies on "autopsy" recorded by A. Momigliano, "Storiografia greca," *Rivista storica italiana* 87 (1975): 45. The presence of women in the circle dominated by *metis* (see Détienne and Vernant, *Cunning Intelligence*, pp. 20, 267) raises problems which I shall discuss in a later version of this article.
46. Hippocrates, *Opere*, pp. 143-44.
47. See P. K. Feyerabend, *Probleme des Empirismus* (Braunschweig, 1981) (*I problemi dell'empirismo* [Milan, 1971], pp. 105 ff.); idem, *Against Method* (London and New York, 1978); and the critical comments by P. Rossi, *Immagini della scienza* (Rome, 1977), pp. 149-50.
48. The *coniector* is a prophet. Here and elsewhere I am following observations made by S. Timpanaro but am putting them in a different (even opposite) perspective: see Timpanaro, *Il lapsus freudiano: Psicanalisi e critica testuale* (Florence, 1974) (in English as *The Freudian Slip: Psychoanalysis and Textual Criticism* [London, 1976; rpt. Shocken Books, 1985]). Briefly, while Timpanaro rejects psychoanalysis because it is closely related to magic, I try to demonstrate that not only psychoanalysis but also the majority of the so-called humane sciences are inspired by a divinatory type of epistemology (see the last part of this essay for its implications). Timpanaro had already alluded to the individualizing explanations of magic and to the individualizing instincts of two such sciences as medicine and philology (*Il lapsus*, pp.71-73).
49. M. Bloch wrote some memorable pages on the "probable" character of

historical knowledge: *The Historian's Craft* (New York, 1962). Its characteristics of indirect knowledge, based on traces, have been emphasized by K. Pomian, "L'histoire de la science et l'histoire de l'histoire," *Annales: E.S.C.* 30 (1975): 935-52, who implicitly reexamines (pp. 949-50) Bloch's observations on the importance of the critical method developed by Maurists (see *The Historian's Craft*, pp. 81 ff.). Pomian's rich study concludes with a brief look at the differences between "history" and "science," but he does not mention the individualizing attitude of various types of knowledge (see "L'histoire," pp. 951-52). On the connection between medicine and historical knowledge, see M. Foucault, *Microfisica del potere: Interventi politici* (Turin, 1977), p. 45, and the text at note 44 above; but for a different viewpoint, see G.-G. Granger, *Pensée formelle et sciences de l'homme* (Paris, 1967), pp. 206 ff. The insistence on the individualizing characteristics of historical knowledge is suspect because too often it has been associated with the attempt to base it on empathy or on an identification of history with art, etc. Obviously, this paper is written from a totally different perspective.

50. On the impact of the invention of writing, see J. Goody and I. Watt, "The Consequences of Literacy," *Comparative Studies in Society and History* 5 (1962-63): 304-45, and, more recently, J. Goody, *The Domestication of the Savage Mind* (Cambridge, 1977). See also E. A. Havelock, *Preface to Plato* (Oxford, 1963). On the history of textual criticism after the invention of printing, see E. J. Kenney, *The Classical Text: Aspects of Editing in the Age of Printed Books* (Berkeley, 1974).

51. The distinction proposed by Croce between "to express" and "to extrinsicate" artistically grasps (even if in a mystifying way) the historical process of the purification of the notion of text which I have attempted to outline here. The extension of this distinction to art in general (obvious from Croce's point of view) is unsupportable.

52. See S. Timpanaro, *La genesi del metodo Lachmann* (Florence, 1963). On page 1 he presents the foundation of *recensio* as the element making a discipline scientific which before the nineteenth century had been an "art" more than a "science" because it was identified with *emendatio*, or conjectural art.

53. See the aphorism by J. Bidez recalled by Timpanaro, *Il lapsus*, p. 72.

54. See G. Galilei, *Il Saggiatore*, ed. L. Sosio (Milan, 1965), p. 38. Cf. E. Garin, "La nuova scienza e il simbolo del 'libro,' " in *La cultura filosofica del Rinascimento italiano: Ricerche e documenti* (Florence, 1961), pp. 451-65, who discusses the interpretation of this and other passages from Galileo proposed by E. R. Curtius from a perspective resembling my own.

55. Galilei, *Il Saggiatore*, p. 264; my italics. On this point, see also J. A. Martinez, "Galileo on Primary and Secondary Qualities," *Journal of the History of Behavioral Sciences* 10 (1974): 160-69.

56. For Cesi and Ciampoli, see the text below; for Faber, see G. Galilei, *Opere* (Florence, 1935), 13:207.

57. See J. N. Eritreo [G. V. Rossi], *Pinacotheca imaginum illustrium, doctrinae vel ingenii laude, virorum* (Leipzig, 1692), 2:79-82. Naudé, along with Rossi, judged Mancini "a great and consummate atheist": see R. Pintard, *Le libertinage érudit dans la première moitié du XVIIe siècle*, 2 vols. (Paris, 1943), 1:261-62.

58. See G. Mancini, *Considerazioni sulla pittura*, ed. A. Marucchi, 2 vols. (Rome, 1956-57). D. Mahon, *Studies in Seicento Art and Theory* (London, 1947), pp. 279 ff., has emphasized Mancini's importance as "connoisseur." J. Hesse, "Note manciniane," *Münchener Jahrbuch der bildenden Kunst*, 3rd ser., 19 (1968): 103-20, is rich in information but too restrictive in his judgment.

59. See F. Haskell, *Patrons and Painters: A Study in the Relations between Italian Art and Society in the Age of the Baroque* (New York, 1971), p. 126; see also the chapter "The Private Patron," pp. 94 ff.

60. See Mancini, *Considerazioni*, 1:133 ff.

61. Eritreo, *Pinacotheca*, pp. 80-81; my italics. Further on (p. 82) another of Mancini's diagnoses which turned out to be correct (the patient was Urban VIII) was called "either divine inspiration, or prophecy" ("seu vaticinatio, seu praedictio").

62. Engravings obviously pose a different problem than do paintings. A general tendency exists today to dismiss the uniqueness of representational art; but opposite tendencies exist, which also confirm uniqueness (of *performance* instead of the work itself: *body art, landscape art*).

63. All this naturally presupposes W. Benjamin, "The Work of Art in the Age of Mechanical Reproduction," in *Illuminations* (New York, 1973), pp. 217-51. Benjamin, however, speaks only of figurative works of art. Their uniqueness, and especially that of paintings, is contrasted to the mechanical reproduction of literary texts by E. Gilson, *Peinture et réalité* (Paris, 1958), pp. 93, and especially pp. 95-96 (I owe this reference to the kindness of Renato Turci). But for Gilson the contrast is intrinsic, and not of a historical character, as I have attempted to demonstrate here. De Chirico's "faking" of his own works shows how the modern notion of the absolute uniqueness of the work of art tends actually to leave out of consideration the biological unity of the individual artist.

64. See a remark by L. Salerno in Mancini, *Considerazioni*, 2: xxiv, n. 55.

65. Ibid., 1:134; at the end of the reference I have changed "painting" to "writing," as sense requires.

66. I am proposing the name of Allacci for the following reasons. In a previous passage, similar to the one cited, Mancini speaks of "librarians, especially Vatican librarians," capable of dating ancient Greek and Latin writings (ibid., p. 106). Both passages are lacking in the shorter redaction, the so-called *Discorso di pittura*, completed by Mancini before November 13, 1619 (ibid., p. xxx). (The text of the *Discorso* is on pp. 291 ff.; the section on the "identification of paintings" is on pp. 327-30.) Allacci was named "scriptor" at the Vatican Library in mid-1619; see J. Bignami-Odier, *La bibliothèque vaticane de Sixte IV à Pie XI* (Vatican City, 1973), p. 129; recent studies on Allacci are listed on pp. 128-31. Moreover, no one in Rome during these years except for Allacci possessed the expertise in Greek and Latin paleography mentioned by Mancini. On the importance of Allacci's paleographical ideas, see E. Casamassima, "Per una storia delle dottrine paleografiche dall'Umanesimo a Jean Mabillon," *Studi medievali*, 3rd ser., 5 (1964): 532, n. 9. Casamassima also suggests the connection between Allacci and Mabillon, referring us for the necessary documentation to the sequel to his article, which, unfortunately, has not appeared. No evidence of dealings

with Mancini emerges from Allacci's correspondence preserved in the Biblioteca Vallicelliana in Rome. The two, however, were members of the same intellectual circles, as demonstrated by their common friendship with G. V. Rossi (see Pintard, *Le libertinage*, 1:259). On the good relations between Allacci and Maffeo Barberini before the latter's pontificate, see G. Mercati, *Note per la storia di alcune biblioteche romane nei secoli XVI–XIX* (Vatican City, 1952) p. 26, n. 1. As I have said, Mancini was Urban VIII's physician.

67. See Mancini, *Considerazioni*, 1:107; C. Baldi, *Trattato* ... (Carpi, 1622), pp. 17 ff. On Baldi, who also wrote on physiognomics and divination, see the entry under his name in the *Dizionario biografico degli italiani*, 5 (1963): 465-67, written by M. Tronti, who concludes by making his own Moréri's disparaging opinion: "On peut bien le mettre dans le catalogue de ceux qui ont écrit sur des sujets de néant." Note that in his *Discorso di pittura*, which he finished before November 13, 1619 (see note 66), Mancini wrote: "The individual properties of writing have been discussed by that noble spirit who, in that booklet of his which is now circulating among us, attempted to demonstrate and explain the causes of these properties, so that, from the manner of the writing he has thought to be able to give information about the temperament and habits of the writer, a curious and beautiful thing, but a little too short." Mancini, *Considerazioni* 1:306-7. The passage poses two difficulties to the identification with Baldi suggested above: (*a*) the first printed edition of Baldi's *Trattato* appeared at Carpi in 1622; thus, in 1619, or just before, it could not have been available as a "booklet ... which is now circulating among us"; (*b*) in his *Discorso* Mancini speaks of a "noble spirit," but in the *Considerazioni* of "fine minds." But both difficulties are resolved in light of the printer's note to the reader in the first edition of Baldi's *Trattato*: "The author of this little treatise, when he wrote it, never gave a thought to whether it would be published or not; but because a certain person, who worked as a secretary, published under his name many writings, letters, and other compositions which belonged to others, I thought it only proper to see that the truth should be made known, and credit be given where it was due." Clearly Mancini first knew the "booklet" of that "secretary," whom I have not succeeded in identifying, and then later also Baldi's *Trattato*, which circulated in manuscript form in a slightly different version from the one that was eventually printed (it can be read, together with other writings of Baldi's, in MS. 142 of the Biblioteca Classense, Ravenna).

68. Mancini, *Considerazioni*, 1:134.

69. See A. Averlino [Filarete], *Trattato di Architettura*, ed. A. M. Finoli and L. Grassi (Milan, 1972), 1:28 (but see in general pp. 25-28). The passage is noted as a foretaste of the "Morellian" method in J. Schlosser Magnino, *La letteratura artistica* (Florence, 1977), p. 160.

70. See, for example, M. Scalzini, *Il secretario* (Venice, 1585), p. 20: "Who becomes accustomed to this form of writing, in a very short time loses the speed and natural openness of the hand." Also, G. F. Cresci, *L'idea* (Milan, 1622), p. 84, who remarks on "those strokes with so many flourishes, which they have boasted of doing in their writing with only one pass of the pen."

71. See Scalzini, *Il secretario*, pp. 77-78: "But if these people who courteously answer, that they write leisurely with graceful line and polish, if they were

called to the service of some prince or lord, who needed, as often happens, to write forty or fifty long letters in four or five hours, and if they were called to his chamber to write, how long would it take them to perform this service?" This tirade is directed against certain unnamed "boastful masters" accused of practicing a slow and tiring chancery hand.

72. E. Casamassima, *Trattati di scrittura del Cinquecento italiano* (Milan, 1966), pp. 75-76.

73. "... this very great book, which nature continually holds open before those who have eyes on the forehead and the brain" (quoted and discussed by E. Raimondi, *Il romanzo senza idillio: Saggio sui 'Promessi Sposi'* [Turin, 1974], pp. 23-24).

74. Averlino [Filarete], *Trattato*, pp. 26-27.

75. See Bottéro, *Symptômes*, p. 101, who traces the lesser use in divination of minerals, vegetables, and, to a certain extent, animals, to their presumed "formal poverty," rather than, more simply, to an anthropocentric perspective.

76. See *Rerum medicarum Novae Hispaniae Thesaurus seu plantarum animalium mineralium Mexicanorum Historia ex Francisci Hernandez novi orbis medici primarii relationibus in ipsa Mexicana urbe conscriptis a Nardo Antonio Reccho ... collecta ac in ordinem digesta a Ioanne Terrentio Lynceo ... notis illustrata* (Rome, 1651), pp. 599 ff.; this is part of the section written by Giovanni Faber, not acknowledged on the title page. On the importance of this book see the perceptive remarks by Raimondi, *Il romanzo*, pp. 25 ff.

77. See Mancini, *Considerazioni*, 1:107, who, in citing a writing by Francesco Giuntino, alludes to Dürer's horoscope. The editor of the *Considerazioni*, 2:60, n. 483, does not specify the work in question; cf., instead, Giuntino's *Speculum astrologiae* (Lyon, 1573), p. 269*v*.

78. See *Rerum medicarum*, pp. 600-627. It was Urban VIII himself who urged that the illustrated description be printed (ibid., p. 599). On the interest in landscape painting in these circles, see A. Ottani Cavina, "On the Theme of Landscape, II: Elsheimer and Galileo," *Burlington Magazine*, 118 (1976): 139-44.

79. See Raimondi's stimulating essay "Towards Realism," in his *Romanzo*, pp. 3 ff. – even if, following Whitehead (pp. 18-19), he tends to reduce unduly the opposition between the two paradigms, one abstract-mathematical, the other concrete-descriptive. On the contrast between classical and Baconian sciences, see T. S. Kuhn, "Tradition mathématique et tradition expérimentale dans le développement de la physique," *Annales: E.S.C.* 30 (1975): 975-98.

80. See, e.g., "Craig's Rules of Historical Evidence, 1699," *History and Theory: Beiheft 4*, 1964.

81. On this theme, hardly touched upon here, see the important book by I. Hacking, *The Emergence of Probability: A Philosophical Study of Early Ideas about Probability, Induction, and Statistical Inference* (Cambridge, 1975). I have found useful M. Ferriani's review article "Storia e 'preistoria' del concetto di probabilità nell'età moderna," *Rivista di filosofia* 10 (1978): 129-53.

82. P.J.G. Cabanis, *An Essay on the Certainty of Medicine* (Philadelphia, 1823).

83. On the subject, see M. Foucault, *The Birth of the Clinic: An Archeology of Medical Perception* (New York, 1973); idem, *Microfisica*, pp. 192-93.

84. See also my *The Cheese and the Worms: The Cosmos of a Sixteenth-Century Miller* (Baltimore, 1980), pp. 58-60.
85. I am returning here, but from a somewhat different perspective, to points made by Foucault in *Microfisica*, pp. 167-69.
86. J. J. Winckelmann, to G. L. Bianconi, April 30, 1763 (from Rome), in Winckelmann's *Briefe*, ed. H. Diepolder and W. Rehm, (Berlin, 1954), 2:316 and 498n.
87. The allusion to "small insights" is found in *Briefe* (Berlin, 1952), 1:391.
88. This is true for more than the *Bildungsroman*. From this point of view, the novel is the true descendant of the fairy tale; see V. I. Propp, *Le radici storiche dei racconti di fate* (Turin, 1949).
89. See E. Cerulli, "Una raccolta persiana di novelle tradotte a Venezia nel 1557," *Atti dell'Accademia Nazionale dei Lincei: Memorie della classe di scienze morali*, 8th ser., 18 (1975); on Sercambi, see ibid., pp. 347 ff. Cerulli's essay on the sources and on the diffusion of the *Peregrinaggio* should be considered, as far as the eastern origins of the story are concerned, in conjunction with the references in note 31, above, and with its indirect flowering, by way of *Zadig*, into the detective story (see the text below).
90. Cerulli (ibid.) mentions a number of translations: into German, French, English and Dutch (both from the French), and Danish (from the German). This list may have to be supplemented on the basis of a work which I have been unable to see: *Serendipity and the Three Princes: From the Peregrinaggio of 1557*, ed. T. G. Remer (Norman, Okla., 1965), who records editions and translations (pp. 184-90). Cf. W. S. Heckscher, "Petites perceptions: An Account of Sortes Warburgianae," *Journal of Medieval and Renaissance Studies* 4 (1974): 131, n. 46.
91. Heckscher, "Petites perceptions," pp. 130-31. Here Heckscher develops an observation from his own "The Genesis of Iconology," in *Stil und Ueberlieferung in der Kunst des Abendlandes*, Akten des XXI Internationalen Kongresses für Kunstgeschichte in Bonn, 1964 (Berlin, 1967), 3:245, n. 11. These two essays by Heckscher, extremely rich in ideas and references, examine the birth of Aby Warburg's method from a perspective which resembles, at least in part, the one adopted here. In a future revision I intend to consider the Leibnizian approach proposed by Heckscher.
92. Voltaire, "Zadig," in *Voltaire's "Candide," "Zadig," and Selected Short Stories*, ed. D. M. Frame (Bloomington, 1966), pp. 110-11.
93. See, in general, R. Méssac, *Le "detective novel" et l'influence de la pensée scientifique* (Paris, 1929), which is excellent, though now partly outdated. On the connection between the *Peregrinaggio* and *Zadig*, see Méssac, pp. 17 ff. and pp. 211-12.
94. "Aujourd'hui, quelqu'un qui voit seulement la piste d'un pied fourchu peut on conclure que l'animal qui a laissé cette empreinte ruminait, et cette conclusion est tout aussi certaine qu'aucune autre en physique et en morale. Cette seule piste donne donc à celui qui l'observe, et la forme des dents, et la forme des mâchoires, et la forme des vertèbres, et la forme de tous les os des jambes, des cuisses, des épaules et du bassin de l'animal qui vient de passer: c'est une marque plus sûre que toutes celles de Zadig." Ibid., pp. 34-35 (quoted from G. Cuvier, *Recherches sur les ossements fossiles* [Paris, 1834], 1:185).
95. See T. Huxley, "On the Method of Zadig: Retrospective Prophecy as a

Function of Science," in *Science and Culture* (London, 1881), pp. 128-48 (a lecture from the previous year to which Méssac, *Le "detective novel,"* p. 37, drew attention). On p. 132 Huxley explained that "even in the restricted sense of 'divination,' it is obvious that the essence of the prophetic operation does not lie in its backward or forward relation to the course of time, but in the fact that it is the apprehension of that which lies out of the sphere of immediate knowledge: the seeing of that which to the natural sense of the seer is invisible." Cf. also E. H. Gombrich, "The Evidence of Images," in *Interpretation*, ed. C. S. Singleton (Baltimore, 1969), pp. 35 ff.

96. See [J.-B. Dubos], *Réflexions critiques sur la poësie et sur la peinture* (Paris, 1729), 2:362-65 (quoted in part by Zerner, "Giovanni Morelli," p. 215n).

97. E. Gaboriau, *Monsieur Lecoq, I: L'enquête* (Paris, 1877), p. 44. On p. 25 the "recent theory" of the young Lecoq is contrasted to the "antiquated practice" of the old policeman Gévrol, "champion of the positivist police method" (p. 20), who stops at appearances and therefore does not succeed in seeing anything.

98. On the long popular success of phrenology in England (long after official science was looking upon it haughtily), see D. De Giustino, *Conquest of Mind: Phrenology and Victorian Social Thought* (London, 1975).

99. "My inquiry led me to the conclusion ... that the anatomy of this civil society ... has to be sought in political economy." K. Marx, *A Contribution to the Critique of Political Economy* (London, 1971), p. 20 (the sentence comes from the preface, written in 1859).

100. See Morelli, *Della pittura*, p. 71. Zerner ("Giovanni Morelli") has maintained, on the basis of this passage, that Morelli distinguished three levels: (*a*) the general characteristics of a school; (*b*) individual characteristics, revealed by hands, ears, etc.; (*c*) mannerisms introduced "unintentionally." Actually (*b*) and (*c*) resemble one another: see Morelli's reference to the "overly fleshy thumbs of male hands" in Titian's paintings, a "mistake" which a copyist would have avoided. *Le opere dei maestri italiani nelle gallerie di Monaco, Dresda e Berlino* (Bologna, 1886), p. 174.

101. An echo of Mancini's writings, analyzed above, could have reached Morelli by means of F. Baldinucci, *Lettera ... nella quale risponde ad alcuni quesiti in materia di pittura* (Rome, 1681), pp. 7-8, and L. Lanzi, *Storia pittorica dell'Italia*, ed. M. Capucci (Florence, 1968). To the best of my knowledge, Morelli never cites Mancini's *Considerazioni*.

102. See *L'identité: Séminaire interdisciplinaire dirigé par Claude Lévi-Strauss* (Paris, 1977).

103. A. Caldara, *L'indicazione dei connotati nei documenti papiracei dell'Egitto greco-romano* (Milan, 1924).

104. Lanzi, *Storia pittorica*, 1:15.

105. E. P. Thompson, *Whigs and Hunters: The Origin of the Black Act* (London, 1975).

106. M. Foucault, *Discipline and Punish: The Birth of the Prison* (New York, 1977).

107. M. Perrot, "Délinquance et système pénitentiaire en France au XIXe siècle," *Annales: E.S.C.* 30 (1975): 67-91, esp. 68.

108. See A. Bertillon, *L'identité des récidivistes et la loi de relégation* (Paris, 1883), p. 24 (reprinted from *Annales de démographie internationale*); E. Locard, *L'identification des récidivistes* (Paris, 1909). The Waldeck-Rousseau law, which

required prison sentences for the relapsed and deportation for the "incorrigible," dates to 1885. See Perrot, "Délinquance," p. 68.

109. Branding was abolished in France in 1832. Both *The Count of Monte Cristo* and *The Three Musketeers* date from 1844; *Les Miserables* is from 1869. The list of ex-convicts who populate French literature of the period could be greatly extended: Vautrin, etc. See, in general, L. Chevalier, *Laboring Classes and Dangerous Classes in Paris during the First Half of the Nineteenth Century* (London, 1973), esp. chs. 2-5.

110. See the problems raised by Bertillon, *L'identité*, p. 10.

111. See A. Lacassagne, *Alphonse Bertillon: L'homme, le savant, la pensée philosophique*, and E. Locard, *L'oeuvre de Alphonse Bertillon* (Lyon, 1914), p. 28 (reprinted from *Archives d'anthropologie criminelle, de médicine légale, et de psychologie normale et pathologique*).

112. Locard, *L'oeuvre de Alphonse Bertillon*, p. 11.

113. See A. Bertillon, *Identification anthropométrique: Instruction signalétiques*, new ed. (Melun, 1893), p. xlviii: "Mais là où les mérites transcendants de l'oreille pour l'identification apparaissent le plus nettement, c'est quand il s'agit d'affirmer solennellement en justice que telle ancienne photographie 'est bien et dûment applicable à tel sujet ici present' ... il est impossible de trouver deux oreilles semblables et ... l'identité de son modelé est une condition necessaire et suffisante pour confirmer l'identité individuelle," except in the case of twins. Cf. idem, *Album* (Melun, 1893), plate 60b (which accompanies the preceding work). On Sherlock Holmes's admiration for Bertillon, see F. Lacassin, *Mythologie du roman policier* (Paris, 1974), 1:93 (who also cites the passage on the ears cited in note 9, above).

114. See Locard, *L'oeuvre de Bertillon*, p. 27. Because of his expertise as a graphologist, Bertillon was consulted in the Dreyfus affair over the authenticity of the celebrated *bordereau*. Because he expressed an opinion clearly supporting Dreyfus's guilt, Bertillon's career was damaged, in the polemical opinion of biographers: see Lacassagne, *Alphonse Bertillon*, p. 4.

115. F. Galton, *Finger Prints* (London, 1892), with a bibliography of the prior publications.

116. See J. E. Purkynê, *Opera selecta* (Prague, 1948), pp. 29-56.

117. Ibid., pp. 30-32, from which the remainder of this paragraph is drawn.

118. See Galton, *Finger Prints*, pp. 24 ff.

119. See L. Vandermeersch, "De la tortue à l'achillée," in *Divination et rationalité*, pp. 29 ff., and J. Gernet, "Petits écarts et grands écarts," ibid., pp. 52 ff.

120. See Galton, *Finger Prints*, pp. 27–28 (and the expression of thanks at p. 4). Galton refers on pp. 26-27 to a prior episode which had no practical consequences, a photographer in San Francisco who had thought he could identify the members of the Chinese community by means of fingerprints.

121. Ibid., pp. 17-18.

122. Ibid., p. 169. For the statement which follows, see Foucault, *Microfisica*, p. 158.

123. The reference here is to L. Traube, "Geschichte der Paläographie," in *Zur Paläographie und Handschriftenkunde*, ed. P. Lehmann, vol. 1 (Munich, 1965 [photographic reprint of the 1909 ed.]). Attention was called to this passage by A. Campana, "Paleografia oggi: Rapporti, problemi, e prospettive di una

'coraggiosa disciplina,' " *Studi urbinati* 41 (1967), n.s. B, *Studi in onore di Arturo Massolo*, 2:1028; A. Warburg, *Die Erneuerung der heidnischen Antike* (Leipzig & Berlin, 1932), whose first essay dates from 1893; L. Spitzer, *Die Wortbildung als stilistisches Mittel exemplifiziert an Rabelais* (Halle, 1910); M. Bloch, *The Royal Touch: Sacred Monarchy and Scrofula in England and France* (London, 1973). The examples could be extended: see G. Agamben, "Aby Warburg e la scienza senza nome," *Settanta*, July-September 1975, p. 15 (where Warburg and Spitzer are cited; on p. 10 there is mention also of Traube).

124. In addition to Campanella's *Political Aphorisms*, which originally appeared in a Latin translation as part of the *Realis philosophia* (*De politica in aphorismos digesta*), see G. Canini, *Aforismi politici cavati dall' "Historia d'Italia" di M. Francesco Guicciardini* (Venice, 1625), on which see T. Bozza, *Scrittori politici italiani dal 1550 al 1650* (Rome, 1949), pp. 141-43, 151-52. See also the entry for "Aphorisme" in the *Dictionnaire* of Littré.

125. Even if it was originally used in a juridical sense; for a brief history of the term, see R. Koselleck, *Critique and Crisis: Enlightenment and the Pathogenesis of Modern Society* (Cambridge, Mass., 1988).

126. I shall deal with this point more fully in a later version of this essay.

127. See Stendhal, *Memoirs of an Egotist*, ed. D. Ellis (London, 1975), p. 71: "Victor [Jacquemont] seems to me a man of the highest distinction – just as a connoisseur (forgive the word) sees a beautiful horse in a four-month-old foal whose legs are still swollen." Stendhal is excusing himself with the reader for using a word of French origin such as *connoisseur* with the meaning that it had acquired in England. See Zerner's remark ("Giovanni Morelli," p. 215, n. 4) that even today there is no word in French equivalent to *connoisseurship*.

128. See the rich and perceptive book by Y. Mourad, *La physiognomonie arabe et la "Kîtab Al-Firâsa" de Fakhr Al-Dîn Al-Râzî* (Paris, 1939), pp. 1-2.

129. See the extraordinary episode attributed to Al-Shâfi'i (ninth century A.D.), ibid., pp. 60-61, which reads like something out of Borges. The connection between the *firâsa* and the feats of the sons of the king of Serendipity has been duly noted by Méssac, *Le "detective novel."*

130. See Mourad, *La physiognomonie*, p. 29, who lists the following classifications for the various types of physiognomics contained in the treatise by Tashköpru Zâdeh (A.D. 1560): (1) the science of wens or moles; (2) chiromancy; (3) scapulimancy; (4) divination by means of footprints; (5) genealogical science by means of the inspection of the members of the body and the skin; (6) the art of finding one's way in the desert; (7) the art of discovering springs; (8) the art of discovering places containing metals; (9) the art of forecasting rain; (10) prophecy by means of past and present events; (11) prophecy by means of involuntary movements of the body. On pp. 15 ff. Mourad proposes an extremely interesting comparison, deserving further study, between Arabic physiognomics and the research of the Gestalt school of psychology on the perception of individuality.

[This essay has provoked numerous comments and rejoinders (including one by I. Calvino in *La Repubblica*, January 21, 1980) which would be superfluous to list here. I shall cite only what appeared in *Quaderni storici* 6, no. 11 (1980): 3-18 (writings by A. Carandini and M. Vegetti); ibid., no. 12, pp. 3-54 (pieces by several individuals and my reply); and *Freibeuter*, 1980, no. 5. Marisa Dalai has made me note, in regard to Morelli, that I should have cited the perceptive observations of J. von Schlosser, "Die Wiener Schule der Kunstgeschichte," *Mitteilungen des Oesterreichischen Instituts für Geschichtsforschung*, Ergänzungs-Band 13, no. 2 (1934): 165 ff.]

Germanic Mythology and Nazism: Thoughts on an Old Book by Georges Dumézil

I should like to thank Kyung Ryong Lee, Arnaldo Momigliano, Adriano Prosperi, Gianni Sofri, and Jean Starobinski for their suggestions and references. Naturally, the responsibility for what I have written is mine alone.

1. See, most recently, Dumézil's statements in 1980 to J. Bonnet and D. Pralon, in F. Desbordes et al., *Georges Dumézil* (Paris, 1981), pp. 20-23. The caesura of 1938 is openly acknowledged (p. 341) even in the critical bibliography which closes out the volume.

2. See G. Dumézil, *Les dieux des Germains: Essai sur la formation de la religion scandinave* (Paris, 1959), p. 1; translated into English as *Gods of the Ancient Northmen* (Berkeley and Los Angeles, 1973), p. xlv.

3. A. Momigliano, "Premesse per una discussione su Georges Dumézil," *Opus* 2 (1983): 331. This issue of *Opus* contains several essays, almost all of which were presented at a seminar on Dumézil held in Pisa in January 1983.

4. Curiously, *Mythes et dieux* is not listed either in the catalogues of the Bibliothéque Nationale (Paris) or in the library of the Sorbonne. In the British Library it is reported as "mislaid." I have located two copies: in the Carolina Rediviva in Uppsala and in the Deutsche Archäologisches Institut, Rome.

5. S. Gutenbrunner, review of *Mythes et dieux des Germains*, by G. Dumézil, *Deutsche Literaturzeitung* 61 (1940): cols. 943-45.

6. M. Bloch, review of *Mythes et dieux des Germains*, by G. Dumézil, *Revue Historique* 188 (1940): 274-76.

7. G. Dumézil, *Mythes et dieux des Germains* (Paris, 1939), pp. 153-57. The comment by C. S. Littleton (*The New Comparative Mythology* [Berkeley and Los Angeles, 1982], p. 63) is scandalously shallow: "It was perhaps ironic that it was in 1939, the year Hitler's legions began their grisly march, that Dumézil first focused his attention upon the Germanic branch of the I.E. speaking world."

8. Dumézil, *Mythes et dieux des Germains*, pp. 79 ff., esp. pp. 90-91.

9. Ibid., p. 157.

10. Ibid., pp. 138-39. On these aspects of Nazi propaganda, see, in general, G. L. Mosse, *The Nationalization of the Masses* (New York, 1975).

11. See what Dumézil himself states in the interview cited above (Desbordes, *Georges Dumézil*, p. 20).

12. See J. Le Goff's introduction to M. Bloch, *Les rois thaumaturges* (Paris, 1983), p. iv, and Bloch's "Pour une histoire comparée des sociétés européennes," in his *Mélanges historiques* (Paris, 1963), 1:16-40.

13. M. Bloch, *Les caractères originaux de l'histoire rurale française* (Paris, 1952), pp. xiv, 46 ff.

14. Bloch, *Apologies pour l'histoire; ou, Métier d'historien* (Paris, 1949).

15. Bloch, *La société feodale: Les classes et le gouvernement des hommes* (Paris, 1940), pp. 47 ff. Dumézil's reference to the *Roi thaumaturges* is in *Mythes et dieux*, p. 53.

16. A. Grenier, review of *Mythes et dieux des Germains*, by G. Dumézil, *Revue des Études Anciennes* 41 (1939): 378-79.

17. *Discours de réception de M. Georges Dumézil à l'Académie Française et réponse de M. Claude Lévi-Strauss* (Paris, 1979), pp. 73-74.

18. See the introduction of F. Jesi to G. Dumézil, *Ventura e sventura del guerriero* (Turin, 1974), pp. xii ff.

19. See J.-Cl. Rivière, "Actualité de Georges Dumézil," *Elements*, Novembre-Decembre 1979, pp. 15-17; G. Dumézil in Desbordes, *Georges Dúmezil*, p. 39; and the passage cited by J. Scheid in *Opus* 2 (1983): 352, n. 1: "What is the 'Indo-European mind'? I can only tell you that everything I have discovered of the Indo-European world would have horrified me. I would not have liked to live in a society which had a *Männerbund* ... or druids."

20. H. Schurtz, *Altersklassen und Männerbunde* (Berlin, 1902); H. Usener, "Ueber vergleichende Sitten und Rechtsgeschichte," in *Verhandlungen der 42. Versammlung deutscher Philologen und Schulmänner in Wien*, 1893.

21. L. Weiser, *Altgermanische Jünglingsweihen und Männerbünde* (Baden, 1927), which also cites M. Zeller, *Die Knabenweihen: Eine ethnologische Studie* (Bern, 1923), a comprehensive survey in which Reik's contribution had already received ample attention: see pp. 120ff.

22. See W. E. Peuckert and O. Lauffer, *Volkskunde: Quellen und Forschungen seit 1930* (Bern, 1951), p. 118, where a distinction is made between Weiser's *bündisch* inspiration and O. Höfler's and R. Stumpfl's, "influenced by the political events" (read: Nazism). W. Emmerich, *Germanistiche Volkstumideologie* (Tübingen, 1968), p. 202, generically groups the positions of the three schools under the label of the school of Much.

23. See W. Laqueur, *Young Germany: A History of the German Youth Movement* (London, 1962).

24. See Weiser, *Altgermanische Jünglingsweihen*, p. 24.

25. Ibid., p. 51.

26. Ibid., p. 48. Weiser returned to this subject in an important essay, "Zur Geschichte der altgermanischen Todesstrafe und Friedlosigkeit," *Archiv für Religionswissenschaft* 30 (1933): 209-27.

27. O. Höfler, *Kultische Geheimbünde der Germanen* (Frankfort a.M., 1934). R. Stumpfl, *Kultspiele der Germanen als Ursprung des mittelalterlichen Dramas* (Berlin, 1936), p. x, mentioned the existence of a second volume and said that he had used it. Höfler noted in the introduction to *Kultische Geheimbünde* (p. xi, n. 1) that the book, which originally was to be entitled *Totenheer-Kultbund-Fastnachtspiel*, was already basically completed in January 1932.

28. Note that Chapter 6 ("Les Guerriers-Fauves") of *Mythes et dieux des Germains*, heavily based on Höfler's work, is taken up again in part in Dumézil's *The Destiny of the Warrior* (Chicago, 1970). See also Höfler's introduction to the German translation of G. Dumézil, *Loki* (Darmstadt, 1959) and Dumézil's contribution to the *Festgabe* for Höfler's seventy-fifth birthday (Vienna, 1976), which contained essays by M. Eliade, S.

Gutenbrunner (author of the review of *Mythes et dieux des Germains* cited in note 5), and others. G. Windengren, *Der Feudalismus im alten Iran* (Cologne and Opladen, 1969), pp. 45 ff., suggests that the work of Weiser and Höfler should be used with caution. By Weiser-Aall, see *Volkskunde und Psychologie: Eine Einführung* (Berlin and Leipzig, 1937), pp. 105-6; by S. Wikander, see *Der arische Männerbund: Studien zur indo-iranischen Sprach- und Religionsgeschichte* (Lund, 1938), pp. 64 ff. See the very favorable review of K. Meuli in *Schweizerisches Archiv für Volkskunde* 34 (1935): 77, and Meuli's considerably more critical opinion in "Schweizer Masken und Maskenbräuche" (1943), now in K. Meuli, *Gesammelte Schriften*, ed. Th. Gelzer, 2 vols., with continuous pagination (Basel and Stuttgart, 1975), p. 227, n. 3. It should be noted that, beginning in 1938, Meuli took a publicly anti-Nazi position: see the biographical appendix by F. Jung, ibid., pp. 1166-67. On Höfler's work (and critical reactions to it), see also A. Closs, "Iranistik und Völkerkunde," in *Monumentum H. S. Nyberg* (Leiden, Teheran, and Liège, 1975), 1:157 ff.

29. Höfler, *Kultische Geheimbünde*, pp. 205-6.
30. Ibid., pp. 277-78. See Emmerich, *Germanistische Volkstumideologie*, pp. 202 ff., for discussions within the orbit of Nazi folklore studies between supporters of the primacy of rite and supporters of the primacy of myth.
31. See N. Cohn, *Europe's Inner Demons* (London, 1975), pp. 107 ff.
32. F. Ranke, "Der Wilde Heer und die Kultbünde der Germanen: Eine Auseinandersetzung mit Otto Höfler" (1940), now in *Kleine Schriften*, ed. H. Rupp and E. Studer (Bern, 1971), pp. 380-408. (Ranke was the only German folklorist to emigrate because he was anti-Nazi: see Emmerich, *Germanistische Volkstumideologie*, p. 159). Höfler replied many years later, restating his old theses, without substantial changes or additions in the documentation: see his *Verwandlungskulte, Volkssagen, und Mythen*, Oesterreichische Akademie der Wissenschaften, Phil.-hist. Klasse, Sitzungsberichte 279 Band, 2 Abhandl. (Vienna, 1973).
33. L. Weiser, *Altgermanische Jünglingsweihen*, pp. 55, 77, 82. I intend to return to these questions in a later work.
34. See Höfler, *Kultische Geheimbünde*, p. 341. On ecstasy, p. 262, n. 337a, is illuminating apropos R. Otto, "Gottheit und Gottheiten der Arier" (1932). On fertility themes, see pp. 87 ff., 286 ff.
35. Thus, Höfler in polemic against F. von der Leyen in *Zeitschrift für deutschen Altertum*, n.s., 73 (1936): 109-15, esp. p. 110. But in the same vein, see also *Kultische Geheimbünde*, p. 15. For some appropriate critical observations, see A. Closs, "Die Religion des Semnonenstammes," *Wiener Beiträge zur Kulturgeschichte und Linguistik* 4 (1936): 665 ff.
36. See K. Meuli, "Die deutschen Masken" (1933), now in *Gesammelte Schriften*, p. 160, where the ritual interpretation later developed by Höfler was already being proposed. The proceedings of the werewolf trial were originally published in *Mitteilungen aus der livländischen Geschichte* 22 (1924).
37. Höfler, *Kultische Geheimbünde*, pp. 345 ff. In a penetrating review, W. Krogmann (*Archiv für das Studium der neueren Sprache*, n.s. 68, Band 90 (1935): esp. 98-100) has noted that Höfler's thesis as a whole was clearly contradicted by this document. I have proposed a completely different interpretation for it in *The Night Battles: Witchcraft and Agrarian Cults in the*

Sixteenth and Seventeenth Centuries (Baltimore, 1983), pp. 28 ff.

38. Höfler, *Kultische Geheimbünde*, p. 357. A similar passage is cited in H. Bausinger's brilliant article, "Volksideologie und Volksforschung: Zur nationalsozialistischen Volksforschung," *Zeitschrift für Volkskunde* 2 (1965): 177-204, esp. p. 189. Höfler reiterated his ideas in a still more explicitly pro-Nazi direction in *Die politische Leistung der Völkerwanderungszeit* (Neumünster, 1939); see especially his concluding pages.

39. The phrase is cited by G. L. Mosse, *The Crisis of German Ideology: Intellectual Origins of the Third Reich* (New York, 1964), p. 216.

40. See Laqueur, *Young Germany*, pp. 109, 193-94. Krebs, chief of the Nazi party in Hamburg, was expelled from the party in 1933.

41. H. Spehr, "Waren die Germanen 'Ekstatiker'?" *Rasse* 3 (1936): 394-400.

42. Bloch, review of Höfler's *Kultische Geheimbünde*, in *Revue historique*, 181 (1937): 437-38 (and cf. pp. 434-35).

43. Mauss's letter is cited in D. Hollier's collection, *Le Collège de Sociologie: Textes de Bataille, Caillois* ... (Paris, 1979), pp. 541 ff. I have made full use of this extremely helpful volume.

44. See Mauss's letter to S. Ranulf cited by S. Lukes, *Emile Durkheim: His Life and Work* (London, 1973), pp. 338-39, n. 71; the original text is published in the superficial essay by S. Ranulf, "Scholarly Forerunners of Fascism," *Ethics* 50 (1939): 16-34.

45. See Hollier, *Le Collège*, pp. 276-77 and passim.

46. Ibid., pp. 23-24.

47. The letter was included in the exhibition in memory of Queneau organized by the Bibliothèque Nationale in 1978, and is mentioned in the catalogue *Raymond Queneau plus intime* (Paris, 1978), n. 383. I cite it from memory.

48. Hollier, *Le Collège*, p. 251.

49. On all this, see the texts reproduced in the appendix, ibid., p. 565 (among which, on pp. 567 ff., is a vulgar attack by Bataille on Georges Sadoul which had appeared in *Commune*, a journal directed by Aragon, among others; both Sadoul and Aragon had to be pardoned by the Communist party for their Surrealist lapses). See also Walter Benjamin's review of Caillois's *L'aridité*, now published in Benjamin's *Gesammelte Schriften* (Frankfort a.M., 1972), 3:549, which concluded: "It is sad to see how a large muddy current is fed from springs situated at a considerable altitude."

50. See Hollier, *Le Collège*, pp. 548-50.

51. Ibid., pp. 421 ff., 323 ff., 447 ff., 164 ff.

52. L. Febvre, "Comment reconstituer la vie affective d'autrefois? La sensibilité et l'histoire," now in Febvre's *Combats pour l'histoire* (Paris, 1953), p. 238.

53. It seems rather astonishing to find as contributors to the *Festschrift* for Herman Hirt (*Germanen und Indogermanen: Volkstum, Sprache, Heimat, Kultur* [Heidelberg, 1936]) the racist publicist H.F.K. Günther or the anthropologist M. Semper (who displayed his own portrait as an example of pure Nordic Aryan race next to that of the Jew Felix Mendelssohn in his essay, "Zur Rassengeschichte der Indogermanen Irans," ibid., 1:341-56, fig. 1) alongside scholars of the level of Dumézil or Benveniste. The presence of Benveniste is doubly surprising since he was Jewish. At any rate, it is worth noting that at the conclusion of his own paper, Benveniste ("Tokharien et Indo-Européen,"

Germanen und Indogermanen, 2:227-40) emphasized the impossibility, on linguistic grounds, of locating the Indo-European *Urheimat* in northern Europe. The editor of the *Festschrift*, H. Arntz, intervened in square brackets to propose the contrary thesis, which had become the official position of Nazi Indo-European studies.

54. Höfler stressed racial ("biological") continuity in *Das Germanische Kontinuitätsproblem* (Hamburg, 1937) alongside the linguistic and the spiritual. Later, he preferred to insist instead on the perpetuity of the archetypes, referring explicitly to M. Eliade: see O. Höfler, *Ueber somatische, psychische, und kulturelle Homologie: Vererbung und Erneuerung*, Oesterreichische Akademie der Wissenschaften, phil.-hist. Kl., Sitzungsberichte, 366. Band, Homologie-Studien zur Germanischen Kulturmorphologie, no. 1 (Vienna, 1980), esp. pp. 38 ff. This concurrence obviously does not mean that interpretations in an archetypal key necessarily have racist implications, but Eliade's youthful leanings in a racist and anti-Semitic direction should not be forgotten. (See F. Jesi, *Cultura di destra* [Milan, 1979], pp. 38 ff.)

55. See F. Desbordes, "Le comparatisme de Georges Dumézil: Une introduction," in Desbordes's *Georges Dumézil*, pp. 45-71, esp. pp. 59-60, who cites as exceptional a reference to a "sometimes almost unconscious" conceptual structure (*L'héritage indo-européen à Rome*, 1949). But in *Mythes et dieux des Germains* Dumézil talked, as we recall, of "spontaneous movement" and of "preestablished congruence between past and present" juxtaposed to cases of "conscious imitation of the past." This very passage has been cited by A. Schnapp as proof of Dumézil's yielding to philo-racist academic fashion; see "Archéologie, archéologues et nazisme," in *Pour Léon Poliakov: Le racisme, mythes et sciences*, ed. M. Olender (Brussels, 1981), pp. 308 and 315, n. 54 (through an oversight the phrase referring to Hitler was omitted from the citation). Actually, that page by Dumézil, although it is ambiguous (and thus, as we have seen, capable of being interpreted in very different ways), does not contain racist statements. Even Schnapp seems to end up admitting this when he observes that Dumézil "has always distanced himself from biological and racist interpretations in the field of Indo-European linguistics" (p. 315, n. 54).

[Now see also a new essay by A. Momigliano, "Georges Dumézil and the Trifunctional Approach to Roman Civilization," *History and Theory* 23 (1984): 312-30, and Dumézil's reply in *L'oubli de l'homme et l'honneur des dieux* (Paris, 1985), pp. 299-318. Dumézil also replied to the present essay: see his "Science et politique: Réponse à Carlo Ginzburg," *Annales: E.S.C.* 40 (1985): 985-89.]

Freud, the Wolf-Man, and the Werewolves

I should like to thank Alberto Gajano, who discussed this research with me.

1. Sigmund Freud, *Collected Papers*, trans. Alix and James Strachey, The International Psycho-Analytical Library, no. 9 (London, 1950), 3:471-605.
2. Ibid., pp. 498-99. Freud had already published the dream in his essay "The Occurrence in Dreams of Material from Fairy Tales," ibid., 4:236-43.

3. See C. Ginzburg, *The Night Battles: Witchcraft and Agrarian Cults in the Sixteenth and Seventeenth Centuries* (Baltimore, 1983; 1st Italian ed., 1966).

4. Ibid., p. 30.

5. See R. Jakobson and M. Szeftel, "The Vseslav Epos," *Memoirs of the American Folklore Society* 42 (1947): 13-86.

6. See C. Ginzburg, "Présomptions sur le sabbat," *Annales: E.S.C.* 39 (1984): 341-54. The connection of the second and third elements with Slavic beliefs in werewolves has already been noted by N. Belmont, *Les signes de la naissance* (Paris, 1971), pp. 108 ff., in a study of symbolic representations of persons born with the caul that reaches conclusions very different from those presented here.

7. Freud, *Collected Papers*, 3:506, 580.

8. Ibid., p. 536.

9. See *Antiche fiabe russe*, raccolte da A. N. Afanasjev, a cura di G. Venturi (Turin, 1955), pp. 95-96. (The fable of the tailor and the wolves does not appear to be included in Afanasjev's *Russian Fairy Tales* [New York, 1945]. – *Trans.*)

10. See Ginzburg, *The Night Battles*, p. 12.

11. See G. Klaniczay, "Shamanistic Elements in Central European Witchcraft," in *Shamanism in Eurasia*, ed. M. Hoppal (Göttingen, 1984), pp. 404-22.

12. See *The Wolf-Man by the Wolf-Man*, ed. M. Gardiner (New York, 1971), and H. P. Blum, "The Borderline Childhood of the Wolf-Man," in *Freud and His Patients*, ed. M. Kanzer and J. Glenn (New York and London, 1980), pp. 341-58.

13. See Freud, *Collected Papers*, 3:501.

14. S. Freud and D. E. Oppenheim, *Dreams in Folklore* (New York, 1958). This essay, found miraculously, appeared posthumously first in 1953.

15. Freud, *Collected Papers*, 3:580-81.

16. *The Complete Letters of Sigmund Freud to Wilhelm Fliess, 1887-1904*, trans. and ed. J. M. Masson, (Cambridge, Mass., 1985), pp. 238-42.

17. A point often made: see, for example, M. Krüll, *Freud and His Father* (New York, 1986).

18. *Letters of Freud to Fliess*, pp. 224, 227.

19. Ibid., p. 225.

20. Ibid., p. 264 (letter dated September 21, 1897).

21. Ibid., p. 227 (letter dated January 24, 1897). On this and the preceding letter, see also J. M. Masson, *The Assault on Truth: Freud's Suppression of the Seduction Theory* (New York, 1984), pp. 105 ff.

22. It appeared in 1925; see *Collected Papers*, 5:181-85. – *Trans.*

23. Freud, *Collected Papers*, 3:577. On this point see also the perceptive remarks by P. Brooks, "Fictions of the Wolf-Man: Freud and Narrative Understanding," in *Reading for the Plot* (Oxford, 1984), pp. 264-85.

24. Freud, *Collected Papers*, 3:575.

25. Ibid., 1:299.

26. See Masson, *The Assault on Truth*, esp. ch. 4. (Cf., however, Krüll, *Freud and His Father*, pp. 68 ff. and passim.) The analytical side of Masson's book is much more convincing than its conclusions. Nevertheless, it is a serious piece of research (as well as a rich repository of unpublished documents) that the

international psychoanalytic community has wrongly attempted to portray as scandalous libel.

27. See Ginzburg, "Présomptions sur le sabbat."

28. See Freud, *Collected Papers*, 3:596. In general, see A. H. Esman, "The Primal Scene: A Review and a Reconsideration," *Psychoanalytic Study of the Child* 28 (1973): 49-81, and more specifically, M. Kanzer, "Further Comments on the Wolf-Man: The Search for a Primal Scene," in Kanzer and Glenn, *Freud and His Patients*, pp. 358 ff., esp. pp. 363-64. On Freud's Lamarckism, see E. Jones, *The Life and Work of Sigmund Freud*, 3 vols. (New York, 1953-57), *ad indicis*.

29. Freud, *Collected Papers*, 3:577-78, 603.

30. See G. Róheim, "Hungarian Shamanism," *Psychoanalysis and the Social Sciences* 3 (1951): 131-69.

31. *The Freud-Jung Letters: The Correspondence between Sigmund Freud and C. G. Jung*, ed. William McGuire, trans. Ralph Manheim and R.F.C. Hull (Princeton, 1974), p. 260.

[A German translation of this essay, followed by a discussion in which R. Schenda, C. Daxelmüller, H. Gerndt, F.-W. Eickhoff, A. Niederer, U. Jeggle, and D. Harmening participated, appeared in the *Zeitschrift für Volkskunde* 82 (1986): 189-225.]

The Inquisitor as Anthropologist

This essay was presented at the conference "Faith, Law, and Dissent: The Inquisition in the Early Modern World," Northern Illinois University and The Newberry Library, October 1985. A slightly different version was read at the annual conference of the American Anthropological Association, Phoenix, November 1988, and at a conference entitled "History, Event, Discourse" at the University of California, Los Angeles, January 1989.

1. On a related subject (but from a different perspective) see R. Rosaldo, "From the Door of His Tent: The Fieldworker and the Inquisitor," in *Writing Culture: The Poetics and Politics of Ethnography*, ed. J. Clifford and G. E. Marcus (Berkeley and Los Angeles, 1986), pp. 77-97, which is based on a comparison of the work of Evans-Pritchard and Le Roy Ladurie.

2. A. Del Col, "La Riforma cattolica nel Friuli vista da Paschini," in *Atti del convegno di studio su Pio Paschini nel centenario della nascita, 1878-1978* (n.p., n.d.), pp. 123-40, esp. p. 134.

3. H. Trevor-Roper, *The European Witch-Craze of the Sixteenth and Seventeenth Centuries* (London, 1969).

4. A. Momigliano, "Linee per una valutazione della storiografia del quindicennio 1961-1976," *Rivista storica italiana*, 89 (1977): 596-608, esp. p. 596.

5. E. E. Evans-Pritchard, *Witchcraft, Oracles, and Magic among the Azande* (London, 1937); A. Macfarlane, *Witchcraft in Tudor and Stuart England* (London, 1970); K. Thomas, *Religion and the Decline of Magic* (London, 1971).

6. H. Geertz and K. Thomas, "An Anthropology of Religion and Magic," *Journal of Interdisciplinary History* 6 (1975): 71-109.

7. R. Kieckhefer, *European Witchcraft Trials* (London, 1976), pp. 8, 27 ff.

8. R. Jakobson, "Language in Operation," in *Mélanges Alexandre Koyré, II: L'aventure de l'esprit* (Paris, 1964), p. 273.

9. M. Bakhtin, *Problems of Dostoevsky's Poetics* (Ann Arbor, 1973).

10. C. Ginzburg, *The Night Battles: Witchcraft and Agrarian Cults in the Sixteenth and Seventeenth Centuries* (Baltimore, 1983).

11. See, for instance, G. E. Marcus and D. Cushman, "Ethnographies as Texts," *Annual Review of Anthropology* 11 (1982): 23-69, as well as the essays in *Writing Culture*. The latest Geertz collection of essays, *Works and Lives: The Anthropologist as Author* (Cambridge, 1988), is also relevant.

12. C. Geertz, *The Interpretation of Cultures* (New York, 1973), p. 19.

13. C. Ginzburg, "Prove e possibilità," postface to N. Z. Davis, *Il ritorno di Martin Guerre* (Turin, 1984), pp. 131 ff.

14. E. Verga, "Intorno a due inediti documenti di stregheria milanese del secolo XIV," *Rendiconti del R. Istituto lombardo di scienze e lettere*, 2nd ser., 32 (1899): 165 ff.

15. Kieckhefer, *European Witchcraft Trials*, p. 22.

16. For a (not always satisfactory) transcript of the two Milanese sentences, see L. Muraro, *La signora del gioco* (Milan, 1976), pp. 240-45. The assumption that the *domina ludi* was called "Herodiades" by ordinary people (p. 148) seems to be unfounded. Kieckhefer does not comment on the inquisitors' identification of Madona Horiente with Diana-Herodiades.

17. J. Herolt, *Sermones de tempore*, sermon 41. I have also examined the following editions: Nuremberg 1480, 1481, 1496; Strasbourg, 1499, 1503; Rouen, 1513.

18. Quoted from J. B. Russell, *Witchcraft in the Middle Ages* (Ithaca, 1972), p. 76.

19. See, among others, A. Endter, *Die Sage vom wilden Jagd* (Frankfort a.M., 1933) and K. Meisen, *Die Sagen vom Wütenden Heer und Wilden Jäger* (Münster i.W., 1935).

20. C. Ginzburg, "Présomptions sur le sabbat," *Annales: E.S.C.* 39 (1984): 341-54.

21. G. Henningsen, "Sicilien: Ett arkaiskt mönster för sabbaten," (Sicily: An Archaic Pattern of the Sabbath), in *Häxornas Europa, 1400-1700: Historiska och antropologiska studier*, ed. B. Ankarloo and G. Henningsen (Lund, 1987), pp. 170-90. An English version of this volume is in press. The paper was originally presented at a symposium on witchcraft and criminal justice held at Stockholm in September 1984.

❧ Index of Names